# MARX'S RELIGION OF REVOLUTION:
## The Doctrine of Creative Destruction

# MARX'S RELIGION OF REVOLUTION:

## The Doctrine Of Creative Destruction

**GARY NORTH**

*Revolutions are the locomotives of history*
Karl Marx (1850)

**THE CRAIG PRESS**
**NUTLEY, NEW JERSEY**
1968

UNIVERSITY SERIES: Historical Studies
Rousas J. Rushdoony, *editor*

Library of Congress Card Catalog Number 68-20162

*Printed in the United States of America*

This book is respectfully dedicated to two profound scholars:
Cornelius Van Til
Ludwig von Mises
Without their contributions, this book would not have been
written.

## THE AUTHOR

Gary North holds the B.A. and M.A. in history from the University of California, Riverside, where he is presently working to complete his Ph.D. He has taught in the University's Western Civilization program, and he has twice been the recipient of Earhart Fellowships for graduate study. Before returning to his graduate studies, he attended Westminster Theological Seminary in Philadelphia, where he received training in the area of Christian apologetics and philosophy, under the guidance of Cornelius Van Til and Robert Knudson.

He is the author of two shorter works, *Inflation: The Economics of Addiction* (1965) and *Monetary Hoarding: The Economics of Survival* (1966), both published by The Pamphleteers, Box 1092, San Carlos, Calif. His articles and reviews have appeared in several periodicals, including *The Journal of Political Economy, The Freeman, Christian Economics, The International Reformed Bulletin, Rampart Journal* (not to be confused with *Ramparts Magazine*), and *Don Bell Reports*. For several years, he has been a regular reviewer for the Riverside (Calif.) *Press-Enterprise* in its book section.

The author's areas of professional academic specialization are the fields of economic history and Colonial America. In the spring of 1966, he was admitted as a member of the Economists' National Committee on Monetary Policy.

# CONTENTS

## I

## MAGIC AND REVOLUTION

Basic to the modern mentality is the belief in magic. Magic is the attempt by man to gain autonomous power, to gain control over the world of man, nature, and the supernatural. In magic, man sees himself as his own god and creator, and total power and control becomes his goal. By means of this total and autonomous power, man expects to govern reality by his own prediction and planning.

The popularity of the Greek mentality to the men of the Renaissance and Enlightenment has been due to the fact that the Greeks combined, it was believed, a scientific technique with a magical faith. A classic example of this Greek perspective is Archimedes, who, to illustrate the power potentially in the principle of the lever, said to Hiero II, monarch of Syracuse, "Give me a place to stand, and I will move the world." This remark has become famous to generations of schoolboys as illustrative of the "genius" of Greece and of the potentialities of "science." The remark, however, is in essence magic, refined and technologically aware magic, but magic nonetheless. "Give me a place to stand!" The assumptions in this presupposition are enormous. Make me a god, and I can move the world. Give me the power to create gold, and I can buy the world. It is one thing for a man to make a lever, and to realize the human possibilities with this mechanism at man's command, but it is another for man to assume unlimited potentialities as the human condition. The scientific achievements of Archimedes were real, but they were set in the context of Hellenic magic.

The Renaissance and Enlightenment restored magic to the world, although the Christian centuries, deeply infected by neoplatonic and Aristotelian thought, were thereby also deeply imbued by magic. The Christian centuries, however, recognized the difference which separated them from antiquity, and the term *Dark Ages* was given to the classical, pre-Christian era. As Peter Gay points out in *The Enlightenment,* "Petrarch removed the label Dark Ages from classical, pre-Christian times and fastened it instead on the Christian era" (p. 74). The modern world saw itself as the era of light, and, not surprisingly, it called itself finally "The Enlightenment." The movement redefined philosophy; it denied the validity of system-making, since man, as his own god, is beyond systems, beyond good and evil. Philosophy for the world of the Enlightenment is, as Peter Gay indicates, "the organized habit of criticism" (p. 130). This criticism is of Christianity in essence: the critique is directed against everything which is hostile to the magical perspective. The critique assumes the reality of the natural world only, denies the Biblical revelation, and posits the autonomy of man.

Karl Marx applied the Enlightenment conception of philosophy with especial consistency. As Marx pointed out, in his *Contribution to the Critique of Hegel's Philosophy of the Right,* the "criticism of religion is the premise of all criticism." This criticism is from first to last an attack on the sovereignty of God in the name of the sovereignty of man; it is an attack on revelation in the name of, not reason as such, but the concept of autonomous reason. It is an attack on Biblical religion in terms of magic and the philosophy of magic.

The philosophy of magic has so deeply entered the modern mind that its insanities pass unnoticed. A classic example of this appears in Ernest Hemingway's *For Whom the Bell Tolls* (1940). The facets of Hemingway's personality which appear clearly in his writings are to a mild degree recognized even in A. E. Hotchner's *Papa Hemingway* (1966). In *For Whom the Bell Tolls,* Hemingway's concept of passionate, romantic sex is magical. For the ancients, magical sex ensured the fertility of the earth. For Hemingway magical sex moves the earth. Pilar declares, "When I was young the earth moved so that you could feel it all shift in space and were afraid it would go out from under you. It happened every night." In several important passages, Hemingway rings the changes on this magical theme. In a passage on Robert Jordan's sexual experience, Hemingway wrote,

10

For him it was a dark passage which led to nowhere, then to nowhere, then again to nowhere, heavy on the elbows in the earth to nowhere, dark, never any end to nowhere, hung on all times always to unknowing nowhere, this time and again for always to nowhere, now not to be borne once again always and to nowhere, now beyond all bearing up, up, up and into nowhere, suddenly, scaldingly, holdingly all nowhere gone and time absolutely still and they were both there, time having stopped and he felt the earth move out and away from under them.[1]

This passage, and others like it, should have provoked nothing but laughter from the millions who read it. It has nothing to do with any man's experience, and its magical sexual mysticism borders on insanity. But it was read with rapt attention, because the readers shared Hemingway's magical view of sex.

But the acceptance of this insane bit of magic is not surprising. The greater magic of revolution is accepted, by Hemingway and the modern world. It is a belief that destruction can be creative, that progress is through chaos, that the principle of social power requires social suicide. The theory of revolution as the means of social progress is pure magic. *Criticism* of religion is carried to its ultimate meaning in the *revolutionary destruction* of religion and the world of Christian faith. This is the essence of "Enlightenment" faith, and it is pure magic. It is not producing Enlightenment but is rather increasing the darkness of the new Dark Ages.

And Karl Marx was a leading architect and planner of the new darkness. The two governing passions of Marx's life were, first, a hatred of Christian society, of Biblical law and order, and, second, a magical belief in the efficacy and power of destruction. The contradictions in his system of economic order are impossible to reconcile. As an economics, it has no future. As a philosophy of magic, Karl Marx's system is impervious to attack, once its presuppositions are granted. The implications of humanism and of anti-Christianity are carried to their logical conclusion, to pure magic. The Marxist belief in the creative power of revolution now extends far beyond the frontiers of Marxism: it is a part of the humanist legacy.

---

[1] Ernest Hemingway: *For Whom the Bell Tolls,* p. 159. New York: Charles Scribner's Sons, 1940.

At the conclusion of World War II, the world powers set in motion, as the principle of progress, the machinery of revolution. In passionate dedication to the City of Man, revolution was encouraged, incited, or engendered in Europe, Asia, Africa, and the Americas. These revolutions, instead of bringing peace and progress to the world, have only increased the darkness of the new Dark Ages and furthered the growing collapse of law, order, and civilization. The humanists are aware of these problems, and they have an answer: more magic, more revolutions, revolution within the revolution. They are confident, of course, that they represent light and civilization. After all, do they not have flush toilets, and have they not invented the atomic and hydrogen bombs? (The ancient Minoan culture of Crete also had its modern plumbing, and much else, in its declining days.) Wisdom was born with them, they believe, these sons of darkness, and they are determined to lead the whole world into the wisdom of creative destruction.

"We have no name; we are *the* people," a tribesman told an enquiring white man, and the modern practitioners of magic are agreed at one point: *they* are *the* people, and the future and the government rests upon their shoulders.

When Hemingway's silly fornicators swore solemnly that "the earth moved" because of their passion, they were in a class with those who expect to move the earth forward by their revolutions. But the earth does not move for either the fornicators or the revolutionists. It responds, not to the magicians but only to the sovereign decree of the triune God. The absurdities of Marx and Hemingway are both amusing and serious. They cannot be met or answered by more humanism, by more magic, but only by Christian scholarship firmly grounded on the Biblical revelation.

In terms of such a faith, and very ably trained in philosophy, history, and economics, Gary North analyzes the implications of Karl Marx and his position. His study is a very important exercise in Christian revisionism. It is an important document in the struggle between *the religion of revolution*[2] and the religion of the Bible. Its analysis of Marx will set the temper of many further studies.

Rousas John Rushdoony
Woodland Hills, California

---

[2] R. J. Rushdoony: *The Religion of Revolution.* Victoria, Texas: Trinity Episcopal Church, 1965.

## II.

## INTRODUCTION

My interest in the Marxian system dates back to the time when I was a sophomore in high school. Since that time there has been a huge outpouring of scholarly books and articles dealing with Marx, especially the so-called "young Marx." I was first introduced to some of this material by Professor Peter Fuss of the Department of Philosophy at the University of California, Riverside, during the course of an undergraduate seminar. Subsequently, I took up the whole subject again in a graduate seminar at Westminster Theological Seminary, Philadelphia, under the guidance of Dr. Robert Knudson. Upon my return to the Riverside campus for further graduate training, I was privileged to take a series of special studies under Donald Lowe of the Department of History, Robert A. Nisbet of the Department of Sociology, and Howard Sherman of the Department of Economics, none of whom is responsible in any way for my conclusions. Nevertheless, without their aid and criticisms, this study would not have been possible. I should also mention the constant encouragement I received from Professor Herbert Heaton, although he was careful to warn me about the morass of material which would face me in such an undertaking. He was so right.

Anyone who has ever looked at even a brief bibliography on Marx and Marxism is aware of the staggering amount of research which has been expended on the man and the movement. It is probably safe to say that in the Western world, the two figures of Marx and Jesus have received the most attention in this century. Why, then, have I decided to add another volume in this already vast ocean of monographs? There are a number of reasons. First, I hope that it will serve as an introduction to some of the major themes in Marx's writings, although many of them will be mentioned only briefly. Second, the book will provide a beginning for anyone who is interested in the flood of scholarly analyses that has appeared in the last century. A beginner normally would not know where to begin; perhaps this will help him. Third, it offers a new way of looking at Marx and his message: not as a secularized Old Testament prophet, but as a modern throwback to the chaos cults of the ancient world. The chief motivation behind the writing of this study, however, was my desire to subject Marx to an evaluation based upon the perspective of that contemporary Calvinist system known as "presuppositionalism." The major exponents of this viewpoint are Professor Cornelius Van Til of Westminster Theological Seminary in Philadelphia and Herman Dooyeweerd of the Free University of Amsterdam.[1] So far as I know, no one writing in English has made this kind of analysis of Marx's thought. I trust that this book will fill the gap.

In no sense, it deserves to be pointed out, is this book a "debate" with Marx. Sidney Finkelstein, writing in the Marxist journal, *Science and Society,* explains why this must be the case: "Philosophies that are incompatible cannot debate one another. There must be some common ground, some problem of life which both accept as crucial and to which the philosophies offer different answers. Otherwise instead of a debate there is simply the revelation of different premises or different concepts of the function of philosophy."[2] Between Christianity and Marxism there can be no meaningful "dialogue." Charles Hodge, the great 19th century Calvinist theologian, put it this way: the last issue of history will be the conflict between "Atheism and its countless forms and Calvinism. The other systems will be crushed as the half-rotten ice between two great bergs."[3] Neither

---

[1] For an introduction to Van Til's writings, see the two books by R. J. Rushdoony, *By What Standard?* (1958) and *Van Til* (1960). Also, see the chapter on "The Neo-Augustinianism of Herman Dooyeweerd" in David Hugh Freeman, *Recent Studies in Philosophy and Theology* (1962). All are published by the Presbyterian and Reformed Publishing Co., Philadelphia.
[2] Sidney Finkelstein, "Marxism and Existentialism," *Science and Society,* XXXI (1967), 59-60.
[3] Charles Hodge, *Princeton Sermons* (London: Banner of Truth Trust, 1958), xv.

the consistent Marxist nor the consistent Christian can hope for a reconciliation between the two systems; it is a question of total intellectual warfare. Members of both sides are convinced that their ultimate triumph is inevitable. The issue is basically a conflict in the realm of faith.

It is interesting to note that in recent years, certain humanists within the churches and outside of them have attempted to reconstruct Marx in their own image. This has been done in order to make Marx appear more palatable to the modern world. For the Christian, however, these efforts have accomplished precisely the reverse; they have exposed the demonic features of a humanism which can embrace something as grotesque as the Marxian system. The orthodox Christian is not convinced by Leopold Senghor, the President of the Republic of Senegal, when he asserts that "Churchmen themselves cannot deny Marx's contribution and they accept his positive values."[4] Nor is there much to be thankful for when we read a statement such as the one made by Santiago Alvarez, a Spanish Marxist: "Thus, logic tells us that the way to test the two positions — the Marxist and the Catholic — is to begin right now joint actions to reconstruct society and to advance, through successive stages, to the creation of a society where both ideologies will be put to the test. So why not make the experiment?"[5] There are many reasons why the experiment

---

[4] Leopold Senghor, "Socialism is a Humanism," in Erich Fromm (ed.), *Socialist Humanism: An International Symposium* (Garden City, N. Y.: Doubleday Anchor, 1966), 54. For a disturbing confirmation of Senghor's suggestion, see the article, "Dialogue: Christ and Marx," *Newsweek* (Jan. 6, 1967), 74, 76. Cf. Christopher Wren, "Can Christians Talk to Communists?" *Look* (May 2, 1967), 36ff.

[5] Santiago Alvarez, "Towards an Alliance of Communists and Catholics," *World Marxist Review,* VIII (June, 1965), 47. See also the report on the conference held between Catholics and Marxists in the spring of 1965: Walter Hollitscher, "Dialogue Between Marxists and Catholics," *World Marxist Review,* VIII (Aug., 1965), 53-58. Hollitscher's statement is to the point: "Humanistic tendencies must be upheld without prejudice — that is the common ground on which atheists and believers can meet for joint action" (56).

should not be made, and some of them are discussed at length in this study.

Marx, like the Devil, must be given his due. He created a vast, compelling intellectual structure, perhaps the greatest of the post-Hegelian attempts to bind together the contradictions of man's self-proclaimed autonomous reason. The attempt failed, but we should be willing to acknowledge his efforts. No modern historian or social thinker can fully escape the influence of Marx's intellect, as Raymond Aron has argued.[6] In a sense, this book takes a stand against all those who think that the whole of Marx's labors were silly. Some of his ideas were silly, and they deserve to be treated as such. For this reason I cannot agree with one critic of this study who wrote: "You should remove the quality of sarcasm from your writing when you write about a great historical figure like Marx." In the history of scholarship, there has been no more sarcastic, vitriolic writer than Karl Marx, and since he established the precedent, who am I to depart from it? But on the whole, I have taken Marx seriously; he is a formidable opponent.

On the other hand, I have taken a stand against those who are unwilling to admit that such an imposing intellectual achievement could have been made by a madman. For Marx, following his humanistic presuppositions to their terrifying ultimate conclusion, did become a sort of lunatic — a man obsessed with the idea of blood, chaos, and revolution. As the Bible says, "The fool hath said in his heart, There is no God" (Ps. 14:1). That Marx said it eloquently makes him no less a fool. The collapse of the system was guaranteed by its starting point: "The criticism of religion ends with the doctrine that *man is the supreme being for man.*"[7] But man is

---

[6] Raymond Aron, *The Opium of the Intellectuals* (N. Y.: Norton, 1962), 105.

[7] Marx, "The Critique of Hegel's Philosophy of Right," (1844), in T. B. Bottomore (ed.), *Karl Marx: Early Writings* (N. Y.: McGraw-Hill, 1964), 52.

not God, and in this fact we find the beginning of the end of the Marxian structure.[8]

---

[8] The beginnings of a new Christian counter-humanist social philosophy can be found in E. L. Hebden Taylor, *The Christian Philosophy of Law, Politics and the State* (Nutley, New Jersey: Craig Press, 1966). The author is building upon the foundation laid by Herman Dooyeweerd, and the book is absolutely indispensable for any Christian who wants to formulate alternative answers to modern secular thought. Its one important weakness is its tendency to over-emphasize the role of the state in the co-ordination of the economic sphere.

*For Marx was before all else a revolutionist. His real mission in life was to contribute, in one way or another, to the overthrow of capitalist society and of the state institutions which it had brought into being, to contribute to the liberation of the modern proletariat, which he was the first to make conscious of its own position and its needs, conscious of the conditions of its emancipation.*

Frederich Engels (1883)[1]

## III.

## THE BIOGRAPHY OF A REVOLUTIONARY

Karl Heinrich Marx, the bourgeois son of a bourgeois father, was born in Trier, in what is now Rhineland Germany, on May 5, 1818. He was a Jew by birth, but in 1824 his father joined the state's official Christian church, and he saw to it that his children were baptized into his new faith. However, the family took its Christian faith just as seriously as it had taken its Jewish faith, i.e., not at all. Marx was a humanist, from beginning to end, and his humanism, unlike his middle class father's humanism, would be taken, step by step, to its revolutionary conclusion. Karl Marx, the grandson of Rabbis, would become the Rabbi of Europe's most important religious movement: revolutionary humanism.

Marx's early years were notable only in the fact that they were so comfortable and so undistinguished. Like the career of his 20th century disciple, Lenin, Marx's pre-college days were marked by his competence and doggedness, but without any signs of originality of

[1] Frederich Engels, "Speech at the Graveside of Karl Marx," (1883), in *Marx-Engels Selected Works* (Moscow: Foreign Languages Publishing House, 1962), II, 168.

thought. He was a good student, especially in languages and in line-by-line dissections of other people's philosophical systems. He was to retain both facilities throughout his life. In 1835, he entered Bonn University, during which time he occupied himself by drinking and dueling, both of which were fundamental pastimes in the education of any young German gentleman.[2] Due to pressures from his father, Marx enrolled the next year in the law school of the University of Berlin. The elder Marx hoped that his son would be subject to fewer distractions at Berlin, since it was known to be very rigorous academically. The German scholar, Ludwig Feuerbach once remarked that "Other universities are positively Bacchanalian compared with this workhouse," in reference to the University, and Heinrich Marx could do no more than to send his son into such an institution.[3] Unfortunately, Marx was easily distracted in Berlin; this time, however, the distractions were primarily intellectual.

Berlin was the center of a group of students and young professors known as the "Young Hegelians," radical followers of the philosopher G. W. F. Hegel (1770-1831). Marx became an intimate member of this "Professors' Club," and most of his time was spent in long philosophical and political discussions in the coffee houses and other meeting places of the little group. In spite of his glowing letters home to his father which were filled with details describing his supposed academic progress — the quantities of work which he claimed to have accomplished are positively staggering — he seemed to advance very slowly, if at all, toward his law degree.[4] Even his asso-

[2] Boris Nicolaievsky and Otto Maenchen-Helfen, *Karl Marx: Man and Fighter* (London: Methuen, 1936), ch. 2. For some illuminating remarks on the close relation between membership in dueling fraternities and success in the 19th century German bureaucracy, see Max Weber's essay, "National Character and the Junkers," in Gerth and Mills (eds.), *From Max Weber: Essays in Sociology* (N. Y.: Oxford University Press, 1946), 386-95.
[3] The quote from Feuerbach is found in Franz Mehring, *Karl Marx* (Ann Arbor: University of Michigan Press, [1933] 1962), 9.
[4] An example of these letters is reproduced in Otto Rühle, *Karl Marx: His Life and Work* (N. Y.: New Home Library, 1943), 15-24. Many of his biographers take these letters seriously, but his father

ciates in the group implored him to hurry on his doctoral dissertation. Finally, in 1841, he submitted his dissertation to another university, the University of Jena, and he was awarded his degree in philosophy (not in law) in the same year.

In 1842, he began to labor at the only type of paying job he would ever hold, that of a journalist. He began to write for the *Rheinisch Zeitung,* one of the liberal papers of the day. It was a small paper, but at least it offered the possibility of rapid advance for a young man who held a doctor's degree. He began in April; by October, the young Marx was editor. Unfortunately, the young man displayed a trait which was to mark him throughout his career: an unwillingness to compromise in the face of overwhelming odds. In March of 1843, the Prussian government ordered it suppressed after April 1. Marx resigned as editor on March 17.

Interestingly enough, at this stage of his career, he was actually opposed to communism as an economic and philosophical system. But within a year he and another young German intellectual, Frederich Engels, were converted to a crude sort of communism. The catalyst in this metamorphosis was Moses Hess, the "communist rabbi," as Marx often called him. Marx later went far beyond Hess in his devotion to the revolutionary cause, and he constructed a far more thorough critique of capitalist society, but the role played by Hess at this early stage of Marx's development cannot be over-estimated.[5]

---

remained somewhat skeptical. For a more reasonable account of what probably took place in these university days, see Leopold Schwartzschild, *Karl Marx: The Red Prussian* (N. Y.: Universal Library, 1947), ch. 3.

[5] Hess had originally encouraged the publishers of the *Rheinische Zeitung* to hire the young Marx. Hess is described by Isaiah Berlin as a communist "missionary," later a Marxist and a Zionist, who spent most of his efforts in gaining adherents to the new faith. See Isaiah Berlin, *Karl Marx: His Life and Environment* (3rd ed.; N. Y.: Oxford University Press, 1963), 72-73. For a more detailed analysis of Hess's thought, see Sidney Hook, *From Hegel to Marx* (Ann Arbor: University of Michigan Press, [1950] 1962), ch. 6.

Another opportunity to enter into the world of journalism presented itself shortly thereafter. Marx took his young bride, Jenny von Westphalen, to Paris, where he and his old "Young Hegelian" associate, Arnold Ruge, set out to edit *Deutsch-Französischen Jahrbücher* [*German-French Yearbooks*]. The first edition was published in February of 1844; it was to be the last, as well. The two men quarrelled, and the breach was never healed. Many of the copies were confiscated by the Prussian government when issues were sent into Prussia. In the *Yearbooks* two of Marx's important early essays appeared: the "Introduction to a Critique of the Hegelian Philosophy of Law," and his reply to Bruno Bauer, "On the Jewish Question," so, from the historian's viewpoint, the endeavor was not totally useless. But given the era in which he lived, Marx was not really the best man to have as an editor, as the radicals in Prussia and France were beginning to learn. Nevertheless, he continued to write for another radical publication, *Vörwarts* [*Forward*].[6]

In 1844, Marx and Engels began a long friendship which was to last as long as both were alive. Engels was the son of a wealthy German industrialist, and he himself did not break off relations with the business until late in his career. He was a man of expensive tastes who enjoyed an evening at the opera or the ballet. He was hardly the man one would expect to find as the collaborator of Karl Marx, the founder of Marxist revolutionary thought. Engels's own work, *The Condition of the Working Class in England in 1844,* was to have a profound effect on Marx; from 1845 on, Marx was to have far more respect for economic research and investigation than he had ever imagined possible in his early "philosophical" days.

The Prussian government put pressure on the French authorities to deport Marx, and in 1845 the little Marx family was exiled to Brussels. In order to avoid any similar experiences, he renounced his Prussian citizenship. For the next two years, Marx was able to devote his time to other affairs. He helped establish radical correspondence societies; he wrote; and he helped organize the League of the Just. The League changed its name in 1847 to the Communist

---

[6] On Marx's early journalism, see Mehring, *Karl Marx,* 32-87.

League; 17 members belonged, none of whom was of proletarian background (it went out of existence in 1851, after the collapse of the revolutions of 1848-50). He and Engels collaborated in writing *The Holy Family* (1845) and *The German Ideology* (1845-46, and published only posthumously in the 1930's). Finally, in 1847, the two worked on their most famous publication, *The Communist Manifesto,* at the request of the Communist League. Engels at first submitted a revolutionary tract modeled after the standard catechisms of the churches of the era, but Marx rejected the idea. The Communist League hoped that it would be ready to influence the masses in the coming revolution, which all the members expected to begin almost momentarily. The revolution came too soon, however; the tract did not appear until February of 1848, just as the uprisings were beginning. The next month saw Marx's expulsion from Belgium.

Marx and his family arrived in London, and he was not to depart from the British Isles for any length of time for as long as he lived. It was in London that he did his research for *Das Kapital,* laboring for long hours in the British Museum each day. He held his only job in Britain as a correspondent and analyst for Dana's *New York Daily Tribune.* It was in England that he and Engels organized, in 1864, the International Working Men's Association (the First International). After his publication of *The Civil War in France* (1871), in which he defended the Paris Commune of 1871, he became known as England's "Red Doctor," yet he never manned a barricade or fired a rifle at government troops; stodgy England never was able to muster up a revolution for him.

For all of his vitriolic attacks on bourgeois institutions and bourgeois morality, Marx was the antithesis of his ideal revolutionary, at least in his private life. He remained legally married to the same woman all his life, and the two were devoted to each other. Though he was hardly a competent breadwinner, he apparently was successful as a father, at least in the eyes of his children.[7] Yet of the three daughters who survived death in childhood, two (including Elanor)

---

[7] See the note by Elanor Marx Aveling on her father's love for his family in Erich Fromm, *Marx's Concept of Man* (N. Y.: Ungar, 1961), 248-56.

committed suicide. But perhaps most important of all was the fact that Karl Marx, the radicals' most brilliant economist, was in poverty and continual debt throughout his life.[8]

Marx's early poverty is understandable, given the fact that he was unwilling to get a regular job (the only one he ever applied for was as a clerk in a railway station, and he was turned down on the basis of his illegible handwriting). Especially in the years 1861-1864 it must have been difficult, for the management of the *New York Daily Tribune* informed him that all available space was henceforth to be used for news concerning the Civil War. But in 1864, Marx received an inheritance from an obscure German follower. The Marx family received £824, a staggering amount of money for the period. Yet Marx was penniless within two years. He insisted that he needed at least £400-£500 annually.[9] It should be borne in mind that an annual income of £400 was a small fortune in 1860. Statistics prior to the 1880's are lacking in precision, but some fairly reasonable estimates of average income have been made. The income of an agricultural laborer in the lowest decile of the population would have been around £31 annually. An average income in 1860 would have been approximately £46 per year. For those in the upper decile, a £72 income would have been typical.[10] While it is true that Marx had heavy debts to pay off, it is hard to believe that he had gone through an £824 inheritance in two years. A man who could not live on an income of £350 per year — five times greater than the *upper* tenth of the British population — certainly can be considered a poor financial administrator, yet this is precisely what Marx received after 1868. Engels sold his share in the family's cotton

---

[8] I am using the terms "radical" and "liberal" in the same sense as Robert A. Nisbet uses them in *The Sociological Tradition* (N. Y.: Basic Books, 1966), 9-16, and as he uses them in his *Community and Power* (N. Y.: Oxford Galaxy, 1962).

[9] Letter to Kugelmann, March 17, 1868: *Letters to Kugelman* (N. Y.: International Publishers, 1934), 65.

[10] Figures dealing with average incomes for British workers are found in A. L. Bowley, *Wages and Income in the United Kingdom since 1860* (Cambridge University Press, 1937), 46.

mill, and Marx received £350 as an annual pension.[11] This was in addition to the £350 paid by Engels to Marx in 1864, and in addition to Engels's gift to pay off Marx's debts, which in 1868 amounted to £210.[12] In other words, Marx had gone through over £1000 of gifts and inheritance between 1864 and 1868, and he had even accumulated another £210 of debt! Yet in 1872, we find him accepting a £15 gift from his American correspondent, Dr. Kugelmann.[13] It is interesting to note that one of the biographies most favorable to Marx refers to Engels's enormous gift as "a definite, if moderate, yearly allowance."[14] Yearly, perhaps; hardly moderate, if contemporary living standards are taken into consideration.

Marx's hostility to bankers and capitalists in general, and Jewish moneylenders in particular, may have stemmed in part from his own inability to make ends meet. In 1866, only two years after his £1150 + windfall, he was searching for a loan at 5%; he was then paying out 20%-30%.[15] His illnesses were expensive, and his attempt to keep his three daughters in bourgeois luxury also drained his finances, but this kind of debt is remarkable. As he wrote to Dr. Kugelmann in 1866, "I am faced with a financial crisis in the *immediate* future, a thing which, apart from the direct effects on me and my family, would also be disastrous for me politically, particularly here in London, where one must 'keep up appearances.' "[16] London's revolutionary circles were apparently afflicted with a severe dose of "bourgeois affectations," and Marx was no exception. It is

---

[11] Letter from Engels to Marx, November 29, 1869. Reprinted in part in Otto Rühle, *Karl Marx,* 359-60.

[12] On the £350 gift in 1864, see Nicolaievsky and Maenchen-Helfen, *Karl Marx: Man and Fighter,* 253. The £210 figure was Marx's estimate of his debts in 1868; letter to Engels, quoted in Rühle, *Karl Marx,* 360.

[13] Letter to Kugelmann, July 9, 1872. Apparently the money was earmarked for "Jennychen." Whether this meant his daughter or his wife, I am not certain. One would assume that it was for his daughter; why the daughter of a man of Marx's wealth needed such gifts is not very clear. *Letters to Kugelmann,* 130.

[14] Nicolaievsky and Maenchen-Helfen, *op. cit.,* 254.

[15] Letter to Kugelmann, Oct. 13, 1866: *Letters to Kugelmann,* 42.

[16] *Ibid.*

ironic that the things which kept him afloat financially were the pawnbrokers and his successful capitalist friend, Engels. The role Engels played was freely admitted by Marx: "He is my most intimate friend. I have *no secrets* from him. Had it not been for him I should long ago have been compelled to take up 'business.' "[17] The thought of Marx taking up business is amusing, given his financial acumen. It is too bad that Marx lived in the 19th century; today he would be supported in a far higher style by any number of private and quasi-private foundations which make it a policy to finance prospective revolutionary writers.

Another feature of Marx's personality was his inability to cooperate with his fellow revolutionaries. Throughout his career, he found himself bickering with former associates and present workers who were, in Marx's mind, rivals. With Engels alone he remained on friendly terms, and Engels was careful always to give Marx the two things which he required: unfailing subservience and money. Otto Rühle, by no means an unfavorable biographer, has not exaggerated when he writes:

> Marx was one of those persons who are overpowered by a perpetual urge towards the highest, the purest, the most ideal. It was not merely his ambition to be the most famous among those who have studied socialist literature, and the most learned of all the critics of economic science; he also wanted to be the most efficient revolutionist, and pre-eminent among the advocates of revolution. He wanted to expound the purest theory, to establish the most complete system of communism. As a preliminary to the demonstration of this superiority, he must prove that the socialist theories of all his predecessors were worthless, false, contemptible, or ludicrous. He had to show that the socialism of the utopists was a crazy-quilt of outworn and questionable ideas. That Proudhon was a suspect intruder into the realm of socialist thought. That Lassalle, Bakunin, and Schweitzer [Johann] were tainted with bourgeois ideology, and had probably sold themselves to the enemy. He, Marx alone, was in possession of the true doctrine. His was the crystal-clear knowledge; his was the philosopher's stone; his the immaculate conception of socialism; his the divine truth. With contemptuous wrath, with bitter mockery

---

[17] Letter to Kugelmann, Oct. 25, 1866: *Letters to Kugelmann,* 44.

and profound hostility, he rejected all other opinions, fought against all other convictions, than his own, persecuted all ideas that had not originated in his own brain. For him, there was no wisdom except his own, no socialism other than the socialism he proclaimed, no true gospel outside the limits of his own doctrine. His work was the essence of intellectual purity and scientific integrity. His system was Allah, and he was its prophet.[18]

Marx's unwillingness to tolerate anything which he regarded as insubordination was the cause of numerous splits within the ranks of the proletarian revolutionary movement in Europe, some of which were avoidable. Even Franz Mehring, the author of the semi-official biography of Marx, has to admit that during the dispute with Lassalle, the founder of the Marxist German Social Democratic Party, Marx was excessively bitter. "In his letters to Engels, Marx condemns Lassalle's activities with a severity which occasionally develops into bitter injustice."[19] Marx's references to him as "a little kike" or as a "Jewish nigger" are certainly not in the best spirit of his own self-proclaimed neutrality.[20]

This brings up the whole question of Marx's supposed anti-Semitism. The question is extremely difficult to deal with, if for no other reason than the fact that it involves a post-mortem psycho-analysis, a questionable academic endeavor at best. How can we know what he thought in an area where his writings are so ambiguous? Those who claim that he was the anti-Semite invariably point to the letters that he wrote to Engels which contained nasty statements about Lassalle. Why would he use the word "Jew" as the ultimate form of contempt? In his essays published in 1844, "On the Jewish Question," what was he attacking, his critics ask, if not the Jewish faith and culture? The answer, at least in part, is that he was attacking bourgeois life in general, using the famous stereotype of the European Jewish financeer as his representative type of the bourgeois man. He saw the Jewish community as an infected, diseased culture

---

[18] Otto Rühle, *Karl Marx*, 382-83; cf. 101, 238.

[19] Franz Mehring, *Karl Marx*, 308.

[20] For a list of these vitriolic references, see Leopold Schwartzschild, *Karl Marx: The Red Prussian*, 251.

— totally bourgeois, and always seeking after money. But the critics' question still remains: why did he single out the Jews?[21]

Sidney Hook has tried to defend Marx on this point: "Although Marx was free of anti-Semitic prejudice, he unfortunately was not over-sensitive to the term 'Jew,' often with unsavory adjectives, as an epithet of abuse."[22] But the fact remains that "Jew" was the word which Marx chose. Otto Rühle has provided as reasonable an answer as one could hope for. Marx, he argues, was acutely aware of the social stigma attached to his own Jewish background. "No one could ever forget that Marx had been born a Jew, for not only was his facial type markedly Hebraic, but his whole aspect shouted a Semitic origin. Baptized or unbaptized, Marx remained a Jew, recognizable as such at the first glance, and burdened therefore with all the odium attaching to his race. One may presume that from early childhood he had been on the defensive, earnestly endeavoring, by means of intelligence and industry, to compensate for the disadvantages of birth." In other words, Rühle speculates, Marx probably suffered from some kind of inferiority complex, and his anti-Semitic references were a form of self-defense: "The reader cannot escape the feeling that he is ostentatiously showing his opposition to Judaism, is demonstratively severing himself from his own race, and by emphasizing his anti-capitalistic tendencies is declaring himself before all the world not to be a Jew."[23]

One curious document should be mentioned in this section. It is at odds with virtually all the information we have concerning Marx's life, yet it cannot be ignored. Most commentators see Marx as a total secularist, whether he was an anti-Semite or not (including the author

---

[21] Jewish conservatives are especially fond of pointing out these apparently anti-Semitic statements. Cf. Max Geltman, "A Little Known Chapter in American History," *National Review* (Oct. 5, 1965), 865-67. Also, Archibald B. Roosevelt and Zygmund Dobbs, *The Great Deceit: Social Pseudo-Sciences* (West Sayville, N. Y.: Veritas Foundation, 1964), ch. 7.

[22] Sidney Hook, *From Hegel to Marx*, 278n.

[23] Otto Rühle, *Karl Marx*, 377. A brief, but similar, analysis is found in Isaiah Berlin, *Karl Marx*, 269.

of this study). But one man, Commander S. M. Riis, claims to have unearthed a long-ignored side of Marx's personality. In an interview which he says took place in 1903, he spoke with a woman who claimed to be Helen (Lenchen) Demuth, who served for many years as Marx's housekeeper. He paid her to relate her remembrances of the daily life in the Marx household:

> After another offer of a schilling, I queried the Demuth woman regarding Marx' religious inclinations. She said: " 'e was a God-fearing man."
>
> I gathered that Marx had often gone on Saturdays to a Jewish temple in Maidenhead section of London. Sometimes, when his ailment had bothered him too severely (using the exact words of the Demuth woman), "he prayed alone in his room, before a row of lit candles, tying a sort of tape measure around his forehead."[24]

Riis does not make any kind of anti-Semitic conclusions about this interview's revelation, nor does he even bother to mention the incident again. He even seems unaware of the magnitude of this information. He just records the incident and goes on. There is no way to confirm the facts involved, whether the woman was really Helen Demuth, whether she was kidding the man, or whether the interview really took place. All other evidence is in opposition to the picture painted by Riis. Yet, if true, it would provide just one more incongruity in the life of this paradoxical figure.

---

[24] S. M. Riis, *Karl Marx: Master of Fraud* (N. Y.: Robert Speller & Sons, 1962), 11.

*Both for the production on a mass scale of this*
*communist consciousness, and for the success of the*
*cause itself, the alteration of men on a mass scale is*
*necessary, an alteration which can only take place in a*
*practical movement, a revolution; this revolution is*
*necessary, therefore, not only because the ruling class*
*cannot be overthrown in any other way, but also be-*
*cause the class overthrowing it can only in a revolution*
*succeed in ridding itself of all the muck of the ages*
*and become fitted to found society anew.*

Karl Marx (1845)[1]

## IV.

## THE COSMOLOGY OF CHAOS

It is always a difficult task to deal with an individual like Karl
Marx, for a number of reasons. Not the least of these problems is
the fact that Marx was a synthesis figure: he was the inheritor of the
revolutionary Jacobin tradition of the French Revolution; he was of
major importance in his development of some of the ideas of classical
political economy; he was one of the founders of economic history,
sociology, and social science in general; and he was the most famous
of the radical left-wing followers of Hegel. Above all, he was the
co-founder (along with Frederich Engels) of "scientific socialism"
or Communism, a system of thought which undergirds, in theory at
least, the civil governments that rule over one-third of the world's
population.

---

[1] Marx and Engels, *The German Ideology* (1845) (London: Lawrence & Wishart, 1965), section on Feuerbach, 86.

In analyzing the Marxian system, it is necessary to look at the background of the philosophical problems that were of greatest concern to him. The central problem which has confronted social philosophers throughout history is the question of law and its relationship to changing conditions in man's universe. For countless centuries, men have attempted to locate permanent standards that can be shown to be both eternal and universally applicable to all human societies. If these laws can once be discovered and codified, they can be relied upon to regulate human society in an orderly and proper manner. The assumption lying behind this search is that mankind is essentially a unified species being, and that the basic human problems and solutions remain the same throughout history and across geographical boundaries. On the other hand, philosophers have also realized that the universe is in constant flux, and human activities do change as men cross over time or national and cultural boundaries. It has proven an impossible task to discover static, universal laws that are relevant for all times and places; theologians have proclaimed such standards, of course, but philosophers have not been able to locate them through the use of "neutral" reason. Cornelius Van Til, the Calvinist philosopher-theologian, has summarized this dilemma very well:

> On the assumptions of the natural man logic is a timeless impersonal principle, and facts are controlled by chance. It is by means of universal timeless principles of logic that the natural man must, on his assumptions, seek to make intelligible assertions about the world of reality or chance. But this cannot be done without falling into self-contradiction. About chance no manner of assertion can be made. In its very idea it is irrational. And how can rational assertions be made about the irrational? If they are to be made then it must be because the irrational is itself wholly reduced to the rational. That is to say if the natural man is to make any intelligible assertions about the world of "reality" or "fact" which, according to him is what it is for no rational reason at all, then he must make the virtual claim of rationalizing the irrational. To be able to distinguish one fact from another he must reduce all time existence, all factuality to immovable timeless being. But when he has done so he has killed all individuality and factuality as conceived of on his basis. Thus the natural man must on the one hand assert that all reality is non-structural

in nature and on the other hand assert that all reality is structural in nature. He must even assert on the one hand that all reality is non-structurable in nature and on the other hand that he himself has structured all of it. Thus all his predication is in the nature of the case self-contradictory.[2]

In Greek philosophy, the dualism between law and "brute factuality" appeared as the "form-matter" controversy (or the "appearance-reality" dualism). Externally existing forms (Ideas) were the basic reality in nature, and these metaphysical forms were to be used as the standards by which order could be imposed upon a recalcitrant fluctuating matter. These metaphysically existing forms were the philosophical corollaries of raw matter which was in total flux; absolutely static laws were to regulate a fluctuating matter which was ruled completely by chance. During the Middle Ages, the dilemma shifted somewhat; the dualism was seen as a conflict between nature and grace. Thomists and later scholastics (including post-Reformation Protestants) divided the reasoning faculty of man into two compartments: natural reason was said to be sufficient for an understanding of natural events, while revelation was needed to comprehend spiritual and supernatural phenomena. Greek philosophical categories were still the foundation of human reasoning in the "natural" sphere (and in practice, the "spiritual" or "grace" side as well was influenced by Greek thought). Finally, the modern form of dualism appeared, ushered in by the Renaissance: the "nature-freedom" division. Man finds himself in a universe which is bounded on the one side by total mystery; nature stands as an irrational force which opposes man, and it subdues man to the control of chance. The laws of nature are unknown, and therefore man faces what appears to be a wholly contingent environment. Yet in discovering the laws of nature, man not only reduces the operation of chance in nature, but he simultaneously reduces the possibilities of his own free action. Man is also a part of nature in the schema of modern philosophy; hence, by restricting the free (i.e., irrational) operations of nature, he must also give up his own freedom. If man is truly

---

[2] Cornelius Van Til, *The Defense of the Faith* (rev. ed.; Philadelphia: Presbyterian and Reformed Publishing Co., 1963), 126-27.

"one with nature" then the laws of nature and the laws of society are both a source of power for him and a threat to his freedom. The power which is granted to man by his knowledge of impersonal law simultaneously reduces man to a machine, a thing in bondage; freedom from bondage in this perspective therefore involves a retreat from law into lawless irrationality. In contrast to the Christian idea that man is free only when he is under divinely inspired and revealed law, the view of modern philosophy is that man can only be free when he is not operating under law.[3] But of course, without law there can be no power, no prediction, and no science.

Kant's contribution was in separating the realms of nature and freedom. As Dooyeweerd writes: "The nature motives were depreciated. The mathematical and mechanistic science-ideal was restricted to an empirical world of sensory phenomena ordered by transcendental logical categories of the human understanding. The autonomous freedom of man does not belong to the sensory realm of nature but to the supra-sensory realm of ethics, which is not ruled by natural laws, but by norms. As in Rousseau, the religious primacy was ascribed to the freedom-motive. But the central seat of human freedom was now sought in the moral aspect of the human will."[4] The basic dualism, however, was not resolved. A link had to be found to reunite the realm of personal ethical norms with the world of empirical reality.

After Kant's critical dualism, we see a new attempt to overcome the separation of the two realms. It was thought that they might be resolved together in the historical sphere, and it is here that we can

---

[3] For a survey of the whole issue of law and freedom in secular philosophy, see Herman Dooyeweerd, *In the Twilight of Western Thought* (Philadelphia: Presbyterian and Reformed, 1960). E. L. Hebden Taylor has provided a thorough treatment of this issue in his important study, *The Christian Philosophy of Law, Politics and the State* (Nutley, New Jersey: Craig Press, 1966), chs. 1-7. R. J. Rushdoony's forthcoming book, *The One and the Many* (Nutley, New Jersey: Craig Press, 1968), should also be consulted.

[4] Dooyeweerd, *In the Twilight of Western Thought,* 50-51. Cf. Isaiah Berlin, *Karl Marx: His Life and Environment* (3rd ed.; N. Y.: Oxford University Press, 1963), 40-53.

see the rise of a new movement, *historicism.* History itself supposedly carries with it its own laws of development, its own principles of interpretation; as historical circumstances change, the laws of history are altered, but in an orderly fashion. Thus man's freedom is re-asserted; he is no longer bound by eternal, fixed laws which bind him into some fixed pattern. Social science, in short, can escape the problem of necessity by redefining itself as an historical science.[5] Yet even in this perspective of historicism, man cannot claim to have regained his freedom, for within any period of time or in any geo-graphical setting, the laws of nature and the laws of society still control him. Within any instant of time, the laws are still total in their control. The fact that they are changing need not reduce their total character; because the laws may be relative between two instants of time does not reduce their absolute authority within each instant. Historicism does not offer an escape for man; it only subjects him to a radical relativism. All his standards are constantly changing through time; his reference points are always shifting. Man still faces the chaos of flux on the one hand and the despotic claims of absolute law on the other. Both claims are made on him simultaneously; they are philosophical corollaries of each other.

These philosophical questions are important, in spite of the fact that they appear to be quite nebulous. The discussions concerning the so-called "New Morality" revolve around this basic question of the permanence of ethical standards. The current "hippie" move-ment is vitally concerned with the whole problem of social norms, contemporary legal codes, and the effects which science has on the freedom of man. Recently, the leader of an underground hippie secret society in San Francisco, "the Psychedelic Rangers," granted an interview to a *Newsweek* reporter. The motto of the Rangers, he said, is this: "The psychedelic baby eats the cybernetic monster." By this, he explained, the group means that the modern LSD-drug culture will sweep over the technological civilization of the West. The crushing burden of bureaucratized, computerized life will be

---

[5] For a positivist's critique of historicism, see Karl R. Popper, *The Poverty of Historicism* (N. Y.: Harper Torchbook, 1961).

liberated by men and women seeking escape through the use of drugs, much as the citizen of Huxley's *Brave New World* used "soma." This hippie expects to have both internal freedom and the wealth provided by mass production: "That doesn't mean back to savagery. It doesn't mean we're going to tear down all the computer systems. It's only a question of the mind being tuned enough, so that it's involved in making things better. And this will result in a civilization that is super-beautiful. We're out to build an electric Tibet."[6] The best of all possible worlds: the mass production of the West and the mystical retreat of the East. Kant's dream is going to be fulfilled in a psychedelic America: there will be a unification of the realm of internal freedom and the cybernetic realm of science.

In the 19th century, the resolution of Kant's dualism was last attempted on a grand scale by the Prussian philosopher, G. W. F. Hegel. He created one of the most complex and total philosophical systems ever constructed.[7] In the same period, the science-ideal was reasserted by the new group known as the positivists, especially St. Simon and Comte. Herbert Marcuse has summarized the viewpoint of the positivist movement:

> The idealistic idea of reason, we recall, had been intrinsically connected with the idea of freedom and had opposed any notion of a natural necessity ruling over society. Positive philosophy tended instead to equate the study of society with the study of nature, so that natural science, particularly biology, became the archetype of social theory. Social study was to be a science seeking social laws, the validity of which was to be analogous to that of physical laws. Social practice, especially in the matter of changing the social system, was herewith throttled by the inexorable. Society was viewed as governed by rational laws that moved with a natural necessity. This position directly contradicted the view held by the dialectical social theory, that society is irrational precisely in that it is governed by natural laws. . . . The positivist repudiation of metaphysics was thus coupled with

---

[6] *Newsweek* (Feb. 6, 1967), 95.
[7] A standard introduction to Hegel's thought is W. T. Stace, *The Philosophy of Hegel* (N. Y.: Dover, 1955).

a repudiation of man's claim to alter and reorganize his social institutions in accordance with his rational will.[8]

It is in Marx's work that we find the next great attempt to unify the various strands of thought, and it is this attempted synthesis that establishes Marx as a major figure in 19th century intellectual history.

Before looking at Marx's system, however, it is necessary to consider briefly Hegel's contribution. He tried to unify the Kantian dualism of human freedom and mechanistic science into an overall philosophy of history. Flux was inserted into the law sphere, while historical factuality became infused with philosophical necessity. History, in Hegel's scheme, is dynamic, non-cyclical, linear; all historical facts are therefore unique. History is developing to a point at which there will be an ultimate reconciliation of the many (facts) with the unity of the one (the Absolute Mind). Unity and diversity will be transcended, and subjective knowledge and objective knowledge will become one supreme form of knowledge. Unfortunately, this will not happen in time, since the historical process is eternal.[9] The final resolution of this dualism serves as a backdrop — a limiting concept — for Hegel's view of history. History, in short, is the self-conscious development of the Spirit, and man is only a means in that development. Man is driven by "the cunning of history." True freedom for man, therefore, consists "in submitting to the inner necessities which are gradually working themselves out in social institutions and not in attempting to force matters in revolutionary action."[10]

The incredible subtleties of Hegel's triadic scheme of historical and logical development have baffled the best of philosophic minds. Some have gone so far as to deny that any "thesis-antithesis-synthesis"

[8] Herbert Marcuse, *Reason and Revolution: Hegel and the Rise of Social Theory* (Boston: Beacon Press, [1954] 1960), 343-44. For an important introduction to the positivists, see F. A. Hayek, *The Counter-Revolution of Science* (Glencoe, Ill.: Free Press, 1955).

[9] Isaiah Berlin, *Karl Marx*, 46-56.

[10] Sidney Hook, *From Hegel to Marx* (Ann Arbor: University of Michigan Press, [1950] 1962), 78.

formula exists in Hegel's system.[11] Others, taking a more moderate approach, admit that the triadic form of reasoning was present in the system, but that no simple generalization can be made about the way in which Hegel used it.[12] In any case, it is probably safe to say that Hegel saw the process of history as the reunification of the Spirit from its alienated condition; it is a dialectical process whereby historical-logical contradictions are overcome by discontinuous "leaps" or syntheses. Louis J. Halle has put it this way: "History, for Hegel, is the dialectical process by which God overcomes his alienation. Replace 'God' with 'Man' and this is what history is for Marx as well."[13]

The basic conservatism of both positivitism and Hegel's thought should be obvious. If history is inexorable, then it does no good to begin a revolutionary movement. In this sense, Comte and Hegel are united, as Hayek has argued:

> Their historical determinism — by which is meant, not merely that historical events are somehow determined, but that *we* are able to recognize why they are bound to take a particular course — necessarily implies a thorough fatalism: man cannot change the course of history. . . . There is no room for freedom in such a system: for Comte freedom is "the rational submission to the domination of natural laws," that is, of course, his natural laws of inevitable development; for Hegel it is the recognition of necessity.[14]

In both cases, men are determined by impersonal forces. Comte sees men controlled by impersonal laws; Hegel sees men controlled by an impersonal, alienated Spirit. Both are opposed to the traditional Augustinian perspective of a world controlled by a *personal* God in whose image man is made. Inherent in both Hegelianism

---

[11] Gustav E. Mueller, "The Hegel Legend of 'Thesis-Antithesis-Synthesis'," *Journal of the History of Ideas,* XIX (1958), 411-14.

[12] J. N. Findlay, *Hegel: A Re-examination* (N. Y.: Collier, 1962), 69-71.

[13] Louis J. Halle, "Marx's Religious Drama," *Encounter,* XXV (October, 1965), 30. This is a very useful introduction to Marx's early thought.

[14] Hayek, *The Counter-Revolution of Science,* 200.

and positivism, however, is a basic possibility of radicalism. If laws can be known by men, then perhaps men can use their knowledge to reorder the world. If the universe does not belong to a personal God who orders it according to His plan and who will bring all things to pass, then man must try to gain control if he is to keep from perishing. The radical side of Hegelian determinism was to become manifest in the 1840's.

Two schools emerged after Hegel's death in the 1830's. One side emphasized the conservative elements of Hegel's system. Taking as their starting point Hegel's dictum that "whatever is real is rational," they argued that the Prussian state was the high point of history at that time (as Hegel himself had argued), and that a revolution would be philosophically unjustified. In contrast to this group were those known as the "left Hegelians" — Bruno Bauer, D. F. Strauss, Arnold Ruge, Ludwig Feuerbach, and Marx — who put stress on the revolutionary implications of the second half of Hegel's statement, "whatever is rational is real." They argued that the irrational, petty, inefficient, and coercive nature of the Prussian state disqualified it as being rational, and therefore its reality was ephemeral. Prussian rule must be criticized unmercifully, and ultimately, Marx concluded, it should be overthrown in favor of a new and rational social environment.

D. F. Strauss launched the intellectual "revolt" with the publication, in 1835, of his *Life of Jesus*. In it he criticized the New Testament documents from the standpoint of a rationalistic historical analysis. The tools of "higher criticism," he argued, demonstrated that the Gospels were filled with many myths which could not be connected with definite historical events. These myths were important as symbols of certain religious truths, but they were not to be considered as history. Strauss did not reject Christianity as a religion, or so he claimed; he "only" asserted that the historic teachings of the faith in regard to the Bible's infallibility were not legitimate in the light of historical investigation.[15]

Bruno Bauer was not willing to let the matter rest at this point.

---

[15] For details concerning Strauss and the other Young Hegelians, see Sidney Hook's *From Hegel to Marx*.

He argued that the Bible was totally false, and that it would be foolish for a thinking man to take it seriously. Religion, in Bauer's view, was nothing more than superstition; it should be replaced by rational thought. Strauss was trying to liberalize Christianity, and not to destroy it (or so Strauss claimed); Bauer was setting forth atheism. As Hook describes the situation, "Strauss' attack cost him at most an academic post. Bauer's works were matters for the police."[16]

Nevertheless, Bauer did not go far enough to satisfy the young radicals of Germany. Feuerbach took Bauer's basic position on the nature of religion and converted it into materialism. He concluded that religion is merely the product of the social needs of mankind. Men project their hopes and values into the void, and they call this projection "God." In his crucial study, *The Essence of Christianity* (1841), he wrote: "The personality of God is thus the means by which man converts the qualities of his own nature into the qualities of another being — of a being external to himself. The personality of God is nothing else than the projected personality of man."[17] In a certain sense, Feuerbach did put his finger on the essence of Christianity. He saw a distinction between faith and love; love united mankind, and this, for Feuerbach, is the very essence of religion. Faith, however, divides men, precisely because it divides men from God: "The essence of religion, its latent nature, is the *identity* of the divine being with the human; but the form of religion, or its apparent, conscious nature, is the *distinction* between them. God is the human being; but he presents himself to the religious consciousness as a distinct being."[18] This, for the humanist, is the unforgivable sin: the Christian denies that man is God, and as a direct result of this blasphemy, the Christian begins to make distinctions between those who believe in God and those who do not: "To believe, is synonymous with goodness; not to believe, with wickedness. Faith, narrow and prejudiced refers all unbelief to the moral disposition.

---

[16] *Ibid.*, 93.
[17] Ludwig Feuerbach, *The Essence of Christianity*, translated by George Eliot (N. Y.: Harper Torchbook, 1957), 226.
[18] *Ibid.*, 247.

In its view the unbeliever is an enemy to Christ out of obduracy, out of wickedness. Hence faith has fellowship with believers only; unbelievers it rejects. It is well-disposed towards believers, but ill-disposed towards unbelievers. *In faith there lies a malignant principle.*"[19]

It was Feuerbach's contention that prior to Christianity, men had a conception of the species as a whole, but that Christianity destroyed this conception of a united humanity. Historically, he was on shaky ground; the distinction which the Greeks drew between Greeks and Barbarians (all those who did not speak Greek) seems to testify to the incapacity of men to consider themselves as a unified whole. Still, his basic point is correct; Christianity in its orthodox form has a vision of a divided humanity: men are either saved or lost, and the distinction is permanent throughout eternity. Thus, as a humanist, Feuerbach was far more consistent than Hegel or Strauss. Hegel originally hoped to defend religion (though not Christian orthodoxy) by means of his philosophical speculations. Feuerbach took Hegel's presuppositions and extended them into a position of radical materialism. In 1850, he went so far as to claim that man is what he eats, but this "vulgar" materialism never had any influence on Marx.

Feuerbach's vision of alienated humanity — alienated because of the perversity of religious beliefs which divide mankind — combined with his materialism to cause a metamorphosis in the minds of the Young Hegelians. Years later, Engels described the impact of his ideas:

> Then came Feuerbach's *Essence of Christianity*. With one blow it pulverized the contradiction, in that without circumlocutions it placed materialism on the throne again. Nature exists independently of all philosophy. It is the foundation upon which we human beings, ourselves the products of nature, have grown up. Nothing exists outside nature and man, and the higher beings our religious fantasies have created are only the fantastic reflection of our own essence. The spell was broken; the "system" was exploded and cast aside, and the contradiction [between nature and the Abso-

---

[19] *Ibid.,* 252.

lute Idea in Hegel's system], shown to exist only in our imagination, was dissolved. One must himself have experienced the liberating effect of this book to get an idea of it. Enthusiasm was general; we all became at once Feuerbachians.[20]

Feuerbachian humanism was to be taken one step farther by Marx and Engels. Religion, Marx saw, was not merely to be criticized with the tools of logic and historical methodology. Religion, said Feuerbach, was merely a factor in life which pointed to man as a species. Man had alienated himself by projecting his ideals into the void, Feuerbach had argued. But why had man done this? Obviously, concluded Marx, because of the alienated social conditions that made up man's environment. Feuerbach, however, offered no solution to man's alienation, since he expected men to escape their alienation merely by adopting a religion of humanistic love for humanity. This was not a solution, Marx believed, since it did not get to the root of the problem; man's oppressive social conditions gave rise to such fantasies, so one must deal with man's environment in order to remove the bases of the religious illusions. Feuerbach's materialism was faulty; it conceived of man as a plastic, observing creature, totally subject to the material reality about him. Marx rejected it in his famous theses on Feuerbach (1845), and in the 11th thesis, he summarized his position: "The philosophers have only *interpreted* the world, in various ways; the point, however, is to *change* it."[21] Marx was to devote the remainder of his life to this twofold task: interpreting the world; and organizing, explaining, and prophesying the revolution which would change it.

---

[20] Frederick Engels, *Ludwig Feuerbach and the End of Classical German Philosophy,* in *Marx-Engels Selected Works* (Moscow: Foreign Languages Publishing House, 1962), II, 367-68. On the impact of Hegelian Transcendentalism and theological Unitarianism in the United States, see the essay, "The Religion of Humanity," in R. J. Rushdoony, *The Nature of the American System* (Nutley, New Jersey: Craig Press, 1965).

[21] Marx, "Theses on Feuerbach," in *Marx-Engels Selected Works,* II, 405. Hook includes a detailed study of the Theses in *From Hegel to Marx,* ch. 8. Also, see S. Diamond, "Marx's 'First Thesis' on Feuerbach," *Science and Society,* I (1937), 539-45.

Marx, in 1842, was not yet a communist, as we have seen earlier. In 1843, Moses Hess converted him to the communist ethic, and he was never to depart from this faith in the next four decades of his life. In the posthumously published writings of this early period in his career, we can see the rough outlines of the themes that were to characterize all of his life's work. However he may have modified this original framework, he was never to abandon its basic premises.

Our chief sources of information for the "early Marx" (age 25-27) are the *Economic and Philosophic Manuscripts of 1844,* unpublished until 1927 and translated into English (apart from a 1949 mimeographed version circulated within a small group of American Marxists) only in the last decade. When these manuscripts are read along with the first writings which he and Engels worked on, *The Holy Family* (1845) and *The German Ideology* (1845-46), they present a picture of Marx which, with only a few notable exceptions, had not been recognized by most modern scholars until very recently.[22]

In the deluge of scholarly articles and books which has been produced as a result of the "discovery" of these 1844 notebooks, one fact has become clear: Karl Marx was a radical humanist in the tradition of the Enlightenment and the French Revolution.[23] Human-

---

[22] For translations of the more important fragments of these writings, see T. B. Bottomore and M. Rubel, *Karl Marx: Selected Writings in Sociology and Social Philosophy* (N. Y.: McGraw-Hill, 1964). In addition to this collection, Bottomore has also edited a complete set of the *Economic and Philosophic Manuscripts of* 1844, along with the essays published in 1844 in the *Deutsch-Französische Jahrbücher:* Bottomore (ed.), *Karl Marx: Early Writings* (N. Y.: McGraw-Hill, 1964). I am using the Milligan translation of the EPM 1844, edited by Dirk J. Struik (N. Y.: International Publishers, 1964).

[23] There has been a virtual Renaissance in Marxian studies due to the publication in English of these early manuscripts. On the question of alienation, see the bibliography included in *Marxism and Alienation: A Symposium* [Marxist] (N. Y.: Humanities Press, 1965). Some of the useful studies of the early Marx are: Erich Fromm, *Marx's Concept of Man* (N. Y.: Ungar, 1961), in which Marx is presented as an early existentialist. In opposition to this

ism can mean many things to different people, but Marx spelled out his humanism in no uncertain terms: "The criticism of religion ends with the doctrine that *man is the supreme being for man*. It ends, therefore, with the *categorical imperative to overthrow all those conditions* in which man is an abased, enslaved, abandoned, and contemptible being. . . ."[24]

This revolutionary impulse is visible throughout his writings, and it characterizes his humanistic perspective. Man is his own highest good; man is therefore his own "ultimate concern," to use Tillich's phrase — his own God. As such, man must be as creative as God, and therefore he must purge his universe of all that is inhuman, and therefore evil and irrational. Man's universe must give glory to its creator, man, and it cannot be permitted to reflect anything that is not humane. Man, in short, is to be the standard of evaluation for all things, including himself. Engels later summarized this goal as the creation of a world in which "man no longer merely proposes, but also disposes," thus claiming as man's right that which the Bible limits to God: "A man's heart deviseth his way: but the Lord directeth his steps" (Prov. 16:9).[25]

---

view are Bartlett and Shodell, "Fromm, Marx and the Concept of Alienation," *Science and Society,* XXVII (1963), who stress Marx's concept of revolutionary action. Loyd D. Easton, "Alienation and History in the Early Marx," *Philosophy and Phenemonological Research,* XXII (1961); Mihailo Markovic, "Marxist Humanism and Ethics," *Science and Society,* XXVII (1963); Donald Clark Hodges, "The Unity of Marx's Thought," *Science and Society,* XXVIII (1964); Daniel Bell, *The End of Ideology* (N. Y.: Free Press, 1962), ch. 15; Donald Clark Hodges, "Marx's Contribution to Humanism," *Science and Society,* XXIX (1965); Erich Fromm (ed.), *Socialist Humanism* (Garden City, N. Y.: Doubleday Anchor, 1966).

[24] Marx, "Contribution to the Critique of Hegel's Philosophy of Right," (1844), in Bottomore (ed), *Karl Marx: Early Writings,* 52. In all cases throughout this study, the italics are Marx's, not mine. In his early studies, Marx was especially liberal in his use of underlining as a means of emphasis.

[25] Frederich Engels, *Herr Eugen Dühring's Revolution in Science* [*Anti-Duhring*] (London: Lawrence and Wishart, 1934), 348. This

In an important chapter on "Socialist Humanism," the Marxist philosopher Maurice Cornforth has defined Marxist humanism, and it indicates the totality of the commitment to man (in opposition to God) in Marxist thought:

> Humanism takes the view which Plato objected to so strongly when it was first put forward by Protagoras, that "man is the measure of all things." Everything else is to be judged in accordance with how it affects men and can be used by men. Everything men do is to be done for the sake of men and to be judged by its effects on men. Men were not created to serve God, but their purpose is to make other things serve men.[26]

### Creation

Marx's humanistic theology necessarily excludes the Christian conception of creation, one of the fundamental pillars of the Christian philosophy of history.[27] Man must be his own creator in the Marxist framework, and Marx made this quite clear: "A *being* only considers himself independent when he stands on his own feet; and he only stands on his own feet when he owes his *existence* to himself. A man who lives by the grace of another regards himself as a dependent being."[28] Marx understood perfectly the implications of the Christian conception of creation and the necessity of divine grace as a sustaining power in the universe; he understood it and rejected it:

> But I live completely by the grace of another if I owe him not only the maintenance of my life, but if he has, moreover, *created* my *life* — if he is the *source* of my life. When it is not of my own creation, my life has necessarily a source of this kind outside of it. The *Creation* is therefore an idea very difficult to dislodge from the popular consciousness. The fact that nature and man

was published originally in 1877-78 in *Vörwarts,* a German radical publication.

[26] Maurice Cornforth, *Marxism and the Linguistic Philosophy* (N. Y.: International Publishers, 1965), 303.

[27] Cf. R. J. Rushdoony, *The Biblical Philosophy of History,* a forthcoming book to be published by Craig Press, Nutley, New Jersey.

[28] Essay on "Private Property and Communism," in *Economic and Philosophical Manuscripts of 1844* (N. Y.: International Publishers, 1964), 144 [cited hereafter as EPM].

exist in their own account is *incomprehensible* to it, because it contradicts everything *tangible* in practical life.[29]

Man cannot even ask where the first man came from, in much the same way that the Christian philosopher cannot question the fact that God created the universe. To question one's philosophical presuppositions is self-contradictory; neither Marx nor the consistent Christian thinker can do this. One cannot challenge one's god, and man is Marx's god: "Who begot the first man, and nature as a whole? I can only answer you: Your question is itself a product of abstraction."[30] In the passage following this last section, Marx set forth some incredibly obscure arguments which were to show that the whole issue of human origin is illegitimate. Then he made this point:

Since, however, for socialist man, the *whole of what is called world history* is nothing but the creation of man by human labour, and the emergence of nature for man, he, therefore, has the evident and irrefutable proof of his *self-creation,* of his own *origins* . . . the quest for an *alien* being, a being above man and nature (a quest which is an avowal of the unreality of man and nature) becomes impossible in practice. *Atheism,* as a denial of this unreality, is no longer meaningful, for atheism is a *negation of God* and seeks to assert by this negation the *existence of man.* Socialism no longer requires such a roundabout method; it begins from the *theoretical* and *practical sense perception* of man and nature as essential beings.[31]

Socialist man does not even need to assert his own being by denying God; he just ignores God from the start. One stands on one's own two feet; how the feet got there, or how the foundation upon which the feet are resting got there, one never bothers to ask. In fact, one should not ask it; the question is a product of abstraction. One who has been forced to read the fantastically abstract discussions

---

[29] *Ibid.*

[30] *Ibid.,* 145.

[31] Here I am using the Bottomore translation of EPM, *Karl Marx: Early Writings,* 166-67. The passage appears in the Struik edition, 145.

found throughout Marx's writings can only wonder why, at this particular point, Marx shied away from abstract thinking.

Karl Marx always prided himself on remaining on "neutral" ground philosophically. He always asserted that he was rigorously empirical and scientific. As he wrote in *The German Ideology* (1845-46): "The premises from which we begin are not arbitrary ones, not dogmas, but real premises from which abstraction can be made in the imagination. . . . These premises can thus be verified in a purely empirical way."[32] Socialism begins, however, with the presupposition that God's existence is not a valid philosophical issue; if He did exist then man and nature could not exist, since they would owe their origin to God, and *by definition* man and nature are *autonomous!* Marx always began with empirical premises only in the sense that he assumed, *a priori,* that all concrete, visible phenomena are self-sustaining, self-creative, and totally autonomous.

The doctrine of creation is central to all philosophical systems, and Marxism is no exception. Marx's whole perspective was based upon the idea that *human creative activity* is the ultimate foundation of all social existence. This is one of the central themes in Marxism, and it can be found in the theoretical volumes of *Capital* just as easily as it can be gleaned from his earlier writings, although perhaps not in such a blatant fashion. *Production* is the sphere of human existence from which all other temporal spheres are viewed; in this sense, it is the Marxist's intellectual "Archimedean point." Again and again, Marx returned to the production theme: "As individuals express their life, so they are. What they are, therefore, coincides with their production, both with *what* they produce and with *how* they produce."[33] If this is true, then his materialistic conception of history has its theoretical justification: "The nature of individuals thus depends upon the material conditions determining their pro-

---

[32] Marx and Engels, *The German Ideology* (London: Lawrence and Wishart, 1965), 31. These manuscripts were not published in the authors' lifetimes.
[33] *Ibid.,* 32.

duction."[34] Human labor, in fact, actually defines mankind as a species:

> Indeed, labor, *life-activity, productive life* itself, appears in the first place merely as a *means* of satisfying a need — the need to maintain physical existence. Yet the productive life is the life of the species. It is life-engendering life. The whole character of a species — its species character — is contained in the character of its life activity; and free, conscious activity is man's species character. . . . The animal is immediately one with its life activity. It is *its life activity*. Man makes his life activity itself the object of his will and of his consciousness. He has conscious life activity. . . . Conscious life activity distinguishes man from animal life activity.[35]

In this perspective, the whole of man's existence is interpreted as a part of this single sphere, *production:* "Religion, family, state, law, morality, science, art, etc., are only *particular* modes of production, and fall under its general law."[36] Meyer has pinpointed the source of this element of Marx's thought: "Marx has appropriated for his system a Promethean image of man the creator, man the provider, man the tamer of his environment. He has identified himself with a glorification of material achievements which, before him, had been an essential part of revolutionary liberalism, part of the ideology of the rising bourgeoisie."[37] Marx, in spite of his emotional attacks against bourgeois ideals, could not escape the influence of the presuppositions of the Enlightenment.[38]

---

[34] *Ibid.*

[35] "Estranged Labor," EPM, 113.

[36] "Private Property and Communism," EPM, 136.

[37] Alfred G. Meyer, *Marxism: The Unity of Theory and Practice* (Ann Arbor: University of Michigan Press, 1954), 75. Cf. Veljko Korac, "In Search of Human Society," In Erich Fromm (ed.), *Socialist Humanism* (Garden City, N. Y.: Doubleday Anchor, 1966), 3.

[38] Donald Clark Hodges has attempted to sever Marx's thought from the Enlightenment, but his arguments are not very convincing. See his essay, "The Unity of Marx's Thought," *Science and Society,* XXVIII (1964). For Marx's attacks on the ideals and institutions

In contrast to Hegel, who conceived of human alienation as a spiritual-intellectual problem, Marx saw it as a social and productivity phenomenon. It is human material labor, not intellectual labor, which is alienated, and the cure for the problem should not be sought in the realm of thought.[39] Marx absolutized the sphere of human labor, and it is not surprising that he should have found the solution to the alienation question in that same sphere.

## Alienation

With this framework of humanism supporting his thinking, Marx's revolt against the society in which he found himself is easy to understand. Industrialization was transforming a rural civilization into an urbanized society, and the transition was not an easy one. While the horrors of the so-called Industrial Revolution have undoubtedly been overemphasized, there was naturally a great deal of personal and social strain involved in the process of urbanization. Men who have worked as farmers all their lives, for example, find it difficult to adjust to the production methods of the factory system.[40] The religious rootlessness of urban life as compared with rural traditional culture is another familiar theme, and need not be reviewed here. Marx realized the impact which urban life would have on the conservative tendencies of a formerly agricultural Europe, and he welcomed the transition: "The bourgeoisie has subjected the country to the rule of the towns. It has created enormous cities, has greatly

---

of bourgeois life, see section II of *The Communist Manifesto,* in *Marx-Engels Selected Works,* I, 48-51. Also, see his essay, "On the Jewish Question," which is far more hostile to bourgeois life as such (especially money) than it is critical of Jews as such. It was written in 1843 and published in 1844; reprinted in Bottomore (ed.), *Karl Marx: Early Writings.*

[39] For a comparison of the alienation concept as held by Hegel and the Marxian concept (plus related topics), see Herbert Marcuse, *Reason and Revolution: Hegel and the Rise of Social Theory.* Cf. Fritz Pappenheim, *The Alienation of Modern Man* (N. Y.: Monthly Review Press, 1959), 83-84.

[40] Cf. Sidney Pollard, "Factory Discipline in the Industrial Revolution," *Economic History Review,* Second Series, XVI (1963), 254-71.

increased the urban population as compared with the rural, and has rescued a considerable part of the population from the idiocy of rural life."[41]  What disturbed Marx was the dehumanizing nature of industrial production, which he identified exclusively with capitalistic, privately owned production. Thus, he and Engels were able to spend hours going through Parliamentary reports and other documents in their search for appropriate "horror stories" about urban life under the rule of the capitalists. This tradition was carried on successfully by the Fabian socialists in England during our century, a fact which might have bothered (or perhaps even amused) Marx; that such bourgeois reformers as the Fabians should have carried on his intellectual labors would never have occurred to him.[42]

The alienation theme appears more often in his earlier writings than in the later ones, although it never disappears entirely in the so-called "mature Marx." For this reason, modern scholars have become fascinated with these early manuscripts. The alienation which they see in the modern world has focused their attention on Marx's handling of the subject. As one commentator has put it: "Surely the outstanding characteristic of contemporary thought on man and society is the preoccupation with personal alienation and

---

[41] Marx, *Communist Manifesto* (1848), in *Marx-Engels Selected Works,* I, 38.

[42] The literature on the "Industrial Revolution" is voluminous. Marx's chapters in *Capital,* vol. I, 10, 15, 25, and Engels's *The Condition of the Working Class in England in 1844* (1845) were very early examples of the "horror story" approach. Conservative thinkers also looked nostalgically back to rural life and its control by the landed aristocrats, and they concluded that industrialism is a curse. As Nisbet has pointed out, "This is why the indictment of capitalism that comes from the conservatives in the nineteenth century is often more severe than that of the socialists." *The Sociological Tradition* (N. Y.: Basic Books, 1966), 26. Fabian writers, especially J. L. and Barbara Hammond, produced semi-popular books describing the "intolerable" conditions of the period. Paul Mantoux's *The Industrial Revolution in the Eighteenth Century* (English translation, 1928) is probably the best of these studies. They tend to de-emphasize such factors as: (1) the lack of capital and savings in the period; (2) the tremendous impact of the population explosion in these centuries, which lowered

cultural disintegration."[43] In the mid-19th century, it was Marx's preoccupation with revolution which fascinated those people who happened to encounter his writings; in the 1880's, his economics interested the scholars; in the 1940's and 1950's, his political philosophy was the important issue. Today, it is unquestionably the alienation theme, possibly because so many of today's scholars feel themselves to be totally alienated from contemporary culture.

In brief, the thesis of this study is quite simple: *Marx's concept of human alienation was used by him as a substitute for the Christian doctrine of the fall of man.* He used the idea in at least two different ways: first, to show the "externalization" of one's life (through the sale of one's labor power); second, in the sense of social estrangement, or the detaching of oneself from other men (interpersonal alienation).[44]

What is the source of man's alienation? This is the most important question which can be raised in regard to Marx's entire philosophy of human history; it was of crucial importance in the development of the original Marxist system. In the one (and the

---

*per capita* income throughout Western Europe (especially in those areas in which no industrialization occurred); and (3) the misallocation of scarce resources caused by state regulations and prohibitions on private industry. See F. A. Hayek (ed.), *Capitalism and the Historians* (University of Chicago Press, 1954), for alternative views of the industrialization of Europe. Also see T. S. Ashton, *The Industrial Revolution* (N. Y.: Oxford University Press, 1964); R. M. Hartwell, "The Rising Standard of Living in England, 1800-1850," *Economic History Review,* Second Series, XIII (1961); John U. Nef, "The Industrial Revolution Reconsidered," *Journal of Economic History,* III (1943); Herbert Heaton, *Economic History of Europe* (rev. ed.; N. Y.: Harper & Row, 1948), chs. 21-24.

[43] Robert A. Nisbet, *Community and Power* (N. Y.: Oxford Galaxy, 1962), 3.

[44] I am here relying upon the helpful suggestion made by Daniel Bell, "The 'Rediscovery' of Alienation," *Journal of Philosophy,* LVI (1959), 933n. Sidney Hook finds at least four definitions: "Marxism in the Western World: From 'Scientific Socialism' to Mythology," in Milorad Drachkovitch (ed.), *Marxist Ideology in the Contemporary World — Its Appeals and Paradoxes* (N. Y.: Praeger, 1966), 19-25.

only) section dealing with the ultimate source of human alienation, Marx refused to explain it in terms of his economic materialism, as one might suppose. Private property did not cause alienated human labor; in fact, the very reverse is true:

> Thus, through alienated labour the worker creates the relation of another man, who does not work and is outside the work process, to this labour. The relation of the worker to work also produces the relation of the capitalist (or whatever one likes to call the lord of labour) to work. *Private property* is, therefore, the product, the necessary result, of alienated labour, of the external relation of the worker to nature and to himself. *Private property* is thus derived from the analysis of the concept of *alienated labour;* that is, alienated man, alienated labour, alienated life, and estranged man.[45]

In order to make his position absolutely clear, he added:

> We have, of course, derived from the concept of *alienated labour (alienated life)* from political economy, from an analysis of the *movement of private property.* But the analysis of this concept shows that although private property appears to be the basis and cause of alienated labour, it is rather a consequence of the latter, just as the gods are *fundamentally* not the cause but the product of confusions of human reason. At a later stage, however, there is a reciprocal influence.[46]

Private property, in other words, was not the cause of man's alienation; originally, man's alienation caused the establishment of private property. Marx never again mentioned the original cause of man's alienated condition, so we must rely on this early essay for our knowledge of his thoughts on the ultimate source of man's plight.

Once private property is seen as a *result* of alienated production, one of the central flaws in Marx's system is revealed. If the original cause is psychological rather than economic, then there is no guarantee that the coming revolution will permanently wipe out alienation merely because it destroys private property. If the "fall into sin" of

---

[45] Bottomore translation, "Alienated [Estranged] Labour," EPM, in *Karl Marx: Early Writings,* 131. In the Struik edition, 116-17.
[46] *Ibid.*

man is psychological, then how can the "salvation" of man be assured by a social revolution? This whole issue will be discussed in detail in relation to Marx's linear concept of history.

Under a system of alienated production, Marx argued, man discovers that his very life forces are being robbed from him. The source of his immediate difficulty is the existence of the *division of labor*. The division of labor is the essence of all that is wrong with man's present condition; for Marx, it is contrary to man's existence as a fully creative being. It pits man against his fellow man; it creates class divisions; it destroys the unity of the species. That Marx should oppose the division of labor with such vehemence is not too surprising. Mankind, in the Marxian perspective, is God; theologically, one cannot permit the Godhead to be divided. In his treatment of French Revolutionary thought, Rushdoony elaborates on this question:

> Tenth, humanity is the true god of the Enlightenment and of French Revolutionary thought. In all religious faiths one of the inevitable requirements of logical thought asserts itself in a demand for *the unity of the godhead*. Hence, since humanity is god, there can be no division in this godhead, humanity. Mankind must therefore be forced to unite. Since Enlightenment philosophy was monistic, this means an intolerance of differences as unessential. National and racial differences, instead of being God-given and possessing richness and dignity to be respected, are to be obliterated. The goal is not communion but uniformity.[47]

Following an analysis remarkably similar to Rousseau's, Marx argued that the division of labor gave rise to social classes; therefore, to eliminate these economic classes — themselves an outward manifestation of man's alienated condition — mankind must abolish the division of labor.[48] Anything that leads to divisions in mankind's unity must be eliminated, by definition.

---

[47] R. J. Rushdoony, *This Independent Republic* (Nutley, New Jersey: Craig Press, 1964), 142.
[48] Jean Jacques Rousseau, *Discourse on the Origin of Inequality,* in G. D. H. Cole (ed.), *The Social Contract and Discourses* (London: Dent, 1966), esp. 195-208. Cf. Robert A. Nisbet, "Rousseau and Totalitarianism," *Journal of Politics,* V (1943), 93-114.

One of Marx's diatribes against the division of labor is found in volume I of *Capital:* "Some crippling of body and mind is inseparable even from division of labour in society as a whole. Since, however, manufacture carries this social separation of branches of labour much further, and also, by its peculiar division, attacks the individual at the very roots of his life, it is the first to afford the materials for, and to give a start to, industrial pathology."[49] Admittedly, industrial activity has sometimes led to such "pathology" — a pathology which is usually accompanied by falling productivity and declining profits, although Marx ignored this fact. In contrast to this Enlightenment view of the division of labor stands the traditional Christian view of man and society. The Christian perspective reverses the Marxian outlook. Men have individual callings precisely because the fall of man has resulted in human depravity; the curse on the earth has limited its productivity drastically, making necessary a social order based upon the specialization of labor. Such specialization is required if productivity is to be increased; if men wish to have more material goods and greater personal services, they must choose callings in which they can become efficient producers. The Christian concept of the calling supports social harmony; the division of labor forces men to restrain their hostilities against each other if they wish to increase their material wealth. In this perspective, the division of labor is an aid to social unity. In the Christian view, as in the very early Marxian, social alienation and social conflict stem from within man himself (Jas. 4:1); given this fact, the division of labor can be seen as a blessing rather than a burden. Without it, men would destroy themselves with even greater ferocity than they have previously demonstrated. Scarcity, which has its origin in the curse of the ground (Gen. 3:17-19), makes social collaboration a necessity. In short, the cause of economic scarcity is not in "deformed human institutions" as all socialists have always claimed; it is basic to the human condition.[50] While this does not sanction total specialization

---

[49] Marx, *Capital* (Chicago: Kerr & Co., 1906), 399. This edition has been reproduced exactly and is available as a Modern Library book.
[50] For a classical liberal's similar treatment of this subject, see Lud-

of production (since man, in the Christian framework, is more than a machine), it does demand that the division of labor be accepted as a positive social benefit.[51]

Marx, however, was utterly hostile to the Christian idea of the calling: "In a communist society there are no painters but at most people who engage in painting among other activities."[52] The division of labor is personified for Marx in the distinction between mental and physical labor: "Division of labor only becomes such from the moment when a division of material and mental labor appears."[53] Since private property and human alienation are reciprocal, we find that the division of labor and private property are also reciprocal: "Division of labor and private property are, however, identical expressions. . . ."[54] Human alienation, private property, and the division of labor are all aspects of the same detestable condition of man in capitalist society.[55]

Man, under capitalism, has become a mere commodity: *"The demand for men necessarily governs the production of men, as of every other commodity. . . .* The worker has become a commodity, and it is a bit of luck for him if he can find a buyer."[56] Marx saw what a totally secularized, urbanized, and "rationalized" capitalist productive system was doing to those workers who labored under it. Instead of blaming the rootless secularism which was dehumanizing the culture of the 19th century, he blamed capitalism's division of labor. This is precisely what one might expect; Marx, like so many

---

wig von Mises, *Socialism* (New Haven, Conn.: Yale University Press, 1951), 60-62.

[51] One of the most profound descriptions of the division of labor is found in St. Paul's first epistle to the Corinthians, chapter 12. In it, he describes the distribution of spiritual gifts to the Christian church in terms of a body: there are hands and feet, eyes and ears, and each has its special function.

[52] *The German Ideology,* 432.

[53] *Ibid.,* 43.

[54] *Ibid.,* 44.

[55] "Meaning of Human Requirements," EPM, 159.

[56] "Wages of Labor," EPM, 65.

secular philosophers, divinized one aspect of the social order: production. Every aspect of man's life was viewed by Marx from this one perspective. "As individuals express their life, so they are," he wrote.[57] Man therefore expresses his very being in his own productive activity. Under capitalism, however, the products of his labor do not belong to him, but to another man, the capitalist. This is the source of man's alienation. He concluded, "as the result, therefore, of the fact that more and more of his products are being taken away from the worker, that to an increasing extent his own labor confronts him as another man's property. . . ."[58] Estranged labor turns the products of his own hands into alien, hostile creations that stand in opposition to him; it tears him from his very species life. It finally results in an estrangement between man and man.[59] While the emphasis on the separation between men did not occur very often in Marx's subsequent writings, the idea that man's labor actually confronted him as an alien force appeared in the later volumes of *Capital*.[60] A laborer is like a complex machine which is slowly wearing out; the profits of the capitalist stem from the *exploitation* (not a very neutral term for a professing "scientist") of his employees' life forces. Under alienated production, a peculiar phenomenon occurs, according to Marx: the more material wealth society produces, the more inhuman it becomes, and the less of one's own life can a person possess. "The less you *are,* the less you express your own life, the greater is your alienated life, the more you have,

---

[57] *The German Ideology,* 32.
[58] "Wages of Labor," EPM, 67.
[59] "Estranged Labor," EPM, 114.
[60] *Capital,* I, 339, 384, 396-97, 462, 625. *Capital* (Chicago: Charles H. Kerr Co., 1909), III, 102, 310, 948. Moscow's Foreign Languages Publishing House has published an inexpensive three volume set of *Capital,* and recently another edition has been issued by International Publishers in New York City. I am using the older Kerr edition throughout, however, since most libraries have this set if they have any at all.

58

the greater is the store of your estranged being."[61] All mankind is being dehumanized under capitalism, including the capitalist:

> Estrangement is manifested not only in the fact that *my* means of life belong to *someone else,* that *my* desire is the inaccessible possession of *another,* but also in the fact that everything is itself something *different* from itself — that my activity is *something else* and that, finally (and this applies also to the capitalist), all is under the sway of an inhuman power.[62]

Here we see one aspect of the inevitable problem of the nature-freedom problem. Man's own creation, which he had hoped would free him from an irrational nature governed by scarcity, now turns upon him and becomes his master, "an inhuman power." Rather than putting the responsibility for this where Dooyeweerd has shown that it belongs — in the antinomies of all secular thought and the societal relations that are based upon it — Marx proclaimed that capitalist relations of production are the sole cause of man's problem. Industrial production, in short, is the expression of alienated mankind in general:

> We see how the history of *industry* and the established *objective* existence of industry are the *open book* of *man's essential powers,* the exposure to the senses of human *psychology.* . . . We have before us the *objectified essential powers* of man in the form of *sensuous, alien, useful objects,* in the form of estrangement, displayed on *ordinary material industry.* . . .[63]

Some reputable scholars have argued that the alienation theme, while important to Marx as a young man, did not really play a very large part in his mature writings. Yet in the posthumously published volume three of *Capital,* we find the same idea expressed in even clearer and more forceful language: "Capital becomes a strange, independent, social power, which stands opposed to society as a thing, and as the power of capitalists by means of this thing."[64] The worker is forced to create an alien force which stands above him:

---

[61] "Meaning of Human Requirements," EPM, 150.
[62] *Ibid.,* 156.
[63] "Private Property and Communism," EPM, 142.
[64] *Capital,* III, 310.

". . . the combination of the labor of a certain individual laborer with that of other laborers for a common purpose, stands opposed to that laborer and his comrades as a foreign power, as the property of a stranger which he would not care particularly to save if he were not compelled to economize with it. It is entirely different in the factories owned by the laborers themselves, for instance, in Rochdale."[65] Capitalistic private ownership, and not industrialism as such, is the culprit in the Marxist system.

Thus, the ultimate hope of mankind lies in the possibility of man's being able to overcome the evils of alienated production. The triumph of mankind will therefore involve the abolition of private property and the abolition of the division of labor. In one of the most utopian passages in Marx's writings, we find outlined his dream for that future paradise; here is the post-revolutionary society, a culture devoid of all human alienation:

> . . . in communist society, where nobody has one exclusive sphere of activity but each can become accomplished in any branch he wishes, society regulates the general production and thus makes it possible for me to do one thing today and another tomorrow, to hunt in the morning, fish in the afternoon, rear cattle in the evening, criticize after dinner, just as I have a mind, without ever becoming hunter, fisherman, shepherd or critic.[66]

It seems fantastic that Marx could assert in all seriousness such an impossible ideal for a society which is to retain the productivity of modern industrialized life. Daniel Bell has even gone so far as to argue that Marx later abandoned any such realization in the "promised land."[67] Bell, however, is forced to appeal to certain passages in the writings of Engels, since Marx never formally repudiated his earlier stand. Engels, we must bear in mind, had a tendency to state

---

[65] *Ibid.*, III, 102.

[66] *The German Ideology*, 44-45.

[67] Daniel Bell, "The 'Rediscovery' of Alienation," *Journal of Philosophy*, LVI (1959), 943. T. B. Bottomore also argues that Marx later grew less utopian in his view of the division of labor. See his essay, "Industry, Work, and Socialism," in Fromm (ed.), *Socialist Humanism*, 395.

the obvious, frequently by-passing the repercussions his statements would have in the overall Marxian scheme. Marx was seldom so straightforward as his fellow worker. In a confusing passage in volume three of *Capital*, he admitted that a certain kind of central direction is necessary "in every mode of production requiring a combination of labors." This direction is to be like that of a conductor leading an orchestra. The evil side of capitalistic centralized direction will, of course, be absent, since "this labor of superintendence arises in all modes of production, which are based on the antagonism between the laborer as a direct producer and the owner of the means of production."[68] Apparently, the abolition of the antagonism between capitalists and laborers will alter fundamentally the very nature of industrial production; he was obviously clinging to the same hope which had captured his imagination three decades earlier. He never bothered to explain just how mass production of consumer goods would be possible in a world in which men could change their occupations two or three times a day.[69]

## Classes and History

Marx's concern with the problems of human alienation, private property, and the division of labor led him very early to a theory of class antagonism. This concept began to take shape in *The German Ideology,* a manuscript written by Marx and Engels (and, apparently, Moses Hess) in 1845-46.[70] Class distinctions ultimately stem from the division of labor:

> The division of labor inside a nation leads at first to the separation of industrial and commercial from agricultural labour, and hence to the separation of *town* and *country* and to the conflict of their interests. Its further development leads to the separation of commercial and industrial labour. At the same time through the division of labour inside these various branches there develop

[68] *Capital,* III, 451.
[69] Cf. Robert Tucker, *Philosophy and Myth in Karl Marx* (Cambridge University Press, 1961), 198-99.
[70] Part of the manuscript appears in Hess's handwriting: Sidney Hook, *From Hegel to Marx,* 186.

various divisions among the individuals co-operating in definite kinds of labour.[71]

Marx could easily have concluded from this that the proletarian class was itself divided into subclasses, but the thought was never entertained by him very seriously. We have already seen that "as individuals produce their life, so they are. . . . The nature of individuals thus depends upon the material conditions determining their production."[72] Thus, the transition is simple: different men have different functions to perform in industrial production, and this gives rise to the creation of separate classes. Social production determines man's very being; this is the foundation of Marx's theory of the "ideological superstructures" of human thought:

> In direct contrast to German philosophy which descends from heaven to earth, here we ascend from earth to heaven. That is to say, we do not set out from what men say, imagine, conceive, nor from men as narrated, thought of, imagined, conceived, in order to arrive at men in the flesh. We set out from real, active men, and on the basis of their real life-process we demonstrate the development of the ideological reflexes and echoes of this life-process. The phantoms formed in the human brain are also, necessarily, sublimates of their material life-process, which is empirically verifiable and bound to material premises. Morality, religion, metaphysics, all the rest of ideology and their corresponding forms of consciousness, thus no longer retain the semblance of independence. They have no history, no development; but men, developing their material production and their material intercourse, alter, along with this their real existence, their thinking and the products of their thinking. Life is not determined by consciousness, but consciousness by life.[73]

Hegel, in other words, was wrong in trying to trace the history of the Universal Spirit in the form of human ideas; these ideas have no independent existence apart from material conditions. By reversing the Hegelian formula, Marx arrived at his conception of *economic determinism,* or as it is also called, the *materialistic conception of*

---

[71] *The German Ideology,* 32.
[72] *Ibid.*
[73] *Ibid.,* 37-38.

*history*. It is epitomized in his phrase, "Life is not determined by consciousness, but consciousness by life." The theory is intimately bound up with his conception of classes. At a point in time, human productive activity was not alienated (this is Marx's "Golden Age"); once alienated labor entered the picture, man became alienated from his fellows, and ultimately these hostile individuals joined with others of similar economic interests and origins. These groupings are economic classes. Classes seek to control society for their own benefit, and this is the origin of the *State*. As he wrote, "the division of labor implies the contradiction between the interest of the separate individual or the individual family and the communal interest of all individuals. . . . And out of this very contradiction between the interest of the individual and that of the community the latter takes an independent form as the *State*. . . ."[74] The class which wishes to control society must therefore "first conquer for itself political power in order to represent its interest as the general interest. . . ."[75]

Now, if ideas, morality, metaphysics, and ethics stem from the nature of the mode of production, then the prevailing ideologies are nothing more than class ideologies — the ideologies of the ruling class. In other words, the prevailing laws and rules that govern any society, as well as the philosophical and theological presuppositions that undergird the rules, are ultimately the products of *class interests*. The idea of a truly general interest or a truly universal philosophy was repellent to Marx; his opposition to the "True Socialists" and the "Utopian Socialists" was based upon his rejection of a universal system of ethics which could serve as a common ground between classes.[76] All morality is class morality.

At the heart of Marx's conception of historical development lies his theory of classes and his corresponding theory of economic determinism. In the famous Preface to the *Critique of Political Economy*

---

[74] *Ibid.*, 44-45.

[75] *Ibid.*, 45.

[76] On the "Utopian Socialists," see the *Communist Manifesto,* in *Marx-Engels Selected Works,* I, 62-64. The critique of "True Socialism" fills a large section of *The German Ideology;* see the section on "True Socialism," esp. 501-03.

(1859), he spelled out his thesis quite bluntly. After restating his familiar idea that the "mode of production of material life conditions the social, political and intellectual life process in general," he went on:

> It is not the consciousness of men that determines their being, but, on the contrary, their social being that determines their consciousness. At a certain stage of their development, the material productive forces of society come into conflict with the existing relations of production, or — what is but a legal expression of the same thing — with the property relations within which they have been at work hitherto. From forms of development of the productive forces these relations turn into their fetters. Then begins an epoch of social revolution. With the change of the economic foundation the entire immense superstructure is more or less rapidly transformed. In considering such transformations a distinction should always be made between the material transformation of the economic conditions of production, which can be determined with the precision of natural science, and the legal, political, religious, aesthetic or philosophic — in short, ideological forms in which men become conscious of this conflict and fight it out.[77]

Marx had no doubt, therefore, concerning the true nature of historical development; as he wrote in the opening sentence of the *Communist Manifesto* (1848): "The history of all hitherto existing society is the history of class struggles." Classes must fulfill their appointed roles in historical development; when the mode of production is altered (due to the contradictions inherent within it), classes rise or fall from power. Feudal society becomes capitalist society; the feudal lord loses his position to the capitalist entrepreneur (though not without a struggle). What Marx had previously seen as the internal alienation within the individual man now becomes the total alienation and warfare between classes, and specifically, two classes: the haves and the have-nots. As Halle has put it: "The real actors in Marx's drama are the two social classes: the proletariat

---

[77] *A Contribution to the Critique of Political Economy,* translated by N. I. Stone (Chicago: Charles H. Kerr Co., 1904), 11-12. This selection is included in *Marx-Engels Selected Works,* I, 363.

and the capitalist. They have now become separate persons, rather than separate aspects of the same person."[78]

The conflicts in history will be reconciled only after the Revolution. Apparently, progress will then be possible even without the "dialectical" conflict between classes. This is a problem in the Marxian system, since the whole premise of historical advancement is based squarely upon the idea of conflict as a dynamic force. Contemporary Marxists have been forced to acknowledge that certain kinds of "progressive differences" may still remain between groups of "unalienated" men after the revolution, thus providing the necessary forces for social advancement.[79] In any case, the proletariat is the engine of social progress in our own age; its revolutionary action will ultimately resolve the contradictions inherent in society, whether within man, among men, between classes, within human thought, or in the productive process.

Philosophy — class philosophy — is one of the tools which the proletariat can use in its war against the fetters of capitalist production, and after the revolution philosophy will cease to be divided, since all classes other than the proletariat will be dissolved. In other words, philosophy is not a mere tool of the mind, a means for merely comprehending the world; *philosophy* is a *weapon*. "Just as philoso-

---

[78] Louis J. Halle, "Marx's Religious Drama," *Encounter,* XXV (Oct., 1965), 36. For a similar analysis, see the Roman Catholic scholar, Gary L. Chamberlain, "The Man Marx Made," *Science and Society,* XXVII (1963), 319. This perspective has been popularized by Robert C. Tucker in his important study, *Philosophy and Myth in Karl Marx.*

[79] Harry Slochower, "The Marxist Idea of Change and Law," *Science and Society,* VIII (1944), 352. Cf. Cavendish Moxon, "Communications," *Science and Society,* VII (1943), 256. As the Fabian writer, G. D. H. Cole, has put it: "Struggle can proceed upon other planes than that of class, and in higher and less brutal forms. But what these forms will be the Marxist neither pretends nor even wishes to know in advance of the event." *The Meaning of Marxism* (Ann Arbor: University of Michigan Press, [1948] 1964), 275.

phy finds its *material* weapons in the proletariat, so the proletariat finds its *intellectual* weapons in philosophy."[80]

At this point, it would probably be wise to return to the original problem which was raised in the introduction to this chapter. The dilemma which confronted Marx was the one which has confounded all secular thinkers who have considered the problem of philosophy: how can we relate the flux of history to general laws which are permanent and which regulate the flux? If we are to understand (and influence) history, then we need standards of evaluation by which we can examine, explain, catalogue, control, and to some extent *predict* history. Marx turned to the historical process itself, and specifically to the economic and social elements of history, in his search of those laws of development. Not logic, not military or political history, not church history, but economic history is supposedly the key to which unlocks the closed door of the mysteries of the past, present, and future. He thought that he had discovered a pattern of development in economic history, a pattern which could be used to predict the future of mankind. It is this "historicist" methodology — the attempt to explain history by means of laws inherent in history itself — which has repelled such positivists as Karl Popper.[81] Popper sees the retreat into history as a denial of the possibilities of the corrective power of human reason:

> There is a wide gulf between Marx's activism and his historicism, and this gulf is further widened by the doctrine that we must submit to the purely irrational forces of history. For since he denounced as Utopian any attempt to make use of our reason in order to plan for the future, *reason can have no part in bringing about a more reasonable world.* I believe that such a view must lead to mysticism.[82]

---

[80] Marx, "Contribution to the Critique of Hegel's Philosophy of Right," in Bottomore (ed.), *Karl Marx: Early Writings,* 59. This essay was originally published in 1844. Cf. Adam Schaff, "Marxism and the Philosophy of Man," in Fromm (ed.), *Socialist Humanism,* 148.

[81] Karl R. Popper, *The Open Society and Its Enemies* (4th ed.; N. Y.: Harper Torchbook, 1964), II, 202-11. Cf. Popper, *The Poverty of Historicism* (3rd ed.; N. Y.: Harper Torchbook, 1961).

[82] *The Open Society and Its Enemies,* II, 202.

This is the issue, of course, as seen from a perspective of the total rationalist. It is the old conflict between total rationalism and total irrationalism, between static law and flux. But Popper himself cannot solve the problem, and he also retreats into a position of irrationalism with his concept of "piecemeal social engineering" which, because it is not total — not worked out according to a systematic preconceived plan — will somehow preserve man's freedom in a technological world. Marx was more of a rationalist than Popper thinks, and Popper is less rationalistic than Popper thinks, but the basic question still remains: how are we to subdue the flux of history to the orderly world of law, while simultaneously preserving human freedom? One can have total law without human freedom, as Roderick Seidenberg predicts, or total anarchy without law, as some of the more anarchistic hippies seem to want, but how is it possible to have both?[83]

Marx constantly attacked the so-called "vulgar economists" because of their notion of static social and economic laws, as well as for their view of a constant human nature. "It is precisely characteristic of vulgar economy that it repeats things which are new, original, deep and justified during a certain outgrown stage of development, at a time when they have become platitudinous, stale, false."[84] Laws in one era are not applicable in another period of time. There can be absolute, inevitable, total law in one period, and this is what enables social scientists to investigate society and make

---

[83] For Seidenberg's terrifying view of the coming ant-hill society, see *Post-Historic Man: An Inquiry* (Chapel Hill: University of North Carolina Press, 1950) and *Anatomy of the Future* (Chapel Hill: University of North Carolina Press, 1961). Seidenberg, in contrast to writers like Huxley, Orwell, and C. S. Lewis, welcomes the coming static universe. Man will sacrifice freedom and change in order to gain total wealth and total technology.

[84] Marx, *Capital*, III, 913. See especially the review of volume I of *Capital* which Marx quoted favorably in the preface to the second edition of the first volume in 1873. Marx clearly agrees with the reviewer's evaluation of his (Marx's) perspective of changing law. See the Unterman edition of *Capital* (N. Y.: Modern Library, n. d.; Chicago: Charles H. Kerr, 1906), I, 22-24. In one brief passage, Marx tried to hold on to a more static conception of law, but even

accurate predictions about what is to come, but these rigid laws are not permanent. One can be certain that the economic laws inherent in capitalist society will not be present in the socialist age to come, in exactly the same way that laws governing feudal economic life are no longer present under capitalism. Each successive age overcomes and transcends the laws of its predecessor. Law, like matter, is in constant flux. Popper, though he has no answer for the problem, has indeed spotted a central flaw in Marx's system. Ultimately, the total rationalism of Marx's "scientific" socialism degenerates into philosophical irrationalism and mysticism. Marx stepped into a position which inevitably implies a total *relativism.* At the bottom of the Marxist system, like the other modern systems of rationalistic society, is the concept of *chance;* the material universe is unsupported by an overall plan (such as we find in Calvinism), nor does it operate by any permanent, universal laws.[85]

Marx's understanding of human society rested on his concept of economic determinism. Yet he was forced to admit that "Economic categories are only the theoretical expressions, the abstractions of the social relations of production."[86] And these social relations of production are constantly changing. How did Marx know that he was analyzing 19th century society with the proper theoretical framework? How could he be certain that, assuming their existence, economic laws were in fact related in some way to the material world

---

here, his relativism was inescapable for him: "No natural laws can be done away with. What can change, in changing historical circumstances, is the *form* in which these laws operate." Marx to Kugelmann, 11 July, 1868: *Letters to Kugelmann* (N. Y.: International Publishers, 1934), 73. This is as close as he ever came to a static conception of law.

[85] The implications of this radical relativism are rejected, without any justification, by Harry Slochower, "The Marxist Idea of Change and Law," *Science and Society,* VIII (1944), 345-55. M. M. Bober has seen this clearly: "In obvious consequence of their basic conceptions, Marx and Engels are apostles of the relativity of ideas." *Karl Marx's Interpretation of History* (N. Y.: Norton, [1948] 1965), 123.

[86] Marx, *The Poverty of Philosophy* (1847) (Moscow: Foreign Languages Publishing House, n. d.), 105.

which he was trying to analyze? How could he even believe in economic laws at all? The answer is simple: he had *faith*. His "empirical neutralism" rested on the most theological foundation imaginable. The contradictions in his thinking are astounding: asserting total rationalism, he drifted into mysticism; proclaiming the powers of prediction, he destroyed the very concept of law which might have supported the possibility of prediction; arguing in favor of an all-encompassing philosophical and social theory, he came to a position of relativism. Only his personal faith enabled him to pass over these fundamental antinomies in his system.

Engels made explicit the relativism of the Marxian outlook: "A system of natural and historical knowledge which is all-embracing and final for all time is a contradiction to the fundamental laws of dialectical thinking; which, however, far from excluding, on the contrary includes, the idea that the systematic knowledge of the external universe can make giant strides from generation to generation."[87] The last clause, it should be pointed out, is a statement of irrational faith; the first clause denies the validity of the second (assuming there is such a thing as logic). One can speak of progress only in terms of a permanent framework; Engels denied the existence of such an eternal standard, and so did Marx. Yet the idea of systematic knowledge implies the existence of a total standard of truth; one can approach such systematic truth only if truth actually exists. Otherwise, man has no grounds for saying that giant strides in knowledge are, in fact, being made. As with Hegel, the idea of eternal truth is merely a presupposed limiting concept, an intellectual backdrop, for Marx and Engels. As Engels wrote:

> If mankind ever reached the stage at which it could only work with eternal truths, with conclusions of thought which possess sovereign validity and an unconditional claim to truth, it would then have reached the point where the infinity of the intellectual world both in its actuality and in its potentiality had been exhausted, and this would mean that the famous miracle of the infinite series would have been performed.[88]

---

[87] Engels, *Herr Dühring's Revolution in Science* [*Anti-Dühring*] (London: Lawrence and Wishart, [1877] 1934), 31.
[88] *Ibid.*, 100.

He was able to ward off the charge of total relativism only by appealing to the concept of the *relative exactness* of the natural sciences. Some of their truths *are* eternal, he claimed, thus effectively negating what he had just written.[89] Even here he was forced to admit that "eternal truths are in an even worse plight in the third, the historical group of sciences."[90] The conclusion was inescapable:

> . . . knowledge here is essentially relative, inasmuch as it is limited to the perception of relationships and consequences of certain social and state forms which only exist at a particular epoch and among particular people and are of their very nature transitory. Anyone therefore who sets out on this field to hunt down final and ultimate truths, truths which are absolutely immutable, will bring home but little, apart from the platitudes and commonplaces of the sorriest kind.[91]

Van Til has argued that total rationalism must always have total irrationalism as a corollary. If man, on the presuppositions of rationalistic, autonomous human thought, can claim to know anything, he must claim to know everything. If all facts are related to all others, then exhaustive knowledge must be a requirement for true knowledge. If something is not known, the thinker cannot be sure that the unknown factor is not somehow influencing the behavior or the nature of the known. Thus, on man's presupposition of autonomy, to know anything truly requires that one must know everything exhaustively. The possibility of exhaustive knowledge, however, is not open to man (not even with the aid of computers); the result is total irrationalism: nothing can be known with certainty. Man loses control of his universe; chance reasserts itself. All of his knowledge may be an illusion; man cannot be sure. All that secular man can do is to retreat into *faith,* and in today's world the brand of faith most popular is pragmatism; if something works, it is acceptable as knowledge. Of course, the idea of "it works" implies permanent standards of proper functioning, and this again introduces the original problem: how can we discover such standards? Do they really

---

[89] *Ibid.,* 101.
[90] *Ibid.,* 102.
[91] *Ibid.,* 103.

exist, and can they be applied to this world? Marx, no less than other autonomous thinkers, could not resolve this issue.

The answer to the question is found in the revelation of God to man, but Marx and his fellow humanists reject this possibility. Rushdoony, following Van Til, explains why the revelation of God in the Bible is basic to all understanding:

> All knowledge becomes possible because God is absolute, autonomous and self-contained. Because He is the source of knowledge concerning Himself, and the basic principle of interpretation for all creation, we do not need to have an exhaustive knowledge of God to have reliable knowledge, nor do we need to know all created facts to have valid knowledge of the universe. Man cannot comprehend all facts with his knowledge, and he therefore cannot know God or creation exhaustively. If it is brute factuality that he deals with, then he has no reliable knowledge, since unrevealed possibilities remain. But since God has no unrealized potentialities, and since God has created all things in terms of His plan and decree, our knowledge can be reliable and valid. The incomprehensibility of God is thus the basis of man's knowledge.[92]

God's eternal decree is the absolute standard, and He has revealed Himself to man. Thus, men have a standard by which they can evaluate the created facts of the universe. Man does not need to claim omniscience in order to justify his knowledge. Thus, he need not become involved in the irrationalism of all secular thought; the fact that he cannot know all things does not doom his thought to chaos.

We have examined Marx's concept of history at some length. What about his theory of classes? Joseph A. Schumpeter has called attention to some of the flaws of Marx's theory of classes. In his important work, *Capitalism, Socialism and Democracy* (1942), Schumpeter showed how Marx never really defined the word "class." He ended the third volume of *Capital* (never completed in his lifetime, but substantially finished in 1867) with these words: "The first question to be answered is this: What constitutes a class?"

---

[92] R. J. Rushdoony, *By What Standard?* (Philadelphia: Presbyterian and Reformed, 1958), 161.

Two paragraphs later, the manuscript breaks off; Marx failed to answer the question in the remaining sixteen years of his life. But the general outline of "owners" and "non-owners" is clear. In our day, Marx wrote, we see only two classes: the proletariat class which owns none of the means of production and the capitalist class which does.

Schumpeter points out that there are other ways of defining a class; economics is only one way of delimiting social groups from each other. For one thing, there is a constant rise and fall of families in and out of the ruling class.[93] For another, such factors as race or military prowess may serve as better models in certain societies than the concept of ownership of capital. One of the problems Marx had in explaining the triumph politically of Louis Napoleon Bonaparte in mid-19th century France concerned just this issue. If the State is the reflection of class supremacy, then how did Bonaparte succeed? He represented all classes, and his greatest strength was among the small peasants, yet the urban bourgeoisie was the class which dominated the economy. Marx tried to argue that "the peasants find their natural ally and leader in the *urban proletariat,* whose task is the overthrow of the bourgeoise order."[94] But this does not do much to explain how Bonaparte III was elected, since the proletariat certainly had no power in France in the 1850's, and even if it had been a powerful class, it certainly had no reason to elect Bonaparte. Why,

---

[93] Joseph A. Schumpeter, *Capitalism, Socialism and Democracy* (N. Y.: Harper Torchbook, 1962), 19.

[94] Marx, *The Eighteenth Brumaire of Louis Bonaparte,* in *Marx-Engels Selected Works,* I, 338. An attempt has been made by Wlodzimierz Wesolowski to re-examine Marx's use of the idea of class rule, and he concludes that Marx's analysis of 19th century French political life was, in fact, consistent with his class theory. I do not find Wesolowski's arguments very convincing. What he has shown is only that Marx the political analyst was more careful and more accurate than Marx the social theorist. In so far as Marx's political analysis was correct, the force of his class theory was weakened. Wesolowski, "Marx's Theory of Class Domination: An Attempt at Systematization," in Nicholas Lobkowicz (ed.), *Marx and the Western World* (Notre Dame University Press, 1967), 53-97.

then, did all classes support him? Marx the political journalist came into conflict with Marx the social theorist. His narrowly defined class theory did not fit the empirical political facts.

Marx had to link his theory of class conflict with his theory of economic determinism if the system were to display theoretical consistency. Schumpeter has seen the absurdity of this link:

> Marx wished to define capitalism by the same trait that also defines his class division. A little reflection will convince the reader that this is not a necessary or a natural thing to do. In fact it was a bold stroke of analytic strategy which linked the fate of the class phenomenon with the fate of capitalism in such a way that socialism, which in reality has nothing to do with the presence or absence of social classes, became, by definition, the only possible kind of classless society, excepting primitive groups.[95]

It was *analytic strategy,* not empirical investigation, which led Marx to make the connection between classes and economic power.

In all of this we can see the desire which led Marx to define classes (and, in his economic writings, commodities) in very special, very limited ways: he wanted to find assurance that his economic determinism would bring the new socialist era into existence. Mankind should not be left in a sea of chance; the new society *had* to come. If this meant that certain limited and even peculiar definitions would have to be applied to complex social phenomenon, then Marx was not one to hesitate. Man has a role to fulfill, a task to complete; he needs the power of rigorous economic determinism to help him in his battle against chance. In a neglected portion of *The German Ideology,* Marx outlined this task:

> In the present epoch, the domination of material conditions over individuals, and the suppression of individuality by chance, has assumed its sharpest and most universal form, thereby setting existing individuals a very definite task. It has set them the task of replacing the domination of circumstances and of chance over individuals by the domination of individuals over chance and circumstances.[96]

---

[95] Schumpeter, *loc. cit.*
[96] Marx, *The German Ideology,* 482.

Several problems are involved here. First, Marx admitted that for him economic determinism is a corollary of a chance universe. The two concepts are mutually exclusive, yet both were held by Marx. If man is to conquer the contingency of nature, he must do so, in the Marxist scheme, by means of industrial power and economic law. Engels, as usual, put the whole issue much more clearly than Marx did:

> Hegel was the first to state correctly the relation between freedom and necessity. To him, freedom is the appreciation of necessity. "Necessity is *blind* only *in so far as it is not understood.*" Freedom does not consist in the dream of independence of natural laws, but in the knowledge of these laws, and in the possibility this gives of systematically making them work towards definite ends. . . . Therefore the *freer* a man's judgment is in relation to a definite question, with so much the greater *necessity* is the content of this judgment determined; while the uncertainty, founded on ignorance, which seems to make an arbitrary choice among many different and conflicting possible decisions, shows by this precisely that it is not free, that it is controlled by the very object it should itself control. Freedom therefore consists in the control over ourselves and over external nature which is founded on knowledge of natural necessity; it is therefore necessarily a product of historical development.[97]

This, however, raises another issue, the question of *elites.* If men — generic, species mankind — are to take control of circumstances, then we must, as Engels put it, gain "control over ourselves." C. S. Lewis, in one of the most important novels of the century, *That Hideous Strength,* has one of the characters in the book raise precisely this question: "Man has got to take charge of Man. That means, remember, that some men have got to take charge of the rest — which is another reason for cashing in on it as soon as one can. You and I want to be the people who do the taking charge, not the ones taken charge of."[98] Marx did not care to deal with this

---

[97] Engels, *Anti-Dühring,* 128.
[98] C. S. Lewis, *That Hideous Strength* (N. Y.: Macmillan, 1947), 37. This book is a theological *1984.* It is available in paperback as the third book in the trilogy of *Perelandra* and *Out of the Silent Planet.*

problem, but modern day analysts of the Soviet and satellite nations have been forced to reckon with it; the "classless" society has created a new class of political elites.[99]

The most fundamental problem, nevertheless, is philosophical: if man is to take control of his universe, and if chance is to be defeated, how can man do this if he is determined by that very chance universe? This was the dilemma Feuerbach had not resolved, and it was Marx's desire to turn Feuerbach's passive man into a person who could change the alienated world. But how can a man who is determined by the world ever accomplish this? At this point, Marx introduced his theory of *reciprocity* or interaction between the substructure of economic production and the superstructure of thought and volition. History, he argued in *The Holy Family* (1845), does not control man at all: *"History does nothing; it 'does not possess immense riches,' it 'does not fight battles.' It is men, real, living men, who do all this, who possess things and fight battles. It is not 'history' which uses men as a means of achieving* — as if it were an individual person — *its own ends. History is nothing but the activity of men in pursuit of their own ends."*[100]

It appears that Marx was inserting the element of human choice into his scheme, in order to preserve human freedom. Unfortunately, in doing so, he reintroduced contingency into his system. Why is

---

[99] Milovan Djilas, in *The New Class* (N. Y.: Praeger, 1957), blames Stalin rather than the socialist economic system as such for the tyranny of Communism. He cannot offer a solution for the problem of bureaucratic elites, except for an appeal to a vague "democratic socialism." Hayek's *Road to Serfdom* (University of Chicago Press, 1944) has disposed of that particular hope. The socialist planning board will inevitably become a part of a "new class." T. B. Bottomore, a Marxist sociologist, has also called attention to the elite issue in his essay, "Industry, Work, and Socialism," in Fromm (ed.), *Socialist Humanism,* 397. On the dangers of a technological elite, see the essay by Mathilde Niel, "The Phenomenon of Technology: Liberation or Alienation of Man?" in *ibid.,* 334-46.

[100] Marx, *The Holy Family,* quoted in T. B. Bottomore and M. Rubel (eds.), *Karl Marx: Selected Writings in Sociology and Social Philosophy* (N. Y.: McGraw-Hill, 1964), 63.

the coming socialist revolution inevitable? How can it be said (as he repeated constantly) that social conditions determine man's thoughts, his will, and his decisions? Yet Marx never wavered from his belief that the coming socialist society *is* inevitable; he never for a moment entertained the thought that the conflagration could be permanently postponed (in most countries, at least). He wrote many thousands of pages of economic analysis to prove the inevitability of the Revolution.[101] He wrote thousands of lines in newspaper articles predicting the collapse of the capitalist system. Marx was no fool; he saw the contradiction involved in this indeterminism, and he returned almost immediately to his determinist scheme: "What is society, whatever its form may be? The product of men's reciprocal activity. Are men free to choose this or that form of society themselves? By no means."[102]

> It is superfluous to add that men are not free to choose their *productive forces* — which are the basis of all their history — for every productive force is an acquired productive force, the product of former activity. The productive forces are therefore the result of practical human energy; but this energy is itself conditioned by the circumstances in which men find themselves, by the productive forces already won, by the social form which exists before they do, which they do not create, which is the product of the former generation.[103]

This circularity is best expressed by Marx's equivocation, "circumstances make men just as men make circumstances."[104] But it

---

[101] Cf. *Capital*, I, 534, 836-37.

[102] Marx to P. V. Annenkov, 28 Dec., 1846: Dona Torr (ed.), *Marx-Engels Selected Correspondence, 1846-1895* (N. Y.: International Publishers, 1935), 7.

[103] *Idem.* Cf. the opening lines of Marx's *Eighteenth Brumaire of Louis Bonaparte* (1852): "Men make their own history, but they do not make it just as they please; they do not make it under circumstances chosen by themselves, but under circumstances directly encountered, given and transmitted from the past." *Marx-Engels Selected Works*, I, 247.

[104] *The German Ideology*, 50.

was Engels's letter to J. Bloch in 1890 which announced with absolute clarity that the Marxist system is unable to overcome this dualism between chance and necessity:

> According to the materialist conception of history, the *ultimately* determining element in history is the production and reproduction of real life. More than this neither Marx nor I have ever asserted. Hence if somebody twists this into saying that the economic element is the *only* determining one, he transforms that proposition into a meaningless, abstract, senseless phrase. The economic situation is the basis, but the various elements of the superstructure: political forms of the class struggle and its results, to wit: constitutions established by the victorious class after a successful battle, etc., juridical forms, and then even the reflexes of all these actual struggles in the brains of the participants, political, juristic, philosophical theories, religious views and their further development into systems of dogmas, also exercise their influence upon the course of the historical struggles and in many cases preponderate in determining their *form*. There is an interaction of all these elements in which, amid all the endless host of accidents (that is, of things and events, whose inner connection is so remote or so impossible of proof that we can regard it as non-existent, as negligible) the economic movement finally asserts itself as necessary. Otherwise the application of the theory to any period of history one chose would be easier than the solution of a simple equation of the first degree.[105]

Ironically, Marx had claimed for his system exactly this kind of mathematical precision in his early days. In 1843 he had written that in the study of political conditions,

> one too easily overlooks the *real nature of relations* and seeks to explain everything as a consequence of the will of persons concerned. There are *relationships* which determine the activities of individual men and separate groups that are as independent of them as breathing. If one places oneself in this real perspective

---

[105] *Marx-Engels Selected Works,* II, 488; *Marx-Engels Selected Correspondence,* 475. Cf. Letter to C. Schmidt, 27 Oct., 1890: MESW, II, 494; MESC, 480. See Marx's similar statement in *Capital,* III, 919. For a contemporary analysis of accidents and necessity, see A. P. Chermenina, "The Concept of Freedom in Marxist-Leninist Ethics," *The Soviet Review,* VI (1965), 50.

. . . one will perceive the effects of relations where upon first view only persons were conceived as actual forces. As soon as it is pointed out that relations necessarily make circumstances, it will not be difficult to determine under which conditions it must actually manifest itself in life and under which it cannot even though there exists a need for it. One could determine this with almost the same certainty as a chemist can determine under which special conditions matter undergoes combination.[106]

Engels categorically asserted that accidents have no lasting importance in determining the course of history. But this is a statement of his faith, not of his irrefutable proof. How can he be certain that such events are so remote or so impossible to measure that they can be regarded as non-existent? He inserts accidents in an attempt to give some room for human freedom in a world determined ultimately by economic factors. But this new contingency does little for man's sense of freedom; he still cannot do much to direct his own path in life, let alone the course of his society. Economic circumstances ultimately appear as final. Besides, as Marx argued, these accidents cancel each other out: "These accidents themselves fall naturally into the general course of development and are compensated again by other accidents."[107] All they can do is accelerate or delay the general course of events.[108] But the insertion of the element of contingency effectively guts the whole system. Marx and Engels went from pillar to post on this issue; they never came to rest at a place

---

[106] Quoted by A. James Gregor, "Marx, Feuerbach and the Reform of the Hegelian Dialectic," *Science and Society,* XXIX (1965), 77. Lichtheim's argument that Marx became deterministic only in his later years is unable to account for such statements as these in his youth. If anything, his qualification of his determinism which we find in *Capital,* III, 919, would indicate that he was less of a determinist in his "mature" period. But it would be most accurate to say, in contrast to Lichtheim, that Marx was both a determinist and an indeterminist throughout his career; both were held in a contradictory dialectical tension. Cf. George Lichtheim, *Marxism: An Historical and Critical Study* (N. Y.: Praeger, 1961), 236-37.

[107] Marx to Kugelmann, 17 April, 1871: *Letters to Kugelmann* (N. Y.: International Publishers, 1934), 125.

[108] *Ibid.*

of total determinism or total indeterminism. R. N. Carew-Hunt has commented on this Marxist dualism:

> If man is to be in any real sense the master of his destiny, it can only be through ideas and opinions. But these belong to the superstructure, and the form they take is determined by the substructure. All they will admit is that an interaction takes place between the two, though upon what principle they do not tell us. But once an interaction has been conceded, the whole thesis is undermined, since we are no longer dealing with a purely economic factor, but with one which has been itself in part determined by non-economic factors. To say after this that the economic factor must always be decisive is meaningless.[109]

Walter Odajnyk has echoed this observation:

> It is the same glaring contradiction in Marxism that keeps coming back again and again: men, ideas, society are determined by operative physical, economic, and social causes, and yet they can be free of all these causes at times, if not always. Marxism holds on to both, for it needs the determinism and it needs causation; but to be realistic as well as revolutionary, it is forced to explain and even to rely upon situations as if determinism and causation did not apply. Thus it must sustain the contradiction within itself for the sake of its existence as a theory.[110]

The "interaction" theory breaks up the original strength of the economic-materialist conception of history. Admittedly, the theory does seem to provide a certain element of human freedom for the system, and contemporary Marxists have used some of these "indeterminist" passages in Marx to try to show that Marx was a man who loved human freedom — a true humanist. Some have even gone so far as to say that Marx never really believed that the socialist revolution was inevitable.[111] But these attempts to make Marx palatable

---

[109] R. N. Carew-Hunt, *The Theory and Practice of Communism* (Baltimore, Md.: Pelican, 1964), 78.
[110] Walter Odajnyk, *Marxism and Existentialism* (Garden City, N. Y.: Doubleday Anchor, 1965), 41.
[111] This approach is taken by John Lewis in his biography, *The Life and Teaching of Karl Marx* (N. Y.: International Publishers, 1965), 136-37, 203-04; György Márkus, "Marxist Humanism," *Science and Society*, XXX (1966), 275-87, esp. concluding remarks.

only destroy the original unity of the determinist vision. Without total determinism, the system loses its compelling quality. As Schumpeter writes, "the glamour of the fundamental truth that surrounds it depends precisely on the strictness and simplicity of the one-way relation which it asserts."[112] If the idea of absolute economic determinism is abandoned, Marxism loses its ideological punch.

In the last analysis, we find that the Marxian theory of classes and the materialist conception of history cannot stand. The antinomies of the system cannot be overcome: man, a creature of his environment, is called upon to transcend that environment and to create a new world. Man lives in a determined world, yet he finds that world inhabited by chance. Like all secular philosophers, Marx saw the origin of all things in chance, and he was never able to eliminate chance from his supposedly deterministic universe. As a result, there is a constant tension between man's freedom and man's determined life; as to which is more prominent depends upon the context of Marx's particular argument: where he tried to escape the implications of economic determinism, he appealed to chance, and where he wished to insure the inevitability of the Revolution, he appealed to determinism.

There is another problem with his theory of classes. Marx was not a systematic thinker, contrary to popular opinion. He was a powerful thinker, and his system is a monumental one, but that is not the same as saying that he was systematic. He changed his definitions in the course of his arguments, and he used familiar terms in peculiar ways (this is especially true in the economic writings). With the exception of the first 200 pages of volume I of *Capital,* in which he developed his theory of surplus value, there is almost no other equally systematic exposition of any theme in all of his works. He would pass over some subject briefly, giving an indication of real insight, but he would only hint at solutions. This is especially true in the case of his theory of the economic substructure of society.

If a man's class membership depended upon his role in the mode

---

[112] Schumpeter, *Capitalism, Socialism and Democracy,* 13.

of production, then it was absolutely vital for Marx to give an accurate definition of "mode of production." Unfortunately, he was not very careful in his usage of the phrase. As a result, a conflict has developed over what exactly the theory implies: did Marx proclaim a strictly technological interpretation of history, or was it a more broad definition? Some scholars take the view that Marx thought that technology alone determined the nature of the society. Others think that Marx believed that all the relations of production — ownership, technology, bureaucracy, and even ideas — must be considered in any "social equation." H. B. Mayo has commented on this confusion:

> Marx himself summarized his theory thus: "the mode of production in material life determines the social, political and intellectual life processes in general"; and speaking of production, said, "this one historical fact is the fundamental determinant of all history." At times he listed the three ingredients as purposive labor activity, subject matter (materials), and the instruments. Sometimes, however, the meaning was broadened to include the methods of exchange and the means of transport, which vary according to whether production is for one's own needs or for the market. . . . The greatest ambiguity of all in this essential phrase has already been mentioned: where are we to put knowledge, science, technology, labor skills — among the modes of production or in the superstructure? If we put them among the former as they ought to be, and as Marx sometimes put them, since scientific knowledge is obviously one of the forces of production, then the unique point of Marxist theory disappears. Marx's fundamental law may then be reduced to the statement that history is made by mankind working with nature. However true this may be, it is certainly not what Marxists usually think they mean. On the other hand, to put science in the strictly determined superstructure, as Marx and Engels sometimes put it, ignores the truth that the materials and tools depend for the most part on knowledge. The very foundation of Marxist theory is sapped by this uncertainty, and hence Marxism can mean different things to different people, just as it meant different things to Marx at different times. Most expositions of Marx are thus forced to make his theories appear more consistent than they really are.[113]

[113] H. B. Mayo, *Introduction to Marxist Theory* (N. Y.: Oxford University Press, 1960), 69-70.

The ambiguities in Marx's own mind account for many of the debates among his followers, and between his followers and his detractors. Marx's theory was supposed to give an account of the nature of historical change, but it fails in its task. What is the source of change: ideas, technology, legal relationships, or some other element? As Mayo puts it: "In the end, then, it comes to this: the forces of production, never clearly defined, are said to determine both the course of history and the entire superstructure of society. In no sense is this an *ultimate* explanation, since how changes occur in the independent variable is as much a mystery as ever. But since the weary mind must somewhere come to rest, Marx took his stand upon spontaneous changes in the elusive modes of production. They are the mysterious self-supported tortoise holding up society and carrying history along on its back."[114]

Thus, we see that the Marxist theory of historical development is a morass of circular arguments and shifting definitions. It is unable to resolve the "nature-freedom" antinomy, and by relying upon pure contingency to provide freedom for man, the necessary Revolution lost its scientific inevitability. Without a consistent class theory to support the Revolution's appearance, it can hardly be said to have been established empirically. Yet Marx never lost faith in the coming cataclysm. It was not made clear exactly how change occurred in the society, but Marx always believed that he had demonstrated that social change is unilinear and points to the ultimate resolution of all human history. What was it that compelled him to hold on to the idea of the coming Revolution with such a religious determination? Why did he spend his whole life trying to show that the proof of the Revolution's inevitability had been found?[115]

---

[114] *Ibid.*, 71.

[115] Mayo has raised some serious objections to Marx's historical methodology in his essay, "Marxism as a Philosophy of History," *The Canadian Historical Review*, XXXI (1953), 1-17. For an enlightening discussion of classes and historical accidents in Marx's writings, see M. M. Bober, *Karl Marx's Interpretation of History*, 67-112.

All roads in Marx's works lead to the Revolution. Whether we examine his theory of human alienation or his philosophy of history, whether we look at his theory of knowledge or his economic analysis, whether politics is the theme or the development of science, all contradictions and difficulties are to be resolved by the coming of the Revolution. It is the beginning of a truly human history; it is the end of fettered production and exploited labor. It is the discovery of human freedom combined with absolute omnipotence and total control over nature. No more absurdities like the division of labor will exist, no more warfare, no more conflict between men or within man. Without the ideal of the Revolution as its goal, Marxism would be little more than a huge mass of economic and historical material — interesting, perhaps, but hardly the basis of a mass movement. When combined with the idea of total revolution, it becomes a new religion, or more accurately, a very ancient religion in a new, pseudo-scientific garb.

Was Marx primarily a scientist, or was he a religious prophet? This debate has divided scholars for over half a century, and it is unlikely that it will be resolved in the near future. T. B. Bottomore, a sociologist whose works are in the Marxist tradition, is one of those who think that Marx is best understood as a scientist; naturally, the Soviet Marxists agree with this evaluation.[116] Robert C. Tucker, Louis J. Halle, Erich Fromm, Karl Löwith, and many others see him as a semi-religious figure, especially as an Old Testament prophetic type. Löwith's description is typical:

> He was a Jew of Old Testament stature, though an emancipated Jew of the nineteenth century who felt strongly antireligious and even anti-Semitic. It is the old Jewish messianism and prophetism — unaltered by two thousand years of economic history from handicraft to large-scale industry — and Jewish insistence on absolute righteousness which explain the idealistic basis of Marx's materialism. Though perverted into secular prognostication, the

[116] Bottomore, "Karl Marx: Sociologist or Marxist?" *Science and Society*, XXX (1964), 11-24.

*Communist Manifesto* still retains the basic features of a messianic faith: "the assurance of things hoped for."[117]

Unquestionably, there is a religious element in Marxism. But to classify him as an Old Testament prophetic figure is to miss the essential nature of the Marxist message. *What Marxism represents is a secular throwback to the chaos cults of the ancient world,* and not a modern school of the prophets.

Marx attempted to overcome the dialectical tension between thought and action; he was aware of the fact that theoretical explanations of the universe are always separated from the actual material events, and he was determined to bridge the gap. Thus, he offered his thesis that in *action* — revolutionary practice — we have the resolution of the dichotomy. In his second thesis on Feuerbach, he wrote that "the question whether objective truth can be attributed to human thinking is not a question of theory but is a *practical* question. In practice man must prove the truth, that is, the reality and power, the this-sidedness of his thinking." Can human thought be said to be valid apart from revolutionary action? Marx utterly denied the possibility: "The dispute over the reality or non-reality of thinking which is isolated from practice is a purely *scholastic* question." He continued the theme in the eighth of these theses. "Social life," he said, "is essentially practical."[118] Statements such as these have led many scholars to conclude that Marx was essentially a pragmatist, and in a certain sense, this is an accurate evaluation.[119] In this pragmatism we can see Marx's relativism at work: theory is always changing, just as matter is in constant flux; only

---

[117] Karl Löwith, *Meaning in History* (University of Chicago Press, 1949), 44. On the Communist Party as a secular church, see Raymond Aron, *The Opium of the Intellectuals* (N. Y.: Norton, 1962), ch. 9.

[118] Marx, "Theses on Feuerbach," (1845), in *Marx-Engels Selected Works,* II, 403-05.

[119] Sidney Hook, in his earlier writings, is an example of this interpretation, although he probably would reject it today. Hook, *Towards an Understanding of Karl Marx* (N. Y.: John Day, 1933); *From Hegel to Marx,* 284-85.

revolutionary practice can unify theory and empirical reality. Lichtheim has put it well: Marx was very much a "pragmatic theorist."[120]

Revolution, however, has more than an intellectual function in Marx's system. Revolution is to create a new society and a new humanity: "In revolutionary activity the changing of oneself coincides with the changing of circumstances."[121] Man can change his own nature, and the nature of the species as well, by changing his environment: "By thus acting on the external world and changing it, he at the same time changes his own nature."[122] As the chronology of the two quotations indicates, Marx held this belief throughout his career. What he had originally conceived as a psychological fall into alienation now was to be healed by an alteration of the environmental substructure of society. He pursued this theme with a religious fanaticism:

> For the creation on a mass scale of this communist consciousness, as well as for the success of the cause itself, it is necessary for men themselves to be changed on a large scale, and this change can only occur in a practical movement, in a *revolution*. Revolution is necessary not only because the *ruling* class cannot be overthrown in any other way, but also because only in a revolution can *the class which overthrows it* rid itself of the accumulated rubbish of the past and become capable of reconstructing society.[123]

---

[120] George Lichtheim, *Marxism,* 129.

[121] *The German Ideology* (1845-46), 230.

[122] *Capital,* I (1867), 198.

[123] *The German Ideology,* 86. This is the same quote which appears at the beginning of this chapter. In this case, however, I am using the translation in Bottomore and Rubel (eds.), *Karl Marx: Selected Writings in Sociology and Social Philosophy,* 65. In the light of this statement by Marx, the conclusion made by H. B. Mayo seems ludicrous: "As we have seen, Marx did not idealize violence as such; his error may be called rather an error of judgment. Believing that the bourgeoisie would not yield their class position without armed resistance, he naturally believed also that overthrow by violence would be necessary, and this is now a prime article of the communist creed." *Introduction to Marxist Theory,* 257.

In an early essay for *Vörwarts* [*Forward*], a revolutionary German periodical, he was equally emphatic: "Revolution in general — the *overthrow* of the existing ruling power and the *dissolution* of existing social relationships — is a *political act*. Without *revolution, socialism* cannot develop."[124] Much later, he wrote: "Force is the midwife of every old society pregnant with a new one."[125] He was to modify this view only slightly on one occasion: England, he said, might possibly avoid revolution in its transition to socialism, but it was not very likely. However, he did not voice this opinion very often, and usually it was said only to members of the International Working Men's Association, a trade union organization which relied heavily on British "bread and butter" union support. His private opinion, which only his intimates saw, was far more explicit: "The Englishman first needs a revolutionary education," he wrote to Engels in 1866. "One thing is certain, these thick-headed John Bulls, whose brainpans seem to have been specially manufactured for the constables' bludgeons, will never get anywhere without a really bloody encounter with the ruling powers."[126] The "bloody encounter" was a matter of religious and philosophical principle with him; the Revolution had to come if man were to free himself from the bondage of an alienated world.

The doctrine of revolutionary practice became for Marx the equivalent of the chaotic license which was at the heart of all pagan cosmologies. The Golden Age could only be recovered through total license, chaos, and degradation: this theme was central to pagan cosmologies, and it was basic for Marxism. The ancients believed in the existence of a primitive age of luxury, wealth, and freedom; this age had been lost.[127] Orthodox Hebrew and Christian theology explains this transition in terms of an ethical fall into sin; man op-

---

[124] Written in 1844, in Bottomore and Rubel, *op. cit.*, 238.

[125] *Capital*, I, 824.

[126] Marx to Engels, 27 July, 1866: *Marx-Engels Selected Correspondence*, 213.

[127] Cf. Hesiod (8th century B.C.), *The Works and Days*, lines 109-201, for an account of the five ages of man: from Gold to Iron. (Lattimore Translation).

posed the law of God and was punished for his disobedience. The fall, in other words, was an ethical rather than a metaphysical phenomenon. The ancients, however, saw the fall as a metaphysical event; the world is in bondage to law and scarcity, and by returning to chaos for a period, society participates in that pre-temporal age of plenty. There is the hope that the Golden Age itself might be restored. Only through participation in the pre-temporal chaos event can society be rejuvenated; only through ritualistic participation can the link be established between cosmic time and the present reality.

In all but the Biblical cosmology, the creation was seen as the imposition of order upon a chaotic matter. Thus, in the festivals and other rituals of chaos, society was thought to have access to that vital matter which existed before form was imposed to stifle its free action. Roger Caillois has explained this pagan cosmology, focusing his attention on the festival:

> It is a time of excess. Reserves accumulated over the course of several years are squandered. The holiest of laws are violated, those that seem at the very basis of social life. Yesterday's crime is now prescribed, and in place of customary rules, new taboos and disciplines are established, the purpose of which is not to avoid or soothe intense emotions, but rather to excite and bring them to climax. Movement increases, and the participants become intoxicated. Civil or administrative authorities see their powers temporarily diminish or disappear. This is not so much to the advantage of the regular sacerdotal caste as to the gain of secret confraternities or representatives of the other world, masked actors personifying the Gods or the dead. This fervor is also the time for sacrifices, even the time for the sacred, a time outside of time that recreates, purifies, and rejuvenates society. . . . All excesses are permitted, for society expects to be regenerated as a result of excesses, waste, orgies, and violence.[128]

---

[128] Roger Caillois, *Man and the Sacred* (Glencoe, Ill.: Free Press, 1959), 164. Cf. Thorold Jacobson's analysis of the meaning of festivals in Henri Frankfort, *et al., Before Philosophy* (Baltimore, Md.: Pelican, [1946] 1964), 213-16. This volume was previously published by the University of Chicago Press under the title, *The Intellectual Adventure of Ancient Man.*

The festival is a ritual recreation of some key event in the life of a society. Perhaps the most famous of the Creation festivals were the Saturnalia, the New Year, and the spring fertility rites. There was an identification with those first days of the universe where no rules bound creation. "It is the Golden Age: the reign of Saturn and Chronos, without war, commerce, slavery, or private property."[129] It was an age of total abundance, but also one of terror, where dark forces were loose in the universe. Both elements were therefore present in the festivals.[130] Here was the primitive conception of the form-mattter controversy or the nature (chaos)-freedom scheme: law was seen both as a limitation on man and simultaneously a barrier against the terrors of the unknown. The function of the excesses was to pour vitality into the world of order: "All living things must be rejuvenated. The world must be created anew."[131] The traditions of the festival have been preserved in modern times in isolated primitive cultures, as well as in many folk customs, such as the Mardi Gras and the Carnival.[132] And Marx's system certainly rested on a cosmology similar to the one described by Mircea Eliade: "This complete reversal of behavior — from modesty to exhibitionism — indicates a ritual goal, which concerns the entire community. It is a case of the religious need for periodical abolition of the norms that govern profane life — in other words, of the need to suspend the law that lies like a dead weight on customs, and to re-create the state of absolute spontaneity."[133]

In a secular form, this tradition of ritual chaos and secrecy has been preserved in the secret societies which are common to all cul-

[129] Caillois, *op. cit.,* 105.

[130] Sir James George Frazer, *The Scapegoat,* vol. IV of *The Golden Bough* (London: Macmillan, 1925), 306-07.

[131] Caillois, *op. cit.,* 101. Cf. A. J. Wensinck, "The Semitic New Year and the Origin of Eschatology," *Acta Orientalia,* Old Series, I (1923), 158-99.

[132] Cf. Mircea Eliade, *Rites and Symbols of Initiation* (N. Y.: Harper Torchbook, 1965).

[133] *Ibid.,* 46. Cf. Eliade, *Patterns in Comparative Religion* (N. Y.: Sheed and Ward, 1958), 398, 402.

tures. This is one of the reasons why they have served so often as sources of revolutionary and conspiratorial activity, especially in the history of Europe.[134] One of the most blatant statements of the philosophy of chaos was made recently by Jeff Nuttall, editor of the underground *My Own Mag,* and the principle mouthpiece for William Burroughs (author of *Naked Lunch,* an underground favorite):

Still, Burroughs, all of us — we're decaying men, for God's sake. We're all decaying, clearly. Playing around with drugs, playing around with every possible sexual deviation. Really, previous ages of decadence would look upon the modern avant-garde with amazement and admiration. We've outdone the lot of them. But the curious, impressive thing is that so many artists are able to go through these things as intelligent men — not as totally unprincipled men. If you go through these things to some purpose, it can be even noble. It's as if, with your own rot, you refuel and invigorate — you fertilize this very scorched earth for those yet to come.[135]

Throughout history and in all societies, we find men who swear allegiance to this demonic philosophy, whatever form it may take. Marx was prefigured by such persons as Mazdak, the revolutionary communist in 5th century (A. D.) Persia, a man who very nearly succeeded in overthrowing the society in which he lived.[136]  In the

---

[134] While they are out of favor in today's historical circles, Nesta Webster's studies contain solid information dealing with the activities and the development of Europe's secret societies. Some of the connections that she establishes between historical events and certain conspiratorial groups are probably questionable on methodological grounds, but much of what she has to say is very important. Historical scholarship always has difficulty in treating secret societies, since they leave few written documents and many of the public data are deliberately misleading. Three of her most important works are *Secret Societies and Subversive Movements* (Hawthorne, Calif.: Omni Reprint, [1923] 1964); *World Revolution* (Waco, Texas: Owen Reprint, [1921] 1964); *The French Revolution* (London: Constable, 1921).

[135] Barry Farrell, "The Other Culture," *Life* (Feb. 17, 1967), 99.

[136] Cf. article on "Mazdak" in James Hastings (ed.), *Encyclopedia of Religion and Ethics* (N. Y.: Scribners, 1951), 508-10.

Assassins of 11th century Arabia (the name is derived from the same root as hashish, which was an integral part of Assassin ritual), a sect of revolutionary Moslems, the same basic perspective was present, and it was imported into the West by Bogomils and Cathars, the dualist sects of the medieval world.[137] The whole list of rationalist secret societies in 18th century Europe — Illuminati, Rosicrucians, Carbonari, Grand Orient Masonry — all contributed to the same revolutionary tradition, though in the name of enlightened and liberated humanity. A classic example of revolutionary French science in the period after the Terror was published in one of the new scientific journals:

> The Revolution has razed everything to the ground. Government, morals, habits, everything has to be rebuilt. What a magnificent site for the architects! What a grand opportunity of making use of all the fine and excellent ideas that had remained speculative, of employing so many materials that could not be used before, or rejecting so many others that had been obstructions for centuries and which one had been forced to use.[138]

The culminating point in this tradition was the French Revolution. It was here that secular humanism, revolutionary fervor, and the secret societies fused into one overwhelming movement.[139] Marx was the inheritor of this tradition, especially of the plot of Babeuf to overthrow the government in 1795. Marx acknowledged his respect for Babeuf's efforts.[140] In fact, Marx's diagram for conspiratorial, revolutionary action which he set forth in his *Address of the Central*

---

[137] Steven Runciman's *The Medieval Manichee* (N. Y.: Viking Press, 1961) gives an account of some of these sects.

[138] Quoted in F. A. Hayek, *The Counter-Revolution of Science*, 109.

[139] The role played by the secret societies is not some wild thesis in the mind of Mrs. Webster; liberals have proudly acknowledged the part which these societies took. Cf. Una Birch, *Secret Societies and the French Revolution* (London: John Lane, 1911). See also Charles William Heckethorne, *The Secret Societies of All Ages* (2 vols.; New Hyde Park, New York: University Books, [1897] 1965) for a sympathetic treatment of these movements.

[140] Marx and Engels, *The Communist Manifesto*, in *Marx-Engels Selected Works*, I, 61. Cf. David Thomson, *The Babeuf Plot* (Lon-

*Committee to the Communist League* (1850) was modeled after the Jacobin organization and Babeuf's secret society.[141] Whatever modifications Marx later made on his original conspiratorial formulations, there can be little question that the framework of his theory of revolution was based upon an ancient cosmology of nature which has had a long history in Western (and Eastern) civilization. Eliade has seen this close relation between Marx and the ancient world:

> Yet Marxism preserves a meaning to history. For Marxism, events are not a succession of arbitrary accidents; they exhibit a coherent structure and, above all, they lead to a definite end — final elimination of the terror of history — "salvation." Thus, at the end of the Marxist philosophy of history, lies the age of gold of the archaic eschatologies. In this sense it is correct to say not only that Marx "brought Hegel's philosophy down to earth," but also that he reconfirmed, upon the exclusively humanistic level, the value of the primitive myth of the age of gold, with the difference that he puts the age of gold only at the end of history, instead of putting it at the beginning too. Here, for the militant Marxist, lies the secret of the remedy for the terror of history: just as the contemporaries of a "dark age" consoled themselves for their increasing sufferings by the thought that the aggravation of evil hastens the final deliverance, so the militant Marxist of our day reads, in the drama provoked by the pressure of reality, a necessary evil, the premonitory symptom of the approaching victory that will put an end forever to all historical "evil."[142]

don: Paul, 1947); Albert Fried and Ronald Sanders (eds.), *Socialist Thought* (Garden City, N. Y.: Doubleday Anchor, 1964), 43-71; Edmund Wilson, *To the Finland Station* (Garden City, N. Y.: Doubleday Anchor, 1953), 69-73. For a defense of Babeuf by one of his contemporaries, see Filipo M. Buonarroti, *Babeuf's Conspiracy for Equality* (London: Hetherington, 1836). Finally, see J. L. Talmon, *The Origins of Totalitarian Democracy* (N. Y.: Praeger, 1960), 167-255.

[141] Marx, *Address* (1850) in *Marx-Engels Selected Works,* I, 106-07. Cf. Ernst Bloch, "Man and Citizen According to Marx," in Fromm (ed.), *Socialist Humanism,* 220-27.

[142] Mircea Eliade, *Cosmos and History: The Myth of the Eternal Return* (N. Y.: Harper Torchbook, 1959), 149.

Eliade could have stated his case even more forcefully. Marx *did* share with the ancients a belief in a past Golden Age, as we have seen; at some point in man's history, albeit a primitive culture, man's world was without alienation. The coming age will be superior, of course, because mankind will also control the former chaos of the environment around him. In his posthumously published manuscripts, *Grundrisse der Kritik der Politischen Ökonomie* (1857-58), Marx sketched some of his ideas on the primitive communal social structure, and as E. J. Hobsbawm has pointed out, Marx's own interests after the publication of *Capital* (1867) were "overwhelmingly concerned with this stage of social development. . . ."[143] Engels shared Marx's interest, and he also pictured a primitive Golden Age in his *Origin of the Family, Private Property and the State* (1884).[144]

The transition between capitalism and the first stage of communism would be heralded by the Revolution, and there is no question that Marx used explicitly soteriological language in describing the coming conflagration. In his essay extolling the Paris Commune of 1871, Marx wrote of a "France, whose salvation from ruin, and whose regeneration were impossible, without the revolutionary overthrow of the political and social conditions that had engendered the Second Empire [of Napoleon III], and under its fostering care, matured into utter rottenness."[145] Marx did not really understand the Commune, but the use he made of it demonstrates that he saw it in terms of political and social regeneration — collective salvation.[146]

---

[143] Eric J. Hobsbawm, "Introduction," in Marx's *Pre-Capitalist Economic Formations* (N. Y.: International Publishers, 1964), 49. This volume contains extracts from *Grundrisse*.

[144] *Marx-Engels Selected Works,* II, 252-55, 263 [cited hereafter as MESW].

[145] Marx, *The Civil War in France* (1871) in MESW, I, 510. On the history of the Commune, see the Marxist version by Lissagaray, *History of the Commune of 1871* (London: Reeves and Turner, 1886), translated by Marx's daughter, Elanor Marx Aveling. For more accurate accounts, see Frank Jellenik, *The Paris Commune of 1871* (London: Victor Gollancz, 1937); Alistair Horne, *The Fall of Paris* (N. Y.: St. Martins, 1965).

[146] Similar statements can be found in the essay: MESW, I, 497, 521.

Revolutionary practice gives the workers a sense of self-realization, since through revolutionary action alone does class consciousness develop. Marx, in 1850, characterized this message: "You have got to go through fifteen, twenty, fifty years of civil wars and national wars not merely to change your conditions but in order to change yourselves and become qualified for political power. . . ."[147] Again, a semi-religious function is accomplished; Caillois's thesis is that only in war and bloodshed can modern man approximate the destruction psychology of the chaos festivals. The communal feeling of collective devotion to a higher cause in modern civilization can be experienced only in warfare.[148] Marx's belief that proletarian consciousness can be achieved only in struggle is very similar to Caillois's position; in this sense, the proletarian revolution has the same religious and psychological function as the festival had in the ancient world.

Engels, in his forthright manner, wrote to Marx in 1857, just as the depression of 1857 was beginning. He had been recuperating from an illness in the United States. His language is clearly religious: "The bourgeois filth of the last seven years had stuck to me to a certain extent after all, if it is washed away now I shall feel another fellow again. The crisis will do me as much good physically as a sea-bathe, I can see that already."[149] The cleansing waters of total chaos: this is the theological foundation of the religion of revolution.

Marx's doctrine of the "dictatorship of the proletariat" reveals a great deal about the function of the Revolution. After the proletarian revolution is achieved, and the working classes seize political power, there will be "a poltical transition period in which the state can be nothing but *the revolutionary dictatorship of the proletariat.*"[150] This will not be the ultimate state, but merely the era of rule by the working classes in which all remnants of bourgeois life will be crushed.

---

[147] Minutes of London Central Committee of the Communist League, 15 Sept., 1850: *Marx-Engels Selected Correspondence,* 92.

[148] Roger Caillois, *Man and the Sacred,* ch. 4.

[149] Engels to Marx, 15 Nov., 1857: *Marx-Engels Selected Correspondence,* 86.

[150] Marx, *Critique of the Gotha Program* (1875), MESW, II, 33.

Engels spelled out in detail what this period would be like, and what the purpose of the proletarian state should be:

> As, therefore, the state is only a transitional institution which is used in the struggle, in the revolution, in order to hold down one's adversaries by force, it is pure nonsense to talk of a free people's state: so long as the proletariat still *uses* the state, it does not use it in the interests of freedom but in order to hold down its adversaries, and as soon as it becomes possible to speak of freedom the state as such ceases to exist.[151]

The transitional period is the one in which the new rulers begin to guide the new society into the world of socialist plenty, but to do this, freedom and bourgeois institutions must be stamped out. It is a period of enforced destruction, as Iring Fetscher has pointed out: Marx's period of "crude communism" would not overcome alienation, and it would even be less progressive in some ways than capitalism.

> There is no connection between this way of abolishing private property and the real appropriation of alienated reality. On the contrary all people would be reduced, according to this notion, to the unnatural simplicity of poor people without needs and wants. "Community [in this case] is only a community of labor and equality of salary paid out by the Communist capital, the community as the universal capitalist." The obvious indication of this kind of brute Communism which Marx understood as a primitive generalization of private property is the *Weibergemeinschaft,* the community of women. This Communism is inhuman, not because it destroys capitalism but because it makes capitalism broader, more radical and more absolute. *It does not transcend capitalism but even lags behind some of the more progressive aspects of private property.* Nevertheless Marx thought at this time that at least from the theoretical point of view this kind of Communism was a stage through which one necessarily had to pass.[152]

Here is one of the dialectical results of the Marxian system: it is simultaneously a call to total revolution against the state and a

---

[151] Engels to A. Bebel, 18-28 March, 1875: MESW, II, 42.
[152] Iring Fetscher, "The Young and the Old Marx," in Lobkowicz (ed.), *Marx and the Western World,* 30.

program to create an absolute state. Marx's ultimate vision was a hope in a society which needed no state, yet it was to take a period of state-planned inhumanity to bring this world into being. Marx tried to compensate the total authoritarianism with a vision of a truly human society to come; this was Marx's "pie on the earth" dream. "But these defects are inevitable in the first phase of communist society as it is when it has just emerged after prolonged birth pangs from capitalist society."[153] The "mature" Marx of 1875 then drew his picture of the coming paradise:

> In a higher phase of communist society, after the enslaving subordination of the individual to the division of labour, and therewith also the antithesis between mental and physical labour, has vanished; after labour has become not only a means of life but life's prime want; after the productive forces have also increased with the all-around development of the individual, and all the springs of co-operative wealth flow more abundantly — only then can the narrow horizon of bourgeois right be crossed in its entirety and society inscribe on its banners: From each according to his ability, to each according to his needs![154]

Marx's basic authoritarianism was perceived by his anarchistic rival, Michael Bakunin. Bakunin had once been able to cooperate with Marx, since they shared an opposition to the bourgeois state, but Bakunin later broke with Marx. He did not share Marx's faith in a total state's ability to abolish the state forever:

> I hate communism because it is the negation of liberty and because humanity is for me unthinkable without liberty. I am not a communist, because communism concentrates and swallows up in itself for the benefit of the State all the forces of society, because it inevitably leads to the concentration of property in the hands of the State, whereas I want the abolition of the State, which under the pretext of moralizing and civilizing men has hitherto only enslaved, persecuted, exploited, and corrupted them. I want to see society and collective or social property organized from below upwards, by way of free association, not from above downwards, by means of any kind of authority whatever.[155]

---

153 *Critique of the Gotha Program*, MESW, II, 24.
154 *Ibid.*
155 Quoted in E. H. Carr, *Michael Bakunin* (N. Y.: Vintage, [1937] 1961), 356. How one can be against private property and also

Some contemporary scholars — e.g., Lichtheim, Halle, Schumpeter — want to play down Marx's revolutionary fervor, especially the call to revolution which he made in his later career. The problem with this interpretation is providing an explanation for his obvious delight with the French Commune of 1871. This "aberation" in the so-called "mature" Marx indicates that his old dream of regeneration through total chaos had merely been waiting for an opportunity to reappear as an intimate part of his social analysis. In an otherwise brilliant article, Halle tries to "demythologize" Marx: Marx was only using the word "revolution" as a religious metaphor, not as an actual form of political action. Sometimes scholars will not take other men at their word; they just cannot believe that another scholar would say such things.[156]

These interpretations of Marx's later "mellowing" are based upon the fact that Marx, at certain stages of his career, was willing to de-emphasize the idea of revolutionary action because of tactical considerations. But his real concern was betrayed by his economic analyses; again and again in his "mature" period, he saw traces of the coming revolution — a revolution which would be ushered in by means of an economic crisis in the world capitalist system. He and Engels welcomed the coming collapse with open arms. As he wrote to Engels in 1857 (supposedly in his "mature" period): "I am working like mad all through the nights at putting my economic studies together so that I may at least have the outlines clear before

property managed by the state is not very clear, but Bakunin certainly saw the latent totalitarianism present in the Marxian system, and for this reason his comments are useful. What exactly he meant by this statement, "I am a collectivist, but not a communist," is a mystery (idem.).

[156] Louis J. Halle, "Marx's Religious Drama," *Encounter,* XXV (Oct., 1965), 37; George Lichtheim, *Marxism.* Lichtheim is probably the most important advocate of the idea that Marx lost his revolutionary outlook after 1850 and became a sort of Social Democrat prototype. Bertram D. Wolfe apparently agrees with Lichtheim on this point: *Marxism: One Hundred Years in the Life of a Doctrine* (N. Y.: Dial Press, 1965), 239n.

the deluge comes."[157] In fact, the two men were continually prophesying the collapse throughout their lifetimes. Engels was still acting as a prophet of doom as late as 1886, although in 1892 he was forced to admit that capitalism was apparently experiencing a revival.[158]

Robert C. Tucker's evaluation seems perfectly justified: "Thus, for Marx, the communist revolution is the means of attaining not material abundance (though that, in his view, will come too) and not justice in the distribution of goods, but the spiritual regeneration of man."[159] Marx held, unquestionably, a religion of revolution. Regeneration through total chaos was his goal, and the proletariat would serve as the priestly class in this ritual so that the whole society might be freed from its alienation.

It was pointed out earlier that Marx's doctrine of alienation was a substitute for the Christian doctrine of the fall of man. In spite of this apparent affinity for a Christian cosmology, Marx's system must be linked more with pagan ancient religion than with Old Testament messianism. This is not really contradictory, since the cosmologies of the ancients were equally substitutes for the idea of the fall. The similarities and distinctions between the pagan and Hebrew-Christian views have already been hinted at previously. The ancients believed in a *metaphysical* fall from chaos into the bondage of order and law. Marx asserted (or so his language indicates) that the fall was originally *psychological,* but that man's alienation became reciprocal with

---

[157] Marx to Engels, 8 Dec., 1857: *Marx-Engels Selected Correspondence,* 225. This letter probably was a response to Engel's letter of 15 Nov., in footnote 149.

[158] Donald M. Lowe, *The Function of "China" in Marx, Lenin, and Mao* (Berkeley: University of California Press, 1966), 18. For other accounts of Marx's continual predictions that never actually materialized into the Revolution, see John Kenneth Turner, *Challenge to Karl Marx,* ch. 6; Bober, *Karl Marx's Interpretation of History,* 305-06, 387-88; Schwartzschild, *Karl Marx: The Red Prussian,* 256-61. The most thorough treatment is found in Fred M. Gottheil, *Marx's Economic Predictions.* (Evanston, Ill.: Northwestern University Press, 1967).

[159] Robert C. Tucker, *Philosophy and Myth in Karl Marx,* 24.

private property at a later date. By changing the environment, man would regain his pre-alienation state, but with his modern technology intact. The Christian view is that the fall was *ethical;* the universe, including man, was cursed as a result of the fall — the alienation between man and the Creator — but the fall itself was ethical. Because man is alienated from God, he is also alienated from his fellow men, since they are made in God's image. The restoration of man and his civilization is not to be accomplished, therefore, by a flight from law, but by a return to covenant obedience in terms of Biblical law. Regeneration is to come through faith in Christ's sacrificial atonement on the cross; this is God's grace to the individual. Any social reconstruction that should result from this *ethical* regeneration of mankind must be in terms of society's obedience to law. Man, in this conception, is truly free only when he is saved by grace (St. Paul's doctrine of the "new man in Christ": II Cor. 5:17) and when he is under God's law. Total perfection is reached only after the judgment brings an end to time; it will not come as a result of the activity of self-proclaimed autonomous men. Thus, the idea of total perfection which is implied in the Marxian scheme is utterly foreign to the orthodox Hebrew-Christian tradition.[160]

There is no question that passages in the Bible do exist that seem to contain a similar hope in total conflagration. The final chapter of Isaiah and the third chapter of the second epistle of St. Peter are examples of this. Judgment in the scriptures is frequently seen in terms of the language of fire and destruction. At times the references deal with the last days of the earth and God's final judgment; in other cases references to the shaking of earthly foundations apply

---

[160] On this point, see B. B. Warfield, *Perfectionism* (Philadelphia: Presbyterian and Reformed Publishing Co., 1958). Raymond Aron has seen the implications of the doctrine of revolution: "Only revolution, because it is an adventure, or a revolutionary régime, because it accepts the permanent use of violence, seems capable of attaining the goal of perfection. The myth of the Revolution serves as a refuge for utopian intellectuals; it becomes the mysterious, unpredictable intercessor between the real and the ideal." *The Opium of the Intellectuals,* 65. Cf. J. F. Wolpert, "The Myth of Revolution," *Ethics,* LVIII (1947-48), 245-55.

only to God's temporal retribution or to a change in God's administration (as from the national covenant with the Hebrews to the universal covenant with the gentile world). For example, Psalm 18 is filled with the language of cataclysmic change, yet David's meaning was clearly allegorical. But one fact dominates all these visions of conflagration: it is God, and only God, who initiates the change. It is expected that faithful men will remain orderly in all the aspects of their lives; they are not to create chaos in order to escape from law (Rom. 13; I Cor. 14:40). It is reserved to God alone to bring his total judgment to the world: "I will overturn, overturn, overturn, it [the crown]: and it shall be no more, until he come whose right it is; and I will give it to him" (Ezek. 21:27).

In contrast to this view stood ancient paganism. It was man who would accomplish this shattering of the foundation. It was man who, by ritual participation in the cosmic time of pre-creation, would restore the Golden Age. It was man who would abolish time and restore eternity to earth. To abolish time and time's curses: here was the goal of the pagan world.

> The wish to abolish time can be seen even more clearly in the "orgy" which takes place, with varying degrees of violence, during the New Year ceremonies. An orgy is also a regression into the "dark," a restoration of the primeval chaos, and as such precedes all creation, every manifestation of ordered form. The fusion of all forms into one single, vast, undifferentiated unity is an exact reproduction of the "total" mode of reality. I pointed out earlier the function and meaning of the orgy, at once sexual and agricultural; at the cosmological level, the "orgy" represents chaos or the ultimate disappearance of limits and, as time goes, the inauguration of the Great Time, of the "eternal moment," of non-duration. The presence of the orgy among the ceremonials shows the *will to abolish the past totally by abolishing all creation.*[161]

---

[161] Mircea Eliade, *Patterns in Comparative Religion,* 399; cf. 400-07 for a full discussion of the subject. "The meaning of the carnivalesque orgy at the end of the year is confirmed by the fact that the chaos is always followed by a new creation of the cosmos. All these seasonal celebrations go on to a more or less clear symbolic repetition of the creation." *Ibid.,* 400.

This, it should be apparent, is the very essence of the Marxian faith. The proletarian class "can only in a revolution succeed in ridding itself of all the muck of the ages and become fitted to found society anew."[162] What Marx wanted was an escape from history. The history of all hitherto existing societies has not been a truly human history, since alienation has dominated them all. As he wrote in the Preface to the *Critique of Political Economy:*

> The bourgeois relations of production are the last antagonistic form of the social process of production — antagonistic not in the sense of individual antagonism, but of one arising from conditions surrounding the life of individuals in society; at the same time the productive forces developing in the womb of bourgeois society create the material conditions for the solution of that antagonism. This social formation constitutes, therefore, the closing chapter of the prehistoric stage of human society.[163]

All earlier societies have been merely "prehistoric." We may call our era "history," but that is a misnomer. What we call history must be abolished if man is to survive. Marx, therefore, appealed to revolutionary chaos to bring an end to this era and to inaugurate true human history. Man must accomplish this, for man is Marx's only god. Eschatology for Marx is the restoration of the society free from alienation and brought into being by man; the escape from the bondage of present history will be achieved.

In linking Marx to the ancient cosmology rather than to the Hebrew-Christian tradition one problem does exist. On the surface, at least, Marx's conception of history is linear; the ancients held a cyclical view of history. This is an apparent contradiction. Marx's view seems to be closer to the Christian viewpoint: history does progress in the Marxian system, and historical facts are important. In this sense, Marx is in the Western tradition; no one who is a part of that tradition can completely escape the influence of Augustine's linear history. It would be odd if Marx had not shared with all Western thinkers some of the premises of Augustine. Nevertheless,

---

[162] Marx, *The German Ideology,* 86.
[163] Preface, *A Contribution to the Critique of Political Economy,* 13; cf. MESW, I, 364.

in several important respects, Marx's history *is* cyclical in nature. If man fell from a primitive society in which there was no alienation, what is to prevent a similar fall back into alienation after the coming revolution has produced the Golden Age? Marx said specifically that private property did not cause the fall into alienation but rather that the reverse was true. Though he assumed that a mere reordering of the social environment will regenerate mankind forever, he could not guarantee that this regenerated state would be preserved. If the original fall was essentially psychological, what is to prevent a similar fall into alienation at some unspecified date in the future? It would seem that this is the implication of Tucker's observation: "And he never seems to have asked himself what would prevent the inhuman force from rising again to estrange man on the yonder side of history."[164] Thus, it seems safe to say that Marx returned, at least in part, to a conception of history which partakes of the old Greek cycles, in so far as he was never able to show that the very logic of his system would not lead back into some kind of cyclical pattern.

With Engels we find some of these themes made explicit. His discussion of the eternal cycle of matter is illuminating. Matter, he wrote, is in eternal motion, "a cycle in which every finite mode of existence of matter . . . is equally transient, and wherein nothing is eternal but eternally changing, eternally moving matter and the laws according to which it changes."[165] In fact, under Engels's earlier assumptions, even the laws of change themselves are changing. It can be argued, perhaps, that a cyclical nature does not necessarily

---

[164] Robert C. Tucker, *Philosophy and Myth in Karl Marx*, 240.

[165] Engels, *Dialectics of Nature,* published posthumously from his notebooks (N. Y.: International Publishers, [1940] 1963), 24. Some important commentators, including Lichtheim and Tucker, do not wish to admit that the later excursions into the study of science that were made by Engels really reflect Marx's perspective. Marx, it is argued, was interested only in human society and social dialectics, not in any mechanical dialectic of nature. Marx's letter to Lassalle, 16 Jan., 1861, throws some light on this subject: "Darwin's book is very important and serves me as a basis in natural science for the class struggle in history." Again, in a letter to Engels, 19 Dec., 1860,

imply a cyclical human history, but when the idea is taken into conjunction with Marx's earlier teachings, it is not beyond reason to conclude that the Marxian conception of history resembles the Greek conception far more than it resembles Augustine's theological, linear history.

We have examined Marx's doctrine of revolution as a cosmological and philosophical theme. This, however, does not explain the historical setting in which Marx placed the inevitable chaos, nor does it give much light on the whole problem of revolutionary tactics. It is to this aspect of the revolutionary format to which we must turn.

Marx never set forth his outline of the Revolution in any one place. Like most of his theories, this one is found throughout his works, and it is not altogether clear as to exactly what he thought the Revolution would be.[166] As to how it was to come into being, he never decided; in fact, conflicting statements concerning the proletarian uprising have been used as a means for distinguishing

he wrote: "Although it is developed in the crude English style, this is the book which contains the basis in natural history for our view." *Marx-Engels Selected Correspondence,* 125, 126. If Marx had been uninterested in any natural dialectic, why was he so taken with Darwin's theory of the eternal struggle in nature? In this regard, I wish to quote from a letter to me from Walter Odajnyk, author of *Marxism and Existentialism* (1965), dated 21 Sept., 1966: "I know that Western commentators — for some curious reason — have attempted to saddle Engels with the sole responsibility for the somewhat embarrassing natural dialectics of Marxism, but I would maintain that it is a logical development of Hegelianism into the material-natural sphere. Marx, for obvious reasons, was more interested in the consequences of an upsidedown Hegelianism in the socio-economic sphere, and to Engels fell the natural order." As Odajnyk goes on to say, Marx was alive at the time of the writing of both *Anti-Dühring* and *Dialectics of Nature.* In reference to the former, Schumpeter writes: "It cannot be denied however that Marx wrote part of ch. x and shares responsibility for the whole book." *Capitalism, Socialism and Democracy,* 39n. The Soviet Marxists, of course, have always accepted Engels's views as basic to Marxism.
[166] Alfred G. Meyer, *Marxism: The Unity of Theory and Practice,* 80.

the younger Marx from the "mature Marx." The year 1850 is usually seen as the point of transition.[167]

In his early years, Marx firmly believed that the forces of material production in capitalism would bring the Revolution to a head. The exploited proletariat class would rise up against the bourgeoisie and take possession of the means of production, the state, and the other organs of bourgeois control. He never fully abandoned this explanation.[168] In 1867 he published volume one of *Capital,* a huge treatise in economics which was supposed to prove that the inner contradictions of capitalist production and distribution would ultimately lead to the Revolution. When that glorious day arrives, "The death knell of capitalist property sounds. The expropriators are expropriated."[169] In the *Communist Manifesto* (1848), he argued that the proletarians must seize control of the capitalist state and use their political power to impose a ten-point program of expropriation against the capitalist order, thus crushing all capitalist institutions and ideas.[170]

One of the most important of the earlier organizational documents was his *Address to the Communist League* (1850). It outlined a program of tactical terroristic activities, using subversion in the tradition of Babeuf's conspiracy. He advised proletarians to use Jacobin-type clubs as the basis of the organizational structure, while maintaining close alliances with the various secret revolutionary societies of the period. A secret, underground government should be established, so that it can seize control of the state when the bourgeois order collapses.[171] Terrorism is useful in stirring up social chaos. In all things pertaining to the proletarian struggle, "Their battle cry must be: "The Revolution in Permanence.""[172]

The changes in Marx's outlook stemmed from the failure of the revolutions in Europe in 1848-50. After this time, he still looked

---

[167] Lichtheim, *Marxism,* 122-29.
[168] Marx, *Wage-Labor and Capital* (1847), MESW, I, 93-105.
[169] *Capital,* I, 837.
[170] *Communist Manifesto,* MESW, I, 53-54.
[171] *Address,* MESW, I, 111. Cf. *The Class Struggles in France, 1848-1850* (1850), MESW, I, 185, 198.
[172] *Address,* MESW, I, 117.

to the contradictions of the capitalist system as the basic cause of the coming struggle, but he began to admit that democratic action might be of real service to the revolutionary cause. If universal suffrage could hasten the collapse, fine, do not hesitate to use it: this was his message to the working class. We have already seen how he admitted that in England and America there might be some small chance to avoid the Revolution in the transition to socialism. He even praised the Ten Hours Act which shortened the working day in England. Of course, in this later period he was trying to gain the support of the English trade unions, and the ballot box appealed to them.[173] As Marx himself realized, he was not wholly forthright in his famous *Address* to the Working Men's Association: "It was very difficult to frame the thing so that our view should appear in a form acceptable from the present standpoint of the workers' movement. In a few weeks the same people will be holding meetings for the franchise with Bright and Cobden. It will take time before the reawakened movement allows the old boldness of speech. It will be necessary to be *fortiter in re, suaviter in modo* [bold in matter, mild in manner]."[174]

Marx's appreciation for the cooperative movement has led Martin Buber to place Marx in the camp of the European utopian thinkers. In his *Paths in Utopia,* Buber argues that Marx wanted to create a sense of communal membership in his post-revolutionary society, and for this reason Marx saw in the co-ops the sign of a coming transformation of society.[175] Marx, in this sense, was a Utopian

---

[173] Marx, *The Inaugural Address of the Working Men's International Association* (1864), MESW, I, 382. Cf. A. Lozovsky (pseudonym for Solomon A. Dridzo), *Marx and the Trade Unions* (N. Y.: International Publishers, 1935), esp. 23-25, 48, 167-70. Lichtheim's interpretation of the document is straightforward: "The *Inaugural Address* is in a sense the Charter of Social Democracy." *Marxism,* 113. Perhaps so, but this does not mean that Marx intended it to be such. As a corrective to Lichtheim's view, see G. D. H. Cole, *The Meaning of Marxism,* ch. 7, esp. 181-90.

[174] Marx to Engels, 4 Nov., 1864: *Marx-Engels Selected Correspondence,* 163.

[175] Martin Buber, *Paths in Utopia* (London: Routledge and Kegan

Socialist, although he had criticized his utopian predecessors for their lack of insight into the nature of capitalist relations of production. His goals, if not his methodology, were utopian. Marx never said exactly what part the co-ops would play in the Revolution; whether their role would be peaceful or revolutionary was never made clear.

There was a fundamental ambivalence in Marx's system: was the primary task of the proletariat political or was it revolutionary and conspiratorial? The streams of Marxism have divided on precisely this issue. In 1872 the general rules of the International Working Men's Association were amended to read: "This constitution of the proletariat into a political party is indispensable to ensure the triumph of the social Revolution and of its goal: the abolition of classes."[176] In a sense, the Marxian scheme had become schizophrenic at this point; both Lenin and Eduard Bernstein could subsequently appeal to Marx (and to Marx's tactical decisions) in support of their two very different positions.[177] Both democratic action and revolution were being affirmed at the same time.[178]

The basic message of the International was still the same as the appeal of the defunct Communist League: ". . . the conquest of political power becomes the great duty of the proletariat."[179] In the 1850 *Address of the Central Committee of the Communist League,* Marx had said that "everywhere workers' candidates are put alongside of the bourgeois-democratic candidates," and he recommended that these candidates should be members of the League whenever possible. Furthermore, "their election is [to be] promoted by all

---

Paul, 1949), ch. 8. For Marx's comments on the co-operative movement, see the *Inaugural Address,* MESW, I, 383; *Capital,* III, 527. It is interesting that a co-op publishing firm was the first company to publish Marx's complete economic writings in this country. This, of course, was Charles H. Kerr & Co.

[176] *General Rules of the I.W.M.A.,* MESW, I, 388.

[177] On Bernstein's socialism and German Social Democracy, see Peter Gay, *The Dilemma of Democratic Socialism* (N. Y.: Collier, 1962). See also Bernstein's *Evolutionary Socialism* (N. Y.: Schoken, [1899] 1961).

[178] Cf. M. M. Bober, *Karl Marx's Interpretation of History,* ch. 13.

[179] *General Rules,* MESW, I, 389.

possible means."[180] Marx was not a Social Democrat in his later years, as Lichtheim would have us believe; he was a revolutionary who was willing to use all means, including the pressure of the ballot, to further his religious goal. Marx would have agreed with Lenin when the latter gave his rule for Party action: one must *"work wherever the masses are to be found."*[181] As Lenin put it, "the revolutionaries who are unable to combine illegal forms of struggle with *every* form of legal struggle are poor revolutionaries indeed."[182] One must use all approaches to bring about social chaos. *Marx was a good tactician: theory was always subordinate to the rule of practice.* The person who fails to understand this basic fact will never understand Karl Marx and those who have followed him.[183]

This conflict between theory and tactics can be seen in Marx's treatment of the Russian question. His system could not allow for a proletarian revolution in any rural, pre-industrial country if theoretical consistency were to be preserved. History's stages cannot be by-passed; feudalism must precede capitalism, and a fully developed capitalism must come before proletarian paradise. He spelled this out very clearly: "No social order ever disappears before all the productive forces, for which their is room in it, have been developed; and new higher relations of production never appear before the material conditions of their existence have matured in the womb of the old society."[184] Russia was an agrarian nation; it had only

---

[180] *Address of the Central Committee to the Communist League* (1850), MESW, I, 114.

[181] Lenin, *"Left Wing" Communism: An Infantile Disorder* (N. Y.: International Publishers, [1920] 1940), 37.

[182] *Ibid.*, 77.

[183] Cf. Lozovsky, *Marx and the Trade Unions,* 114; G. D. H. Cole, *The Meaning of Marxism,* tries to argue that Marx's "flexibility" involved no departure from consistent theory (50). How this "flexibility" is to be kept from becoming pure relativism, Cole does not make clear (nor did Lenin or Marx).

[184] Preface to *A Contribution to the Critique of Political Economy* (1859), 12. He repeated this idea in *Capital,* III, 1030. For obvious reasons, the Marxist writer Maurice Dobb has tried to argue that Marx really never taught that the stages were chronological. He

abolished serfdom in 1861. How could a proletarian revolt possibly succeed there? There was virtually no proletariat to create it. Yet both Marx and Engels came to the conclusion that Russia could have its Revolution apart from the economic foundations required for such an event. In 1875 Engels wrote that the Russian communal land system, the *mir,* could serve as the foundation for a new society, if only there were a revolution in the West immediately following.[185] The preface to the *Communist Manifesto's* Russian edition (1882), co-authored by Marx and Engels, asserted the same thing.[186] In a letter written by Marx in 1877, he had announced: "If Russia continues to pursue the path she has followed since 1861, she will lose the finest chance ever offered by history to a nation, in order to undergo all the fatal vicissitudes of the capitalist regime."[187]

It is not altogether clear as to why Marx and Engels saw fit to abandon their theoretical framework in order to make room for the possibility of a Russian Revolution. It may have been that Marx was impressed by the fact that the Russian radicals were very often open followers of Marx. Russia was the first country in which a wide distribution of *Capital* was experienced. (The Czar's censors thought that such a large, ponderous volume would not be read by anyone.) Buber has seen in this admission by Marx a desire on his part to achieve the kind of communal society which he had always dreamed of: the *mir* seemed to be just this sort of ideal society.[188] Whatever

---

was only concerned with the development of the increasing individualization of man as he progressed away from tribal unity. Dobb, "Marx on Pre-Capitalist Economic Formations," *Science and Society,* XXX (1966), 319-25. He is supported in this interpretation by another Marxist, Eric J. Hobsbawn, "Introduction" to Marx's *Pre-Capitalist Economic Formations,* 36. The reason for all this hedging is that Marx's historical schema is not supported by the historical facts, and Russia and China in the 20th century are the final refutation of the Marxist version of historical stages.

[185] Engels, *On Social Relations in Russia* (1875), MESW, II, 58.

[186] Cf. *Marx-Engels Selected Correspondence,* 355.

[187] Marx to the Editor of the *Otyecestvenniye Zapisky,* late 1877; *ibid.,* 353.

[188] Buber, *Paths in Utopia,* 90-94.

the reason, the "stage theory" of economic and social evolution was dealt a hard blow by the founders of the Marxian system.

What, then, becomes of the all-encompassing theory of capitalist development? What happens to the inevitable sweep of man-made history on the march? Marx answered one criticism of his Russian compromise in this fashion:

> He feels himself obliged to metamorphose my historical sketch of the genesis of capitalism in Western Europe into an historico-philosophic theory of the *marche general* [general path] imposed by fate upon every people, whatever the historic circumstances in which it finds itself, in order that it may ultimately arrive at the form of economy which will ensure, together with the greatest expansion of the productive powers of social labour, the most complete development of man. But I beg his pardon. (He is both honouring me and shaming me too much.)[189]

It is almost beyond belief! The system is now nothing more than "an historical sketch of the genesis of capitalism in Western Europe." The system, as anything more than a general survey of European history, is now officially gutted by its author! It is fantastic that so much labor and energy, so much poverty and sickness, should have been self-imposed by Marx in order to bring forth such a pitiful mouse.

G. D. H. Cole, who was either unfamiliar with this letter or else did not take it seriously, sees Marx's universal history as a powerful, but unfortunately inaccurate, hypothesis. He raises a very legitimate question:

> They could have rested content with a formulation of the law of development limited to the particular civilization which they were trying to influence. Whether, formulated in this narrower way, their theory would have exercised as powerful a spell as it has in fact exercised may be doubted; for its universalism was undoubtedly not the least of its attractions and played a large part in converting it from a rationalistic doctrine into a belief which could be held with the intensity of a religion.[190]

---

[189] Marx to Editor of *O. Z., op. cit.,* 354.
[190] Cole, *The Meaning of Marxism,* 82; cf. 209.

Without the inevitability doctrine, the system loses its forcefulness; without its universality, the same thing is true. Marx drew his view of society and history in large, compelling sweeps of his pen, and as a result, a new religion swept over Europe and Asia. Yet whenever they found themselves in some intellectual trap of their own making, Marx and Engels quibbled their system away in obscure letters to their associates. It was dishonest intellectually, for Marx did not really think that his vision of humanity was less than universal. In 1871 he wrote to Kugelmann: "The struggle of the working class against the capitalist class and its state has entered upon a new phase with the struggle in Paris. Whatever the immediate results may be, a new point of departure of world-historic importance has been gained."[191] The great Revolution was coming, period. But anything which competed with that hope was superfluous for Marx; even theoretical consistency was not to stand in the way of the Revolution, *any* kind of Revolution, even a rural-communal one in backward Russia. At this point, Marx's total religious commitment to the ideal of revolution should be obvious. The Revolution had become a passion for him, a truly holy goal, and everything — family, wealth, time, and even theoretical consistency — had to be sacrificed to it.

The Marxist message is, above all, a call to *revolution;* the society must be *turned over* if it is to be made whole again. In opposition to the Marxian perspective, the traditional Christian message has been a call to *repentance;* individual men must *turn around* from the path of destruction. Marx, in spite of his apparent moralism — almost a Victorian moralism — always denied being a moralist.[192]

---

[191] Marx to Kugelmann, 17 April, 1871: *Letters to Kugelmann,* 125. Some kind of total revolution was vital for Marx, but what kind would it be? Raymond Aron has found at least three wholly different concepts of the Revolution in Marx: a Blanquist conspirational one, an evolutionary one, and the idea of the Permanent Revolution. Aron, *The Opium of the Intellectuals,* 47.

[192] *Capital,* I, chs. 10, 15, 25. On his Victorian moralism, see his comments on a society which permits men to work in close contact with women: *Capital,* I, 283, 434, 536.

"The communists do not preach morality at all."[193] What reason would he have for moralism in a "scientific" system? The capitalist society is doomed and the socialist society is inevitable. Capitalism cannot be reformed by an ethical appeal; good societies are not made by making men "good": ". . . capitalist production comprises certain conditions which are independent of good or bad will. . . ."[194] The Christian appeal to individual repentance, for the Marxist, is an absurd waste of time and energy; capitalist society must be destroyed, since it cannot be reformed. For the Marxist, the very rational goal of the good society can only be brought into being through the use of an irrational Revolution; it is not ethical reconciliation with God, but metaphysical chaos that the Marxist desires.[195] Raymond Aron has commented on this Marxian corollary of both reason and irrationalism:

> On the face of it, Revolution and Reason are diametrically opposed; the latter suggests discussion, the former, violence. Either one argues and ends up by convincing one's opponent, or one renounces argument and resorts to arms. Yet violence has been and continues to be the last resort of a certain rationalist impatience. . . . The error is to attribute to the Revolution a logic which it does not possess, to see it as the logical end of a movement which is based on reason, and to expect it to produce benefits which are incompatible with its very essence. It is not unprecedented for a society to return to the path of peace, after a revolutionary explosion, with a positive balance sheet. But revolutionary means remain on balance contrary to the ends envisaged.[196]

Paradise can be achieved only by total, irrational (or hyper-rational) destruction.

---

[193] *The German Ideology,* 267.

[194] *Capital,* III, 476.

[195] For a Christian treatment of the problem of alienation and repentance, see John Murray, "The Reconciliation," *The Westminster Theological Journal,* XXIX (1966), 1-23.

[196] Raymond Aron, *The Opium of the Intellectuals,* 94, 96.

Marx thought of himself as an optimist. However bad the conditions of life might be under capitalism, and however tyrannical things might become under the initial dictatorship of the proletariat, there is still hope. A new age is coming, Marx believed, and with it would come a new mankind. He never spelled out the details of all the elements of life in the "kingdom of freedom," but he did give a few hints:

> *Communism* is the *positive* abolition of *private property,* of *human self-alienation,* and thus the real *appropriation* of *human* nature through and for man. It is, therefore, the return of man himself as a *social,* i.e., really human, being, a complete and conscious return which assimilates all the wealth of previous development. Communism as a fully developed naturalism is humanism and as a fully developed humanism is naturalism. It is the definitive resolution of the antagonism between man and nature, and between man and man. It is the true solution of the conflict between existence and essence, between objectification and self-affirmation, between freedom and necessity, between individual and species. It is the solution of the riddle of history and knows itself to be this solution.[197]

As we have already seen, the division of labor is to be abolished in this communist-humanist-naturalist Golden Age. While Engels may have abandoned this hope, it was certainly a fundamental tenet of the early Marxist credo. Given this premise, "the communist revolution, which removes the division of labor, ultimately abolishes political instiutions. . . ."[198] If the division of labor gave rise to classes, and if class power was exercised by means of the state, then the abolition of the division of labor would naturally eradicate the need both for classes and the state. If a class can be said to exist, it is only the proletarian class, and therefore there will be no need

---

[197] Marx, "Private Property and Communism," EPM, Bottomore translation in *Karl Marx: Early Writings,* 155. Cf. EPM, 135, in the Milligan translation. The latter contains a key typographical error and is generally unclear.

[198] *The German Ideology,* 416.

for an instrument of class oppression, since there is no rival class to suppress.

When, in the course of development, class distinctions have disappeared, and all production has been concentrated in the hands of a vast association of the whole nation, the public power will lose its political character. Political power, properly so-called, is merely the organized power of one class for oppressing another. . . . In place of the old bourgeois society, with its classes and class antagonisms, we shall have an association in which the free development of each is the condition for the free development of all.[199]

Marx deliberately limited his definition of a class to include little more than a group's economic function in the production system. He limited the idea of the state to that of an arm of oppression of a ruling class. Thus, he could assert that "a vast association of the whole nation" would replace the state. The unity of the new society will abolish the division of labor and therefore it will abolish the dichotomy between individual interests and the general, communal interests. No state is needed in this schema.

Engels may have been bothered by the idea of "the association," although he used it on occasion. In his dialogue against the anarchists, "On Authority" (1874), he denied that it is possible to have an organization without a division between leadership and subordination. "Yes," he paraphrased their reply, "but here it is not a case of authority which we confer on our delegates, *but of a commission entrusted!*" And he replied, quite appropriately: "These gentlemen think that when they have changed the names of things they have changed the things themselves."[200] Precisely; Marx had done just exactly what Engels castigated the anarchists for doing: he had merely given the functions that a state must have over to a new entity called an "association." Marx was careful to define the state strictly as an instrument of class oppression; he did not admit that a state has many administrative functions that must be performed by it apart from any consideration of class interests. Law and law

---

[199] *Communist Manifesto,* MESW, I, 54.
[200] Engels, "On Authority," MESW, I, 638.

112

enforcement are examples of such functions. Unless one can assume that there will be no sin in the Golden Age, then society needs a state (Rom. 13:1-7).

What about economic production in the final society? Marx admitted that there would probably be many problems of production and especially distribution during the period of the dictatorship of the proletariat; this is merely the "first phase of communist society as it is when it has just emerged after prolonged birth pangs from capitalist society."[201] As we have already seen, Marx did not expect great things from it. However, in the "higher phase of communist society," the rule of economic justice shall become a reality: "From each according to his ability, to each according to his needs!"[202] This will be easy to accomplish, since the vast quantities of wealth which are waiting to be released will be freed from the fetters and restraints of capitalist productive techniques.[203] As Mises points out, "Tacitly underlying Marxian theory is the nebulous idea that natural factors of production are such that they need not be economized."[204] Maurice Cornforth, the Marxist philosopher, confirms Mises's suspicion that Marxists see all scarcity as a product of institutional defects rather than as a basic fact of the created order of the universe (cf. Gen. 3:17-19):

> The eventual and final abolition of shortages constitutes the economic condition for entering upon a communist society. When there is socialized production the products of which are socially appropriated, when science and scientific planning have resulted in the production of absolute abundance, and when labour has

---

[201] Marx, *Critique of the Gotha Program* (1875), MESW, II, 24.

[202] *Ibid.*

[203] Marx quoted favorably a passage to this effect written by the socialist William Thompson: *Capital,* II, 370. On Thompson's importance in socialist thought, see Alexander Gray, *The Socialist Tradition: Moses to Lenin* (N. Y.: Longmans, Green & Co., 1946), 269-77.

[204] Ludwig von Mises, *Socialism,* 164. Cf. Bober, *Karl Marx's Interpretation of History,* 289; Meyer, *Marxism,* 82; Berlin, *Karl Marx,* 150.

been so enlightened and organized that all can without sacrifice of personal inclinations contribute their working abilities to the common fund, everyone will receive a share according to his needs.[205]

A critical problem for the whole question of communist planning is how production is to be directed. By what standards should the society guide the allocation of scarce resources? Whatever Marx believed, resources are not in infinite supply, and therefore society must plan production.[206] Automobiles do not grow on trees. Someone must decide how many automobiles should be produced as compared with how many refrigerators. Planning is inherent in all production, and Marx realized this: "Modern universal intercourse can be controlled by individuals, therefore, only when controlled by all."[207] But how can they "all" register their preferences? If there is no private property (and, therefore, no free market economy), and if there is no state planning — no political planning — then who decides what goods are produced and which ones are not? As the laissez-faire advocate, Murray Rothbard, has argued:

> Rejecting private property, especially capital, the Left Socialists were then trapped in an inner contradiction: if the State is to disappear after the Revolution (immediately for Bakunin, gradually "withering" for Marx), then how is the "collective" to run its property without becoming an enormous State itself in fact even if not in name? This was the contradiction which neither the Marxists nor the Bakuninists were ever able to resolve.[208]

---

[205] Maurice Cornforth, *Marxism and the Linguistic Philosophy,* 327.
[206] Even if all material goods were somehow free from the laws of scarcity, men still lack *time.* They are not immortal. Because of this, men must establish certain orders of preference concerning the goods and services that they consume over time, thus giving rise to the factor of *interest* on one's money. For a discussion of this, see Eugen von Böhm-Bawerk, *The Positive Theory of Capital* (4th ed., 1921), Book IV (South Holland, Ill.: Libertarian Press, 1959). Cf. Mises, *Human Action,* chs. 18 and 19.
[207] *The German Ideology,* 84.
[208] Murray N. Rothbard, "Left and Right: The Prospects for Liberty," *Left and Right,* I (1965), 8. See the similar remarks of Abram L. Harris, "Utopian Elements in Marx's Thought," *Ethics,* LX (1949-50), 93-94.

The necessity of productive planning implies scarcity: production is necessary only because all people do not have everything they want at exactly the moment when they want it. Raw materials must be fashioned into goods or indirectly into services; these goods must be shipped from place to place. These things involve time (interest on the investment of capital goods) and labor (wages). *Production*, in short, demands *planning*. Society is never faced with a problem of "to plan or not to plan." The issue which confronts society is the question of *whose* plan to use. Marx denied the validity of the free market's planning, since the market is based upon the private ownership of the means of production, including the use of money. Money, for Marx, was the greatest curse of all non-communist societies. It was his fervent hope to abolish the use of money forever.[209] At the same time, he denied the possibility of centralized planning by the state. How could he keep his "association" from becoming a state? The Fabian writer, G. D. H. Cole, has seen what the demand for a classless society necessitates: "But a classless society means, in the modern world, a society in which the distribution of incomes is collectively controlled, as a political function of society itself. It means further that this controlled distribution of incomes must be made on such a basis as to allow no room for the growth of class-differences."[210] In other words, given the necessity for a political function in a supposedly state-less world, how can the Marxists escape the criticism once offered by Leon Trotsky: "In a country where the sole employer is the State, opposition means death by slow starvation. The old principle: who does not work shall not eat, has been replaced by a new one: who does not obey shall not eat."[211] The Marxists, for that matter, cannot even answer the issued raised by Engels:

---

[209] Marx, "On the Jewish Question," in Bottomore (ed.), *Karl Marx: Early Writings,* 32-40.

[210] Cole, *The Meaning of Marxism,* 249.

[211] Trotsky, *The Revolution Betrayed* (1937), 76, quoted by Hayek, *The Road to Serfdom,* 119. Cf. Abram Harris, "The Social Philosophy of Karl Marx," *Ethics,* LVIII (April, 1948), pt. II, 32.

If man, by dint of his knowledge and inventive genius, has subdued the forces of nature, the latter avenge themselves upon him by subjecting him, in so far as he employs them, to a veritable despotism independent of all social organization.[212]

Thus, we are brought full circle. The "nature-freedom" scheme reasserts itself once again. Either man is controlled by an irrational nature or by a despotic, ultra-rational social system of man's own creation. Walter Odajnyk describes the Marxian view of man — a creature always dominated by his environment, yet somehow the master of his own fate: "He is now something in between a free being and a machine responding to the laws governing its operations — a sort of elaborate IBM machine, which has a degree of operational independence."[213]

In a lengthy passage near the end of the third volume of *Capital*, Marx dealt with the problem as well as he could; he did his best, but he failed:

In fact, the realm of freedom does not commence until the point is passed where labor under the compulsion of necessity and of external utility is required. In the very nature of things it lies beyond the sphere of material production in the strict meaning of the term. Just as the savage must wrestle with nature, in order to satisfy his wants, in order to maintain his life and reproduce it, so civilized man must do it in all forms of society and under all modes of production. With this development the realm of natural necessity expands, because his wants increase; but at the same time the forces of production increase, by which these wants are satisfied. The freedom in this field cannot consist of anything else but of the fact that socialized man, the associated producers, regulate their interchange with nature rationally, bring it under their common control, instead of being ruled by it as by some blind power; that they accomplish their task with the least expenditure of energy and under conditions most adequate to their human nature and most worthy of it. But it always remains a realm of necessity. Beyond it begins that development of human power, which is its own end, the true realm of freedom, which, however, can flourish only upon that realm of necessity as its

---

[212] Engels, "On Authority," MESW, I, 637.
[213] Walter Odajnyk, *Marxism and Existentialism,* 116.

basis. The shortening of the working day is its fundamental premise.[214]

Marx went around the issue without ever confronting it directly: how can society regulate its interchange with nature in a rational manner, thus bringing it under society's common control, while still maintaining the freedom of man within that society and within that "rationalized" universe? The material realm of production, Marx admitted at last, "remains a realm of necessity." Only beyond production can mankind find true freedom, yet the whole foundation of the Marxian system is that man is man *only* in the sphere of free, voluntary productivity.[215] After struggling with one of the most profound philosophical problems which can confront the secular thinker, and after raising the whole question of production in the future society, Marx resolved the issue with these words: "The shortening of the working day is its fundamental premise." The paucity of the answer is staggering, incredible! If so much misery had not been launched by Marx's labors for the forces of revolution, and if so many lives had not been destroyed in the name of Marx, that answer would be amusing in its pathetic quality.

## Conclusion

When self-proclaimed autonomous man asserts his absolute independence from God, he simultaneously asserts his absolute dependence on some aspect (or synthesis of aspects) in the world of creation. Man must have some principle of authority, and if God is not that ultimate source, then man must seek to deify some aspect of the supposedly autonomous universe. What inevitably results, as Dooyeweerd and Van Til have argued, is that man's thought becomes subject to inescapable contradictions. As Dooyeweerd has put it:

For a Christian there can be no question of the inner antinomy [contradiction] that Humanism has to experience on seeing how

---

[214] *Capital*, III, 954-55.

[215] On the contradiction within Marxism between free, unspecialized production and mechanized factory life, see Robert C. Tucker, "Marx as a Political Theorist," in Lobkowicz (ed.), *Marx and the Western World*, 130-31.

human personality, claiming to be autonomous in its self-sufficient freedom, is being enslaved by its own rational creations. The Divine world-order is not itself antinomic when it avenges itself on every deification of temporal meaning on account of this apostasy in the opening process. No more is it antinomic when it causes philosophical thought to entangle itself in inner antinomies, as soon as this thought supposes it can ignore the Divine order.[216]

Karl Marx was not able to escape these contradictions. He deified human thought, and subjected it to the dialectical processes of continual contradiction. He viewed all things from the point of view of the sphere of human production, and subjected that sphere to the contradictions of the "nature-freedom" dualism. In the name of a society without a state, he created a system which was to become totally state-dominated. He hoped to crush all states, yet as Nisbet has seen, "Marx expressed his admiration for the centralization of the French Revolution that had, like a 'gigantic broom,' swept away all the localism, pluralism, and communalism of traditional French society."[217] How could Marx be anything but a statist and an authoritarian? He was a thorough revolutionary, and as Engels wrote, "A revolution is certainly the most authoritarian thing there is; it is the act whereby one part of the population imposes its will upon the other part by means of rifles, bayonets and cannon — authoritarian means, if such there be at all; and if the victorious party does not want to have fought in vain, it must maintain this rule by means of the terror which its arms inspire in the reactionaries."[218] Thus, Marx the professing anarchist necessarily became in practice Marx the totalitarian. This is the fate of all humanistic schemes:

> Humanistic law, moreover, is inescapably totalitarian law. Humanism, as a logical development of evolutionary theory, holds fundamentally to a concept of an evolving universe. This is held to be an "open universe," whereas Biblical Christianity, because of its faith in the triune God and His eternal decree, is said to

---

[216] Herman Dooyeweerd, *A New Critique of Theoretical Thought,* (Philadelphia: Presbyterian and Reformed, 1955), II, 361-62.

[217] Robert A. Nisbet, *The Sociological Tradition,* 138.

[218] Engels, "On Authority," MESW, I, 639.

be a faith in a "closed universe." This terminology not only intends to prejudice the case; it reverses reality. The universe of evolution and humanism is a closed universe. There is no law, no appeal, no higher order, beyond and above the universe. Instead of an open window upwards, there is a closed cosmos. There is thus no ultimate law and decree beyond man and the universe. In practice, this means that the positive law of the state is absolute law. The state is the most powerful and most highly organized expression of humanistic man, and the state is the form and expression of humanistic law. Because there is no higher law of God as judge over the universe, over every human order, the law of the state is a closed system of law. There is no appeal beyond it. Man has no "right," no realm of justice, no source of law beyond the state, to which he can appeal against the state. Humanism therefore imprisons man within the closed world of the state and the closed universe of the evolutionary scheme.[219]

Undoubtedly, Marx was a mighty proponent for the cause of autonomous man. Man is to stand alone, on his own foundation, and create a new world, a paradise on earth. Man is his own God, and he has God's very power of creation; man is totally creative. Yet Marx's blueprint for action was a call to total destruction. Creative destruction: this was, Berlin has argued, "a magnificent realization of his favourite paradox: 'The passion for destruction, too, is a creative passion.' "[220] Here, too, is the philosophy of the chaos cults of the ancient world. Godless man has a passion for destruction, even as the Bible declares: ". . . all they that hate me love death" (Prov. 8:36b). This passion is not part of the biblical heritage, and for this reason the attempt to link Marx to the Old Testament prophetic tradition is really erroneous. Though Marx's system may, in certain instances, resemble in a superficial way the biblical cosmology, on the whole it stands in open contrast to orthodoxy. Halle writes that "Marxism met the city man's need for a new body of belief. It met the need for a religion of the

---

[219] R. J. Rushdoony, "Humanistic Law," introduction to Hebden Taylor, *The New Legality* (Nutley, New Jersey: Craig Press, 1967), vi-vii.
[220] Isaiah Berlin, *Karl Marx,* 261.

industrial age."[221] To some extent, this is true enough, but it misses the point; the cult of chaos has met the emotional needs of apostate men for countless generations. Marx's contribution was his clothing of this revolutionary cult with the language of Germanic logic and contemporary secular science.

The Bible affirms a wholly divergent cosmology. Man is not his own creator; he did not create himself "ex nihilo" — out of nothing. Man is a creature who must operate under law, and he lives in a universe which also operates under law. Because he is under God's law, man can stand over creation as God's vicegerent. Marx, however, could not admit that man's authority is derivative; like the self-proclaimed autonomous men at the Tower of Babel, he announced the creative power of man apart from God: "And they said, Go to, let us build us a city and a tower, whose top may reach unto heaven; and let us make us a name [i.e., define ourselves without reference to God], lest we be scattered abroad upon the face of the earth" (Gen. 11:4). "Ye shall be as gods," the Tempter promised, and Marx believed the promise. In affirming the powers of man for total creation, he launched the forces of absolute destruction. Man's capacity for self-delusion seems boundless, but man has been warned of the results of such self-deception, and the Marxists shall be the recipients of their proper reward: "Bread of deceit is sweet to a man; but afterwards his mouth shall be filled with gravel" (Prov. 20:17).

---

[221] Louis J. Halle, "Marx's Religious Drama," *Encounter,* XXV (Oct., 1965), 37. For a brief but interesting discussion of the appeal of Marxism as an ideology, see Mihaly Csikszentmihaly, "Marx: A Socio-Psychological Evaluation," *Modern Age,* XI (1967), 272-82.

*But in the measure that history moves forward, and
with it the struggle of the proletariat assumes clearer
outlines, they no longer need to seek science in their
minds; they have only to take note of what is happen-
ing before their eyes and become its mouthpiece. . . .
From this moment, science, which is a product of the
historical movement, has associated itself consciously
with it, has ceased to be doctrinaire and has become
revolutionary.*

Karl Marx (1847)[1]

## V.

## THE ECONOMICS OF REVOLUTION

Writing a brief, critical chapter on Marx's economic system is
very much like kicking a dead horse. So many of the criticisms are
ancient, familiar ones, that it seems like such a waste to go over
them once again. For the most part, non-Marxists find little of
relevance in Marx's economics, except for a few scattered observations that were not necessarily bound up with his overall critique of
capitalist society. E. R. A. Seligman, who accepted much of the
Marxian perspective concerning the nature of historical development,
expressed his doubts over a half century ago about the validity of
the actual economic theory which Marx presented. What he wrote
then is echoed today by most of today's non-Marxist scholars:

We need to lay stress on Marx's philosophy, rather than on his
economics; and his philosophy, as we now know, resulted in his
economic interpretation of history. It chanced that he also
became a socialist; but his socialism and his philosophy of history
are, as we shall see later, really independent. One can be an
"economic materialist" and yet remain an extreme individualist.

---

[1] Marx, *The Poverty of Philosophy* (Moscow: Foreign Languages
Publishing House, [1847] n.d.), 120.

The fact that Marx's economics may be defective has no bearing on the truth or falsity of his philosophy of history.[2]

The focus of interest in this century has been on other aspects of Marx's thought: philosophy, politics, or his early sociological writings; the complex labyrinth of his economic system has been left, primarily, to those writing texts on the history of economic doctrines. Yet his approach to economic questions is important, since it throws at least some light on his overall outlook. For this reason alone it would be useful to examine the Marxian economic system, and there are others.

One thing must be stressed from the outset: in spite of Marx's claims to the contrary, he was not even remotely a totally empirical, neutral observer. He came to his studies with a whole host of presuppositions about the nature of capitalist society, and his often use of violent language reflects his deep moral hostility to the world of Europe in the middle years of the 19th century. Abram L. Harris has pinpointed this basic fact: "But Marx's investigation of the facts of economic life was subordinate to his main purpose, which was to prove that the transformation of capitalism was inevitable and a necessary condition of human progress. Marx's absorbing interest was a theory of social and economic progress, and not a theory of economy."[3] György Márkus, writing in the Marxist periodical, *Science and Society,* agrees with Harris: "He was not an unbiased viewer of history, but a *revolutionist* interested in the possibility of humanistic transformation."[4] Marx had very definite ideas about how the truly human society should treat the individual, and these ideas in turn were based upon numerous assumptions about the nature of man, the function of civil government, and the basis of historical development. "From this point of view," Tucker has commented, "*Capital* is the attempted proof of a preconception. . . .

---

[2] E. R. A. Seligman, *The Economic Interpretation of History* (N. Y.: Columbia University Press, [1907] 1961), 24.

[3] Abram L. Harris, "Utopian Elements in Marx's Thought," *Ethics,* LX (1949-50), 79.

[4] György Márkus, "Marxist Humanism," *Science and Society,* XXX (1966), 287.

The first purpose of *Capital* was to demonstrate how and why things must inevitably come to 'such a pass'."[5] The Revolution had to come if society were to be regenerated; the capitalist system, therefore, must be an outworking of an inevitable history, and it must result in a final conflagration. Karl Marx was determined to find in economic theory and history the proof of his presupposition.[6]

In addition to Marx's cosmological presuppositions, he was also a product of his times intellectually and methodologically. His economic tools were those of classical political economy — particularly those of Ricardo — and these tools imposed serious limitations on his analysis of the capitalist economy.[7] By the time the "marginalist revolution" in economics came about in the 1870's, Marx had already written and published two full volumes of economic analysis (including volume one of *Capital*), and he had the basic manuscripts of several further thick volumes. Thus, the new ways of looking at economic events that were sketched by Menger, Jevons, and Walras

---

[5] Robert C. Tucker, *Philosophy and Myth in Karl Marx* (Cambridge University Press, 1961), 204-05. Cf. Charles Gide and Charles Rist, *A History of Economic Doctrines* (Boston: D. C. Heath, 1948), 461n; Henry B. Mayo, *Introduction to Marxist Theory* (N. Y.: Oxford University Press, 1960), 228.

[6] On a preliminary draft of this manuscript, one commentator wrote: "I thoroughly disagree. Marx was very careful and honest with *facts,* and had no more biases than any other social scientist. His whole philosophical method was deeply empirical." Apparently, the critic regards the mere amassing of footnotes as proof of one's empiricism. In the second place, the comment implies that other social scientists are not particularly biased, an idea so absurd that it staggers the imagination. Anyone who thinks science is neutral needs to read Thomas S. Kuhn's *The Structure of Scientific Revolutions* (University of Chicago, 1962). Neutrality in the sciences is a myth. That a full professor in a major American university could operate under this myth is almost unbelievable. We all have our *a priori* assumptions, and his seems to be that social scientists do not have any.

[7] See the article by Donald Clark Hodges for a Marxist's admission of this limitation: "The Value Judgment in *Capital*," *Science and Society*, XXIX (1965), 296-311. Cf. the debate in "Communications," *ibid.*, XXX (1966), 206-27.

came too late in Marx's life to make any impression on him. It was too late for him to have revised his works, even assuming that he might have desired to do so; his health was failing, and after the publication of *Capital* in Germany in 1867, he never returned to his labors in the area of economics.[8]

Marx had certain insights into the nature of capitalism that went beyond the boundaries of classical economic reasoning. He had a sort of intuitive grasp of certain tendencies of 19th century economic life, and he was able to make some profound observations in regard to the probable development of capitalism. Some of them proved to be terribly inaccurate, but others were more successful. As the late Joseph Schumpeter has pointed out in his excellent study, *Capitalism, Socialism and Democracy* (1942), Marx often drew accurate conclusions from false premises; he was right for the wrong reasons.

### The Labor Theory of Value

The labor theory of value was one of the most fundamental doctrines of classical political economy. Given Marx's almost theological concern with man as creator, it is not surprising that he failed to abandon this particular economic principle. He placed it at the core of his system. Unfortunately for his system, it was wrong.[9]

---

[8] For a discussion of the shift in outlook which divided classical economics from the modern perspective, see any standard textbook on the history of economic thought, e.g., Lewis Haney, *History of Economic Thought* (N. Y.: Macmillan, 1949, 1962), 581-634. Another very useful survey for this purpose is Alexander Gray, *The Development of Economic Doctrine* (N. Y.: Longmans, Green & Co., 1948).

[9] A few pro-Marxist economists may not like this evaluation, of course, but the fact remains that modern economics no longer can integrate it into any useful model of economic reality. Even Joan Robinson, who tends to favor much of Marx's analysis, has had some trouble in retaining the labor theory. She argues that it really was not fundamental to Marx's criticism of capitalism. It is unlikely that Marx would have agreed with this "helpful" revision, and if he had accepted it, he would have been forced to reorganize vast quanti-

Marx began volume one of *Capital* with a series of definitions relating to commodities. He first noted that any economic good has both "use-value" and "exchange-value." Use-value, he said, "is independent of the amount of labour required to appropriate its useful qualities" (I, 42). A thing can be useful to men, in other words, even if no one has expended any labor in creating it; a mountain stream or unimproved land are examples. But exchange value, according to Marx, is something else again; exchange value is the congealed form of human labor, since human labor is the only means of creating value. Marx offered the old Aristotelian argument that for an exchange to take place, there must be a common element of equal quantity in each of the exchanged items. "The two things must be equal to a third, which is itself neither the one nor the other. Each of them, so far as it is exchange value, must therefore be reducible to this third" (I, 43-44). The common element cannot be use-value, he hastened to add, because "the exchange of commodities is evidently an act characterized by a total abstraction from use-value" (I, 44). Use-value makes possible an exchange, since people will not bother to enter a market in order to exchange useless goods, but use-value is not the basis of the exchange. Then what is? He concluded that the exchanged objects each must contain equal quantities of human labor. It is not a question of any physical or aesthetic qualities inherent in any particular economic good: ". . . there is nothing left but what is common to them all; all are reduced to one and the same sort of labour, human labour in the abstract" (I, 45).[10]

---

ties of his published and unpublished writings. Cf. Robinson, *An Essay on Marxian Economics* (N. Y.: Macmillan, [1942] 1957), ch. 3. In reply, see G. F. Shove, "Mrs. Robinson on Marxian Economics," *Economic Journal,* LIV (1944), 48-49. Hodges, *op. cit.,* wants to abandon the Marxian language of "value": Marx became, in his words, "trapped in the language of Smith and Ricardo" (311).

[10] In all quotations, I am using the Kerr editions of the three volumes of *Capital.* Volume I: 1906; II: 1909; III: 1909. Volume I is available in a Modern Library edition.

Fundamental to the Marxian economic system is a belief that things will not be exchanged unless the common element, human labor, is present in each good to be exchanged. This, however, is a fallacious concept, and it was dropped by modern economics after the marginalist-subjectivist schools gained predominance in the late 19th century. Exchanges take place when each of the exchanging parties values the other's good more than he values his own. Far from some common element being present, it is the essence of exchange that the exchanged goods be unequal in the eyes of the potential traders. It does no good to reply, as one economics professor scrawled on the first draft of this manuscript, "you are talking psychology, not economics." It was the very essence of the postclassical revision that one must provide a cogent explanation for economic affairs in terms of human action and human decisions. Naturally the explanation is "psychological," since the foundation of economic reasoning is centered on men's decisions to act in the sphere of economics. Any explanation which does not take account of psychological causation in economic affairs is subject to the fallacy Marx was always concerned with, the "fetishism of commodities," i.e., ascribing to economic events a life of their own apart from the human and social relations which make the events possible. Marx's explanation of the exchange phenomenon is a classic case of "economic fetishism": he looked at the commodities instead of trying to explain the phenomenon in terms of the economic actors. The idea of some metaphysical equality in the exchanged items is wholly superfluous, and any conclusions drawn from it can hardly fail to be irrelevant at best, and probably wrong and highly misleading.[11]

[11] For an early exposition of the subjective nature of economic exchange and the necessary inequality involved in these psychological judgments, see Carl Menger, *Principles of Economics* (Glencoe, Ill.: Free Press, [1871] 1950), ch. 4. Cf. Eugen von Böhm-Bawerk, *The Positive Theory of Capital* (4th ed.; South Holland, Ill.: Libertarian Press, [1921] 1959), Book III, 121-256. Marx hinted at the truth involved in this type of analysis in *Capital*, I, 97, but he nevertheless rejected Condillac's very similar discussion of exchange: I, 177. On the absolute necessity of psychological reasoning in economic science, see Ludwig von Mises, *Epistemological Problems of Economics*

Once Marx had accepted the validity of the "common substance" hypothesis, he began to draw certain conclusions: "We have seen that when commodities are exchanged, their exchange value manifests itself as something totally independent of their use-value. But if we abstract from their use-value, there remains Value as defined above. Therefore the common substance that manifests itself in the exchange value of commodities, whenever they are exchanged, is their value" (I, 45). Apart from the difficulty of understanding his own jargon, Marx faced an immediate problem: "How, then, is the magnitude of this value to be measured? Plainly, by the quantity of the value-creating substance, the labour, contained in the article" (I, 45). "The quantity of labour," he went on to say, "is measured by its duration," but this necessarily must assume that all human labor is homogeneous. This he was willing to admit: "The labour, however, that forms the substance of value, is homogeneous human labour, expenditure of one uniform labour-power" (I, 45-46). He continued in this vein:

> The total labour-power of society, which is embodied in the sum total of all the values of all commodities produced by that society, counts here as one homogeneous mass of human labour-power, composed though it be of innumerable individual units. Each of these units is the same as any other, so far as it has the character of the average labour-power of society, and takes effect as such; that is, so far as it requires for producing a commodity, no more time than is needed on an average, no more than is socially necessary. The labour-time socially necessary is that required to produce an article under normal conditions of production, and with the average degree of skill and intensity prevalent at the time (I, 46).

What about skilled labor? "Skilled labour counts only as simple labour intensified, or rather, as multiplied simple labour, a given quantity of skilled labour being considered equal to a greater quantity

(Princeton: Van Nostrand, 1960); Mises, *Human Action* (New Haven, Conn.: Yale University Press, 1949), chs. 1 and 2. See also Israel M. Kirzner, *The Economic Point of View* (Princeton: Van Nostrand, 1960), ch. 7; Murray N. Rothbard, *Man, Economy and State* (Princeton: Van Nostrand, 1962), chs. 1-3.

of simple labour" (I, 51). But how are we to determine the size of the "labor multiplier"? Marx was extremely vague on this point, and for good reason. His analysis rested on the assumption that there is such a thing as homogeneous, average, socially necessary human labor, and that a common unit of measurement can examine quantitatively the varying degrees of intensity of the common labor. In point of fact, however, such an "average labor" exists only as a mental abstraction; there is nothing like it in the real world, and therefore there is no common unit of its measurement. Marx was virtually forced to admit this in his *Poverty of Philosophy* (1847) when he wrote: "Is your hour's labour worth mine? That is a question which is decided by competition."[12] Competition according to what standard? In effect, he was saying that the free market must decide according to its laws of competition. Yet if the labor theory is true, then the market must respond to the labor embodied in the product; the value of the labor in a product should not be determined by the forces of free competition on an open market.

Throughout this discussion, the focus has been on "the commodity." This Marx defined as a strictly social category, an economic good produced by human labor *for the purpose of exchange on the market*. "A thing can be useful," he wrote, "and the product of human labour, without being a commodity. Whoever directly satisfies his wants with the product of his own labor, creates, indeed, use-values, but not commodities" (I, 48). Commodities are produced, not for direct consumption, but for a market. Economic goods — scarce items which are valuable and therefore could command a price — are not necessarily commodities: "In order to produce the latter, he must not only produce use-values, but use-values for others, social use-values" (I, 48). This, it must be pointed out, is a very peculiar way of defiining a commodity. It has a very definite flaw, since on this definition it is impossible to explain the phenomenon of rent. Many economic goods have neither been produced by human labor nor produced for any market, yet they command a price. Marx struggled unsuccessfully with this problem:

---

[12] Marx, *Poverty of Philosophy*, 51.

The waterfall, like the earth in general, and like any natural force, has no value, because it does not represent any materialized labor, and therefore it really has no price, which is normally but the expression of value in money. Where there is no value, it is obvious that it cannot be expressed in money. This price is merely capitalized rent. The ownership of land enables the landowner to catch the difference between the individual profit and the average profit (III, 759).

The problem is not solved by an appeal to land-ownership. If it is true that the waterfall "really has no price," then how does it command a price? If it is true that "where there is no value, it is obvious that it cannot be expressed in money," then why is it expressed in money? By definition, the waterfall contains no value, since value was defined by Marx as congealed labor time (as distinct from use-value), yet he was forced to admit that a waterfall may, in reality, command a price anyway. There is clearly a contradiction here. It stems from his strangely narrow definition of "commodity" which for him did not mean just an economic good, but only an economic good produced by human labor for a market. The 19th century economist, Eugen von Böhm-Bawerk, commented on this strange definition:

> From the beginning he only puts into the sieve those exchange-able things which contain the property which he desires finally to sift out as "the common factor," and he leaves all others outside. He acts as one who urgently desiring to bring a white ball out of an urn takes care to secure this result by putting in white balls only. That is to say he limits from the outset the field of his search for the substance of the exchange value to "commodities," and in doing so he forms a conception with a meaning narrower than the conception of "goods" (though he does not clearly define it), and limits it to products of labor as against gifts of nature. Now it stands to reason that if exchange really means an equalization, which assumes the existence of a "common factor of the same amount," this common factor must be sought and found in every species of goods which is brought into exchange, not only in products of labor but also in gifts of nature, such as the soil, wood in trees, water power, coal beds, stone quarries, petroleum reserves, mineral waters, gold mines, etc. To exclude the exchangeable goods which are not the products of labor in the search for the common factor which lies at the

root of exchange value is, under the circumstances, a great error of method.[13]

As if he had not created enough confusion, Marx further modified his labor theory of value: "If the thing is useless, so is the labour contained in it; the labour does not count as labour, and therefore creates no value" (I, 48). In other words, he admitted that if too much of some commodity has been produced, and if the market is unable to absorb all of this product at a given price (e.g., linen), then the labor which has been expended on this product does not count: ". . . our friend's product is superfluous, redundant, and consequently useless" (I, 120). Almost as superfluous as the labor theory of value, one is tempted to add. Now, Marx argued, it is supply and demand — the market's pricing mechanism — that will determine the value of human labor, and not the other way around (as he had previously maintained). The whole argument is unable to account for prices or values in terms of human labor, yet the labor theory of value is the very foundation of Marx's economic critique of capitalist society.

### Exploitation: Surplus Value

As we have seen, Marx argued that there must be an equality of exchange value in any objects that are traded. If there is no equality of value, then by Marx's definition no exchange can take place. Given this assumption, an important issue immediately arises: if all the products entering into exchange contain equal values, then what is the source of the capitalist's profits? The capitalist, Marx said, begins with an amount of money, M; he converts money into capital, C; at the end of this process of exchange, he takes in more money than he started out with, M'. The system of M-C-M' is basic to the

---

[13] Böhm-Bawerk, "Unresolved Contradiction in the Marxian Economic System," in *The Shorter Classics of Böhm-Bawerk* (South Holland, Ill.: Libertarian Press, 1962), 261. This is the Alice Macdonald translation of an essay first published in 1896 after the posthumous third volume of Marx's *Capital* was released. Its more common title is *Karl Marx and the Close of His System* (N. Y.: Augustus Kelley, 1949). It should probably be translated as "Upon the Completion of the Economic System of Karl Marx."

capitalist structure; without it, there would be no motivation for the capitalist to enter into business. It is imperative that the economist explain this apparent impossibility: the capitalist begins with a given amount of money, and after entering into the market returns with more than he began with, yet at every stage of production and exchange the capitalist is forced to exchange equal values with equal values.

Marx had an ingenious explanation, although its basic elements had been offered by earlier economists: the idea of surplus value. He believed that he had discovered the only commodity which, when purchased at its full value, is able to produce for the capitalist more value than it had cost. That commodity is *labor power*. Labor power, like all other commodities, has an exchange value. Its exchange value, Marx said, is equal to the value necessary for its production. Labor power is also governed by the labor theory of value; the labor which is necessary to create labor power determines its value. Marx put it this way: *"What, then, is the cost of production of labour power? It is the cost required for maintaining the worker and of developing him into a worker. . . . The price of his labour* will, therefore, be determined by the *price of the necessary means of subsistence."*[14] This includes more than just the worker's own personal needs; it includes the needs of his family, since the worker must be replaced eventually by other laborers.

> . . . in calculating the cost of reproduction, whereby the race of workers is enabled to multiply and to reproduce wornout workers by new ones. Thus the depreciation of the worker is taken into account in the same way as the depreciation of the machine.
>
> The cost of production of simple labour power, therefore, amounts to the *cost of existence and reproduction of the worker.* The price of this cost of existence and reproduction constitutes wages. Wages so determined are called the *wage minimum.* This wage minimum, like the determination of the price of commodities by the cost of production in general, does not hold good for the *single individual* but for the *species.* Individual workers, millions

---

[14] Marx, *Wage-Labour and Capital* (1847), in *Marx-Engels Selected Works* (Moscow: Foreign Languages Publishing House, 1962), I, 88.

of workers, do not get enough to be able to exist and reproduce themselves; *but the wages of the whole working class* level down, within their fluctuations, to this minimum.[15]

Marx's picture of millions of workers actually starving in mid-19th century European society was exaggerated (unless he was talking about those countries which had not yet experienced industrialization, e.g., Ireland). Conditions were certainly not pleasant by 20th century middle class American standards, but western culture, apart from Ireland, has avoided starvation during the last two centuries. Nevertheless, his point is clear: the worker under capitalism is forced to accept a minimum wage, by definition. This is the very basis of capitalism, Marx said; given the labor theory of value, which cannot be abandoned in Marx's opinion, there is no other conclusion possible. The minimum subsistence wage is not the product of evil capitalists as such; it is a basic definition of the system as a whole. The labor theory of value absolutely requires that all commodities be exchanged at their value, and the value of labor power, Marx said, is the cost necessary for its minimum reproduction. This, in short, is Marx's version of the "iron law of wages."

The capitalist enters into the labor market and hires laborers. When his employees enter the factory, the process of production begins. Now, let us assume for a moment that it takes six hours for the "average" laborer to produce goods equal in value to those goods necessary to keep him and his family at their subsistence level. At this point, the laborer has created enough value to balance the value of his wages. But the process of production does not cease at this point. The capitalist is in a position to "exploit" the laborer, to use Marx's highly unneutral term. The laborers are not permitted to return home at this time; they can be kept on the job for, say, another six hours (at least this was true in Marx's era). He is forced to add his labor power to additional products, and this added labor (i.e., value) becomes the property of the capitalist who employs him. The value which he creates in the extra six hours is therefore

[15] *Ibid.,* 88-89.

132

surplus value — value which is a surplus over the laborer's minimum subsistence wage. The extra laboring time is therefore the source, the *only* source, of the capitalist's profits. Here is the mystery of capitalism's inner mechanism; here is the secret of its existence. All the requirements have been fulfilled: equals have been exchanged for equals, and yet there has been the creation of profits. "Every condition of the problem is satisfied, while the laws that regulate the exchange of commodities, have in no way been violated. Equivalent has been exchanged for equivalent. For the capitalist as buyer paid for each commodity, for the cotton, the spindle and labour power, its full value" (I, 217).

In analyzing the process of production, Marx divided the capital into two kinds: (1) *constant* capital, which includes machinery, raw materials, and buildings; and (2) *variable* capital, the wages of labor. The latter he called variable because labor, for Marx, is the only commodity from which it is possible to extract more value than it originally cost. Raw materials and machinery, on the other hand, can contribute only that quantity of value which is exactly equivalent to the value of the depreciation and wear of the materials involved. In other words, constant capital adds no *new* value to the process; labor power can. As it is used up by wear and tear, constant capital adds the value of the stored-up human labor which it contains, but any surplus value has already been extracted by the capitalist who employed the laborers who produced the machinery originally; there is no way of extracting further surplus value from a machine. Profits come solely from exploited *living* human labor, i.e., from the variable capital.

This, however, raises a serious problem. If all profits stem from the employment of human labor, then it follows that greater profits can be made in businesses that are labor intensive. The more machinery one employs in the production process, the less profits should be available, since there are fewer laborers present to exploit. Marx stated this explicitly when he wrote that "it is self-evident that the greater the variable capital, the greater would be the mass of value produced and of surplus value" (I, 334). If this analysis is correct, then we should expect to see very little constant capital (machinery and tools of production) employed by the capitalist class, since labor-saving machinery reduces the available human laborers in the "exploitation" system. Yet what we do see is precisely the reverse: the most profitable industries tend to be those in which large quantities of constant capital are employed. The law of surplus value has led to a contradiction between observation and theory, as Marx had to admit. "This law clearly contradicts all experience based on appearance" (I, 335). Marx tried to devise an explanation based on the increase in productivity which machinery provides. Laborers are able to earn their subsistence wages in a shorter period of time, and the capitalist is therefore able to increase the effective amount of time spent in labor for his profits. But this explanation, as we shall see later, comes into conflict with his discussion of the falling rate of profit under capitalism.

The *rate* of surplus value is the ratio of the time spent in laboring for the capitalist over the time the laborer works, in effect, to produce his own minimum subsistence wage. Surplus value, S, is divided by the wage, V. The rate is thus $\frac{S}{V}$.

The capitalist can extract surplus value in either or both of two ways. First, he can lengthen the working day. All of the labor produced in the additional hours thus extracted returns to the capitalist's account. Second, he can intensify the working day by adding new machinery or by speeding up the machinery on hand. This will increase the output of the laborers per hour, and thus they will earn their minimum wage in a shorter period of time; they are actually working longer hours for their employer. The first system Marx called *absolute* surplus value; the second he called *relative* surplus value. Actually, there is a third way: the capitalist can hire the wives and children of the laboring force. Since the subsistence wage paid to the workers is a *family* subsistence wage, he can pay each member less wages if all are working, thus increasing the percentage of time each spends working for him. This would probably be classified under relative surplus value.

Marx believed that he had unlocked the mystery of capitalism's system of production. The M-C-M' riddle was solved. All profits arise from the fact that the value of labor power itself is less than the value of the total amount of products produced by that labor power. *Surplus value,* in short, is simply *unpaid labor* (I, 637). Capitalism operates on the basis of *theft.*

## The Falling Rate of Profit

By explaining profits in terms of his surplus value concept, Marx was led inevitably to a series of questionable conclusions. The most important of these was his belief that the rate of profit in the capitalist system is bound to fall in the long run. This is an inescapable tendency, he argued, given the constant pressure of competition which forces the capitalist to cut his production costs by expanding output, thus enabling his company to sell its products at prices lower than his competition can afford to sell them. This expansion of output clearly requires a greater use of constant capital — raw materials, machinery — proportionate to human labor.

This brings up the whole question of the so-called "organic composition of capital." A greater organic composition of capital means simply that more constant capital is being used in the production process. As more and more machinery and raw materials are added, the percentage of human labor power involved in the process necessarily falls. In other words, there is proportionately less human labor power available for exploitation, and therefore profits must fall, since living labor is the only source of capitalism's profits.[16]

---

[16] Algebraically, the organic composition of capital is expressed by the fraction $\frac{c}{c+v}$. As C rises, the fraction approaches the value of one, or 100% constant capital. The labor factor, V, therefore carries a smaller weight in the fraction. As V gets smaller, the source of capitalism's profits dries up. For a full discussion of this "law" or tendency, see *Capital,* III, ch. 3. The rate of profit is expressed by the fraction $\frac{s}{c+v}$. As C increases, if S (surplus value) and V (wages) remain constant, the value of the fraction clearly decreases,

Capitalism, in Marx's system, is caught in a fundamental contradiction: capitalists are impelled to act in a fashion which will ultimately destroy their very mode of existence. In order to increase their profits, they must increase production; in order to increase production, they must add constant capital; and the addition of constant capital increases the organic composition of capital, thus causing a fall in the rate of profit. This tendency for the rate of profit to fall can be offset by other tendencies which can temporarily compensate for the fall, but ultimately the profits of capitalist must decrease to a level incompatible with the maintenance of the system.[17]

## Capitalist Accumulation

The scramble for profits motivates the capitalist to expand the size of his industry and thus take advantage of the economies of scale — up to a point, increased plant capacity can achieve lower costs per unit. After this point is reached, costs per unit will rise at such a rapid rate that it will not pay the capitalist to invest any more capital into the production plant itself. Marx, however, virtually ignored this latter possibility; he generally took the attitude that the economies of scale are, for all practical purposes, unlimited. He never bothered himself with the very real problem of optimum plant size.[18]

In his frantic search for profits, the small businessman will inevitably be crushed, Marx thought. The small businessman cannot

since its denominator is increasing because of the increase of C. The rate of profit is therefore falling. This assumes, of course, that S is constant, or at least not rising fast enough to offset the rate of the rise in C.

[17] The offsetting tendencies are discussed in *Capital,* III, ch. 25. For a critical discussion of this "law" of Marxian analysis, see David McCord Wright, *The Trouble With Marx* (New Rochelle, N. Y.: Arlington House, 1967), ch. 5.

[18] On this whole subject, see George Stigler, "The Economies of Scale," *Journal of Law and Economics,* I (1958). Cf. Joe S. Bain, "Economies of Scale, Concentration and Entry," *American Economic Review,* XLIV (1954). See the remarks by Abram L. Harris, "The Social Philosophy of Karl Marx," *Ethics,* LVIII (April, 1948), pt. II, 31.

afford to invest the huge sums of capital necessary to increase his company's production. This being the case, the small competitor cannot lower the costs of his products without suffering losses, and he will be driven out of business. Marx gave no attention to the possibility that many kinds of economic activity may be more suited to the smaller enterprise than to a huge, complex, highly bureaucratic, industrialized establishment. The area of personal services is one example, and the service industries have shown a tremendous capacity for growth in this century.[19] It is true, of course, that ours is the age of huge firms, but much of this growth has been the result, not of higher efficiency, but of political intervention and the state's inflationary policies.[20] Even with the growth of the large firms, the tendency of large manufacturing firms to subcontract jobs to smaller organizations, when coupled with the growth of the service

---

[19] For a survey of the literature dealing with the growth of the service industries in the United States, see William Regan, "Economic Growth and Services," *Journal of Business,* XXXVI (1963). Cf. George Stigler, *Trends in Employment in the Service Industries* (A Study by the National Bureau of Economic Research [Princeton University Press, 1956]). In 1870, something like 20% of the American working force was employed in the service industries; by 1950, the figure was over 50%. Most of this change was not due to a falling off of employment in manufacturing industries, but due rather to the decline of the number of those connected with agriculture. See Stigler, *Service Industries,* 5-6.

[20] On the effects of state-sponsored inflation, see my pamphlet, *Inflation: The Economics of Addiction* (Box 1092, San Carlos, Calif.: The Pamphleteers, 1965), 7-10. Inflation tends to encourage the centralization of production, driving out firms which had been competitive in the earlier, non-inflationary period. As I have written elsewhere, "Eventually, the misallocation of scarce resources promoted by the inflation will harm both the laborers and the manufacturers, as prices soar beyond the means of all but the most influential companies (politically) and the members of the strongest labor unions." See my article, "Domestic Inflation versus International Solvency," *The Freeman,* XVII (Feb., 1967), 68-69. This kind of enforced political centralization has nothing to do with the processes of the free market, but on the contrary, is in violent opposition to the market.

industries, has more than compensated for the concentration of capital into the hands of a few big capitalists.

In explaining the constant tendency toward the accumulation of capital, Marx wrote: "The battle of competition is fought by the cheapening of commodities. The cheapness of commodities depends, *ceteris paribus* [other things being equal — G.N.], on the productiveness of labour, and this again on the scale of production. Therefore, the larger capitals beat the smaller" (I, 686). To some extent, this is accurate. But beyond certain limits, the newer, smaller capitalists who have new approaches to the problem of production and marketing, are able to compete successfully with the older, larger units. This presupposes, however, that the state does not interfere in the market's processes in order to grant a favorable position to the larger companies, such as took place in the United States at the turn of the century.[21] In this case, big business was able to preserve its monopoly status, but not because of any inherent laws of the capitalist system; it required the intervention of the state to secure big business's preferred position.

Along with the accumulation of larger and larger capitals, Marx said, would go the concentration of capital into the hands of fewer and fewer capitalists. "Capital grows in one place to a huge mass in a single hand, because it has in another place been lost by many" (I, 686). This is Marx's explanation for the growth of monopolies. The whole problem of monopoly was one which had not been explored to any extent before Marx began to write. He argued that monopolies are basic creations of the capitalist order. They result from "cut-throat" competition among the capitalists, and therefore they cannot be stopped by any kind of piecemeal social legislation. If anything, Marx argued, monopolies are aided by such things as factory acts: the limitations placed on the employment of cheap labor by women and children imposed on the factory owners the necessity of adding even more machinery to increase production (I, 519). Smaller capitalists are placed at an extreme disadvantage

[21] Gabriel Kolko, *The Triumph of Conservatism* (Glencoe, Ill.: Free Press, 1965).

under such conditions, since the bourgeois state has cut off some of their cheap labor supply, and only the larger and richer capitalists can afford to replace these workers with expensive machinery. The tendency in the direction of monopoly is therefore unstoppable under capitalism.

Undoubtedly, when two contemporary Marxists like Paul Baran and Paul Sweezy sit down and try to find evidence of the tendency toward the accumulation and concentration of capital in modern life, they are able to locate considerable supporting data.[22] There are any number of non-Marxists who have viewed with alarm just this tendency.[23] But there are serious differences of opinion among professional economists in regard to the extent of this concentration, the effects it has on the overall economy, the underlying causes of it, and the solutions to its more unfavorable effects. Some reputable investigators have concluded, for example, that one of the major contributors to the formation of monopolies is the government itself.[24] In his balanced treatment of the whole question of monopoly, Edward S. Mason has drawn a conclusion which, had it been a forecast a century ago, Marx would have rejected as utter bourgeois nonsense:

> The studies of trends of both general and market concentration have yielded useful negative conclusions. It is clear now, as it

---

[22] Paul Baran and Paul Sweezy, *Monopoly Capital* (N. Y.: Monthly Review Press, 1965). Cf. "Marxism and Monopoly Capital: A Symposium," *Science and Society,* XXX (1966), 461-96.

[23] Cf. Adolph A. Berle and Gardiner C. Means, *The Modern Corporation and Private Property* (N. Y.: Macmillan, [1932] 1956); Arthur Robert Burns, *The Decline of Competition* (N. Y.: McGraw-Hill, 1934). For views counter to these, see G. Warren Nutter, *The Extent of Enterprise Monopoly in the United States, 1899-1939* (University of Chicago Press, 1951); George Stigler, *Five Lectures on Economic Problems* (London: Longmans, Green & Co., 1949), lecture 5. For a number of different perspectives presented in one volume, see Edwin Mansfield (ed.), *Monopoly Power and Economic Performance* (N. Y.: Norton, 1964).

[24] Walter Adams and Horace M. Gray, *Monopoly in America: The Government as Promoter* (N. Y.: Macmillan, 1955); Kolko, *The Triumph of Conservatism;* Murray N. Rothbard, *Man, Economy and State,* II, ch. 10.

was not clear before, that there is no inevitable historical force at work that must produce, over any extended period of time, an increase in the per cent of economic activity accounted for by the largest firms either in American manufacture or in the economy as a whole.[25]

## Increasing Misery of the Proletariat

This is one of the more familiar themes in Marx's economic analysis. It is familiar in the sense that it has become a cliché within Marxist circles; it is *not* familiar in the sense that anyone is really certain as to what Marx meant exactly by the phrase. Like so many of his teachings, this one was set forth by Marx only in scattered places, and never in any systematic fashion. Commentators are forced to sift through many seemingly contradictory passages in their attempt to find some semblance of order in his idea of "increasing misery."

One view which many scholars (especially the more vociferous critics) have argued is that Marx meant that the increasing misery is to be *absolute* under capitalism: things must inevitably get worse for the proletariat as capitalism develops. There can be no question about the fact that Marx did write several passages which definitely teach just such a doctrine. For example, in the *Communist Manifesto* (1848), he and Engels wrote: "The modern labourer, on the contrary, instead of rising with the progress of industry, sinks deeper below the conditions of his own class. He becomes a pauper, and pauperism develops more rapidly than population and wealth."[26] Again, in *Value [Wages], Price and Profit* (1865), we read: "The general tendency of capitalist production is not to raise, but to sink

---

[25] Edward S. Mason, *Economic Concentration and the Monopoly Problem* (Cambridge, Mass.: Harvard University Press, 1957), 42-43. Solomon Fabricant put it this way: "All the doubts that can be raised [concerning the data] do not destroy, rather they support, the conclusion that there is no basis for believing that the economy of the United States is largely monopolistic and has been growing more monopolistic." See his essay, "Is Monopoly Increasing?" *Journal of Economic History,* XIII (1953), 93.

[26] Marx and Engels, *The Communist Manifesto,* in *Marx-Engels Selected Works,* I, 45 [Hereafter cited as MESW].

the average standard of wages."[27] Certainly, it would not be deliberately misleading to argue, as many have done, that Marx did believe that the condition of the workers was clearly going to decline absolutely.[28]

On the other hand, many commentators have taken the position that Marx actually taught a doctrine of *relative* increasing misery, i.e., that the standard of living might be rising somewhat even for the working class, but rising far more slowly than production would warrant. Most of the wealth would go either into the capitalists' accumulation or into their personal consumption budgets. This has been the view of many Marxists since the time of Karl Kautsky; it is apparently the view of an increasing number of non-Marxist scholars.[29] Perhaps the most explicit statement of the relative increasing misery thesis is found in *Wage-Labour and Capital* (1847): "If capital is growing rapidly, wages may rise; the profit of capital rises incomparably more rapidly. The material position of the worker has improved, but at the cost of his social position. The gulf that divides him from the capitalist has widened."[30] Owing to an increase

---

[27] Marx, *Value* [*Wages*], *Price and Profit*, MESW, I, 447; cf. 446; *Capital*, I, 707-09.

[28] Some of those who have taken this position are M. M. Bober, *Karl Marx's Interpretation of History* (N. Y.: Norton, [1948] 1965), 213-21; G. D. H. Cole, *The Meaning of Marxism* (Ann Arbor: University of Michigan Press, [1948] 1964), 113-18; John Kenneth Turner, *Challenge to Karl Marx* (N. Y.: Reynal & Hitchcock, 1941), ch. 4; Joseph Schumpeter, *Capitalism, Socialism and Democracy* (N. Y.: Harper Torchbook, [1942] 1962), 34-35.

[29] M. Dobb, *On Marxism Today* (London: The Hogarth Press, 1932), 10; Ronald L. Meek, "Marx's 'Doctrine of Increasing Misery'," *Science and Society*, XXVI (1962), 422-41; Thomas Sowell, "Marx's 'Increasing Misery Doctrine'," *American Economic Review*, L (1960), 111-20. Sowell argues that Marx did hold to the absolute increasing misery doctrine before 1850 or so, but in the context of this chapter, I have tried to indicate that he also wrote in terms of it after 1850. Cf. Sowell, *ibid.*, 113; Abram L. Harris, "The Social Philosophy of Karl Marx," *Ethics*, LVIII (April, 1948), pt. II, 24-27.

[30] Marx, *Wage-Labour and Capital*, MESW, I, 98; cf. 94.

in the productivity of capital, it might be possible for both the laborer and the capitalist to improve their respective standards of living. But, as he wrote in *Capital,* "even in such case, the fall in the value of the labour-power would cause a corresponding rise of surplus-value, and thus the abyss between the labourer's position and that of the capitalist would keep widening" (I, 573). While the proletarians may find that their material standard of living may have an occasion to rise, they will be at a psychological disadvantage. Their pitiful successes will be so tiny in comparison to the increase in wealth within the capitalist class.

Bober, who is of the opinion that Marx held to an absolute increasing misery doctrine, has challenged this opposing interpretation: "But we must remember that this psychological misery applies only to 'the most favorable case,' the special phase of accumulation."[31] It then becomes a question concerning Marx's attitude towards the possibility of capitalism continuing the expansion of economic goods and services. It leads, in short, to Marx's theories concerning capitalist crises, capitalism's inherent contradictions, and the coming collapse of the system. These will be discussed at some length later. But on the whole, it would be safe to say that Marx's writings give evidence of both doctrines, depending upon the purpose of the particular document in question. For propaganda purposes, it is impressive to assert the absolute misery doctrine; yet Marx as a careful scholar was determined to cover himself: if there were some increase in the proletariat's wealth, it would naturally require an explanation. However, the attempt to show that Marx matured in his approach — that he held an absolute increasing misery doctrine before 1850, but not after — is hopeless. Marx's writings before 1850 show that he asserted both views, and the same is true for his later writings. There is a certain tendency for scholars to attempt to make Marx look more consistent than he ever was, and as a result we find these men drawing rather fixed lines between the young, revolutionary Marx and the older, more mature Marx. Such hard and fast lines do not fit; Marx may have emphasized certain

---

[31] Bober, *Karl Marx's Interpretation of History,* 215.

arguments in one period as compared to ~~later or~~ earlier one, but the dialectical thinking of his youth never left him. He was forever arguing for conflicting positions throughout his four decade career.

Whichever doctrine is really more representative of his overall system (I personally would favor the relative misery thesis), one Marxian scholar, Ronald Meek, has admitted that Marx certainly did not foresee the startling rise in the standard of living of Western, industrial laborers. The economic progress of the past century has made either of the arguments rather superfluous. Other explanations should be found, Meek thinks, to give an account of this unforeseen improvement — the Lenin imperialism thesis, for example — but the increasing misery doctrine has served its purpose as a piece of propaganda, and it should now be dropped. Marx was correct, Meek argues, in his general predictions concerning capitalism, but this particular dogma should be replaced by something more realistic. He calls for a major revision or revisions in the Marxian economic approach.[32]

In his arguments in favor of his increasing misery doctrine, Marx laid great stress on what he called the "Industrial Reserve Army." It was made up of all those laborers who had been thrown out of their jobs because of the increased mechanization of industry. This reserve army of the unemployed would help to hold down wages, thus making it almost impossible for trade union organizations to organize effectively, especially during periods of economic stagnation and crisis (I, 689-703). The ranks of this army would be increased by petty bourgeois elements which would also be sent into bankruptcy by the crushing competition of the huge capitalist industries. Thus, larger and larger masses of men would face abject poverty and deprivation, while at the same time their presence within the economy would help to make conditions worse for those of their fellow proletarians who happened to be employed. The problem with this whole thesis, other than the fact that such an army has never materialized, has been pointed out by the Fabian socialist scholar, G. D. H. Cole:

---

[32] Ronald L. Meek, "Marx's 'Doctrine of Increasing Misery'," *Science and Society,* XXVI (1962), 422-41, esp. concluding remarks.

. . . Marx nowhere explained why, if the capitalist class managed to rise to power, in most countries, not by catastrophic revolution overthrowing the previous ruling class, but rather by a gradual process of encroachment and adaptation of the established social structure, increasing misery should be the means to the conquest of power by the proletariat, whereas increasing prosperity had been the weapon of the *bourgeoisie*. Yet the view is plainly paradoxical; for, on the face of the matter, the increase of misery would be much more likely to weaken and dispirit a class than to aid it in the prosecution of the class struggle. . . . In effect, if Marx had been right, the probable outcome would have been the collapse of Capitalism under conditions in which the proletariat would have been too weakened by its misery successfully to establish an alternative system. In these circumstances, if there had been no other aspirant to the succession, a collapsing Capitalism would have been the likeliest to be succeeded, not by socialism, but by sheer chaos, and by the dissolution of the entire civilization of which Capitalism had been a phase.[33]

Cole, of course, favored a gradual transition to socialism, and thus was hostile to Marx's openly revolutionary approach. But whatever Marx "really meant" by the doctrine of increasing misery, it seems safe to say that it is no longer a tool of economic analysis in the contemporary Marxist critique of capitalist society. Even the idea of relative increasing misery fails to explain the great advances made by members of the working class in improving their standard of living over the last 100 years. Capitalism simply has not brought deprivation to Western workers. A good Fabian would give the credit to the role of the state and trade unions in forcing capitalism into reforms. A good free market advocate would point to the rising per capita private investment of capital and to the tremendous increases in productivity which such investment has created, in spite of the tampering of the market's actions by the civil government. But both sides would reject Marx's analysis, and even contemporary Marxists are unhappy with it. Those workers who live under capitalism are just not that miserable, if by misery one is referring to their material conditions.

---

[33] Cole, *The Meaning of Marxism*, 113-14.

144

Karl Marx, however profound some of his individual conceptions may have been, was not a systematic thinker. He would take an idea, explore it along one path, and then go on to another line of thought. All too frequently, he failed to tie his speculations into a coherent, systematic whole. As a result, it is difficult to guess exactly what he had in mind concerning any particular subject. Nowhere is his "scattershot" approach more evident than in his explanation (or, more accurately, his explanations) of capitalism's inherent crises. His statements on the subject are found throughout his economic writings, and it is difficult, perhaps impossible, to be certain which one was most fundamental in his own mind.

The most obvious capitalist flaw, for Marx, is the tendency toward the falling rate of profit. As we have already seen, this is caused by the fact that capitalists are forced by competitors to increase the quantity of constant capital in their respective production processes, and this in turn diminishes the proportion of variable capital — living labor — in the process. Living labor is the one source of profits under capitalism; hence, the rate of profit must fall, inevitably, as the ratio of constant capital increases. In other words, Marx argued, we should expect to see two simultaneous tendencies: the falling rate of profit and the increasing misery of the proletariat. Unfortunately for his consistency, the two are in contradiction with each other.

In so far as wages are pushed down to the minimum subsistence level, the proletariat suffers from the misery which the capitalist system inflicts upon it. But when wages are forced lower, the capitalist obviously reaps a profit; there is an increased quantity of surplus value available to him, since there is a greater quantity of unpaid labor present in the production process. On the other hand, if the increased output of the particular capitalist's industry succeeds in what it aims at, i.e., a greater share of the market than his competitors can attain, the laboring classes achieve a higher standard of living, since they can purchase more consumer goods than they previously could with whatever wages they receive. The price of commodities must fall, since each commodity, by Marx's definition, contains a smaller proportion of human labor than before; commodities contain less value, since the average socially necessary labor time embodied in them is falling as the output of the capitalist system increases (III, 264-65). Where capitalist profits are falling, theoretically due to the increased use of productive machinery, the standard of living is rising, and vice versa. The two "inevitable" tendencies offset each other; they are mutually contradictory in the long run.

Marx explicitly stated that the two should be simultaneously achieved under capitalism: "The falling tendency of the rate of profit is accompanied by a rising tendency of the rate of surplus-value, that is, the rate of exploitation" (III, 281). He attempted to explain the contradiction elsewhere, but his argument is hardly convincing (III, 255, 259). It was based primarily on the idea of technological unemployment — the Industrial Reserve Army — a phenomenon which has not yet come into existence as a major economic factor. While some economists do fear that automation may create such a technological unemployment situation in our time, even they are usually more concerned with the problem of the excess leisure time which these unskilled workers will have on their hands, rather than any fear of some kind of mass starvation. It is assumed that the vastly increased production of consumer goods will provide for those who cannot work.[34] Other economists do not think that automation will have such an effect on the labor market; if anything, automation should increase the number of employed persons, since the additional wealth generated by automated production can be used for retraining programs, educational advance, and the expansion

[34] Many of these visionary economists propose a guaranteed annual income to all people irrespective of whether they work for a living or not. Cf. Robert Theobald (ed.), *The Guaranteed Income* (Garden City, N. Y.: Doubleday, 1966); "The Triple Revolution," included in Erich Fromm (ed.), *Socialist Humanism: An International Symposium* (Garden City, N. Y.: Doubleday Anchor, 1966), 441-61. Perhaps the most ridiculous exposition of this position is Richard Elman's *The Poorhouse State* (N. Y.: Pantheon, 1966). An alternative view is Henry Hazlitt's "Income Without Work," *The Freeman,* XVI (July, 1966). Also see Genesis 3:17-19.

of the service industries.[35] In either case, a huge army of unemployed laborers accompanying capitalism's expansion of output is not a group which is going to be thrown into abject poverty in this century, at least not by the mere operation of private capital investment by today's citizens.

In addition to his theory of the declining rate of profit, Marx also employed a theory of overproduction to condemn capitalism's business cycles. Because of this built-in overproduction feature, capitalism is incurably cyclical: booms will always bust.

> The stupendous productive power developing under the capitalist mode of production relatively to population, and the increase, though not in the same proportion, of capital values (not their material substance), which grows more rapidly than the population, contradict the basis, which, compared to the expanding wealth, is ever narrowing and for which this immense productive power works, and the conditions, under which capital augments its value. This is the cause of crises (III, 312-13).

This is not very lucid language, but he expressed himself more concisely elsewhere. Actually, he argued that capitalism on the one hand produces too much, while on the other hand it produces too little. As he wrote, "conflict must continue to ensue between the limited conditions of consumption on a capitalist basis and a production which forever tends to exceed imminent barriers. Moreover, capital consists of commodities, and therefore the overproduction of capital implies an overproduction of commodities" (III, 301). Yet on the very next page he wrote: "It is not a fact that too many necessities of life are produced in proportion to the existing population. The reverse is true. Not enough is produced to satisfy the wants of the great mass decently and humanely" (III, 302). Not all of the population can be employed, he argued, and therefore they

---

[35] Cf. Yale Brozen, *Automation and Jobs* (Selected Papers of the Graduate School of Business Administration, #18, University of Chicago, 1966), or see his article, "Automation and Jobs," *U. S. News and World Report* (March 8, 1965); Tom Rose, "Why Automation?" *The Freeman*, XV (July, 1965). For a very optimistic view of automation, see Eric Hoffer, "Automation is Here to Liberate Us," *New York Times Magazine* (Oct. 24, 1965).

cannot obtain minimum supplies of consumer goods and services. Finally, he concluded: "It is not a fact that too much wealth is produced. But it is true that there is a periodical overproduction of wealth in its capitalistic and self-contradictory form" (III, 303). Clearly, capitalist society is the worst of all possible worlds: it cannot produce enough while it simultaneously produces too much. This is truly dialectical reasoning.

How did he account for such blatant contradictions in capitalism? Basically, he relied on a rejection of Say's Law to explain capitalist crises: in contrast to Say, who had argued that production creates its own demand and therefore there can be no long-run glut of commodities on the market, Marx said that there *must* be such a glut. This periodic glutting of the market will continue, and it will increase in intensity. It will ultimately destroy the capitalist system. Production and consumption will not balance each other, and this will lead to overinvestment in capital goods, further depressing the rate of capitalist profits (III, 294-95). There must be an absolute overproduction of capital. The smooth working of the capitalist system is thus a myth; it is really, Marx taught, a patchwork of glaring contradictory tendencies which will ultimately blow apart.

For certain purposes, however, Marx did accept the validity of Say's Law. He admitted that "it is a mistake to say that the consumption of necessities does not grow with their cheapening" (III, 769). How, then, could a glut arise on the open free market? Will not the capitalists simply lower the prices of their goods until they are all sold? It is certainly more advantageous to receive some money (even at a loss) than no money whatsoever. Marx had already admitted that prices do fall when production increases (III, 98-103, 265). Yet the glut of goods, including, apparently, capital goods, must continue, and Engels added in a parenthetical note that the glut was worse in the 1890's than it had been in Marx's day (III, 518). The obvious question is simply this: why do the capitalists refuse to lower their prices sufficiently to clear the market of unsold goods? Say's Law assumed that capitalists would do so; if they refused, naturally a glut would result. Why would they continue to produce the kinds of goods which the market would not absorb at the given prices?

Marx asserted that gluts could result on the market because buying and selling are separate links in the chain of production, and the two links can be broken. This produces a crisis: "No one can sell unless some one else purchases. But no one is forthwith bound to purchase, because he has just sold . . . if the split between the sale and the purchase becomes too pronounced, the intermediate connection between them, their oneness, asserts itself by producing — a crisis" (I, 127-28). Or again: "The chain of payments due at a certain time is broken in a hundred places, and the disaster is intensified by a collapse of the credit system. Thus violent and acute crises are brought about, sudden and forcible depreciations . . ." (III, 298). But why should the chain break? He never answered this very clearly, but his assumption seems to have been that the prices of goods are set by entrepreneurs who for some mysterious reason are so stubborn that they refuse to admit that they have seriously misforecast the state of the market, and who are unwilling to lower the prices of their products when faced with gluts at the original price level. The assumption of flexible prices was basic to Say's formulation of the law of markets, but for some reason, Marx argued, capitalists are totally irrational — totally unaware of the way to avoid complete losses — and that Say's original assumption is therefore wrong.[36] The market's pricing mechanism, for some

---

[36] Bernice Shoul has argued that Marx did accept the validity of Say's Law in his general analysis of capitalism. He did so, she asserts, in order to demonstrate the coming collapse of capitalism in terms of his theory of the falling rate of profit. By accepting Say's Law, he supposedly was able to criticize capitalism in terms of its own presuppositions. Therefore, Shoul de-emphasizes Marx's obvious rejection of Say's Law when he denied that the pricing mechanism can balance supply and demand. As a matter of fact, Marx in some places assumed the validity of Say's Law, and in other cases, when it suited his particular argument, he rejected it. Why Shoul refuses to see that Marx held both views is a mystery. Perhaps it is her refusal, like so many other scholars who are sympathetic towards Marx's labors, to see what glaring contradictions were

reason which he never was able to explain, ceases to function in its allocation of scarce resources. It refuses to respond to changed conditions, and the market is unable to clear itself of all the goods offered for sale. Production, contrary to Say, has not created its own consumption (II, 397-98). The basic question still remains: why not?

He blamed part of the trouble on the hoarding by capitalists (Keynes, in this century, was to use a similar argument): "In order to accumulate capital, he must first withdraw a part of the surplus-value from circulation which he obtained from that circulation in the form of money, and must hoard it until it has increased sufficiently for the extension of his old business or the opening of a sideline. So long as the formation of the hoard continues, it does not increase the demand of the capitalist. The money is then inactive" (II, 137). He made, however, one absurd assumption: "Credit is not considered here. And credit includes the depositing, on the part of the capitalist, of accumulating money in a bank on payment of interest as shown by a running account" (II, 137). Yet no modern capitalist enterprise actually sets aside a pile of money for some future investment. It is either deposited in a bank or else it is invested in some short-term security or bond. In some cases large corporations actually enter the loan market with excess capital (General Motors' GMAC time payment plan is an example). But no capitalist actually hoards cash. Marx's explanation of the crisis in terms of hoarding is meaningless; the only time when men hoard paper money is at a time when they expect a rapid fall in the price level. This may accentuate a depression, of course, but it cannot cause one; Marx fails to explain why, at one instant, all capitalists would hoard their paper. The only other major source of hoarding is the hoarding of specie metals which goes on during a period of mass inflation. This does little to affect the price level, however, since the percentage of money metals in the

present in the system of such a supposedly brilliant thinker. Bernice Shoul, "Karl Marx and Say's Law," *Quarterly Journal of Economics,* LXXI (1957); reprinted in Joseph J. Spengler and William R. Allen, *Essays in Economic Thought: Aristotle to Marshall* (Chicago: Rand McNally, 1960).

economy dwindles rapidly in any inflation.[37] In any case, these inflationary periods are never characterized by gluts of goods; they are periods of shortages of durable goods in comparison with demand. Finally, even on the assumption that hoarding would temporarily decrease demand, why would it break the "chain of exchange"? Why would not prices lower to compensate for the new conditions, thus clearing the market? If the market is free to raise or lower its prices, then hoarding cannot explain the existence of trade cycles.[38]

Marx's most cogent explanation of the cause of overinvestment, i.e., malinvestment, are found in the sections of *Capital* dealing with the role of credit in the economy. He blamed the overproduction on the expansion of the credit system: ". . . there has been a general overproduction, promoted by credit and the inflation of prices which goes with it" (III, 578).

> So long as the process of reproduction is in flow and the reflux assured, this credit lasts and extends, and its extension is based upon the extension of the process of reproduction itself. As soon as the stoppage takes place, in consequence of delayed returns, overstocked markets, fallen prices, there is a superfluity of industrial capital, but it is in a form, in which it cannot perform its functions. It is a mass of commodity-capital, but it is un-salable. It is a mass of fixed capital, but largely unemployed through the clogging of reproduction. Credit is contracted, 1) because this capital is unemployed, that is, stops in one of its phases of reproduction, not being able to complete its metamor-phosis; 2) because confidence in the continuity of the process of

[37] See my study, *Monetary Hoarding: The Economics of Survival* (Box 1092, San Carlos, Calif.: The Pamphleteers, 1966), 22-23.

[38] For an indirect refutation of Marx on this point, and an explicit refutation of Keynes, see W. H. Hutt, "The Nature of Co-Ordination Through the Price System," chapter 4 of his monumental book, *Keynesianism: Retrospect and Prospect* (Chicago: Regnery, 1963). Cf. F. A. Hayek, *Prices and Production* (London: Routledge and Kegan Paul, 1935); Murray N. Rothbard, *Man, Economy and State,* II, 679-87. If the market is not free to raise or lower prices, then it is no longer a free market, and therefore the "inevitable tendencies" of capitalism toward a crisis due to a breakdown of the exchange mechanism are not, in fact, inevitable under capitalism, but only under some form of state interventionism.

reproduction has been shaken; 3) because the demand for commercial credit decreases. . . . Hence, if the expansion is disturbed, or even the normal exertion of the process infringed, credit also becomes scarce; it is more difficult to get commodities on credit. It is particularly the demand for cash payment and the caution observed toward sales on credit which are characteristic of that phase of the industrial cycle, which follows a crash (III, 567).

Surprisingly enough, this explanation of crises resembles the neo-Austrian trade cycle theory set forth in this century by the free-market advocates, Ludwig von Mises and F. A. Hayek.[39] Mises has developed the arguments of the 19th century "Currency School" of economists, and it is at least possible that Marx was influenced by this group of economic thinkers. In any case, Marx believed that the credit system is a flaw basic to capitalism, but not to socialism. "As soon as the means of production have ceased to be converted into capital (which includes the abolition of private property in land), credit as such has no longer any meaning" (III, 713). This is a strange assertion; credit's function, that of making capital available for industry through savings, certainly is important in any economic system, even if the state or the "association" does the saving. However, Marx may have had in mind only the idea that fractional reserve banking would cease under socialism. He ridiculed all non-specie metal monetary systems (a fact which may come as a surprise to many readers), since he believed that unbacked paper credit or currency is a basic fraud of capitalism. Since all fractional reserve banking is based upon an expansion of currency and credit beyond the available gold and silver reserves, the system must be condemned (I, 144; III, 537). His criticism went far deeper than this, however; Marx argued that under communism no money would exist at all. Money is the very symbol of the evils of capitalism — the very sign of alienated production — and one of the glories of full communism

---

[39] Mises, *Human Action,* ch. 20. Cf. his book, *The Theory of Money and Credit* (New Haven, Conn.: Yale University Press, [1912] 1951), 357-66. For a study of the depression of 1929-39 written in terms of the neo-Austrian theory of the trade cycle, see Murray N. Rothbard, *America's Great Depression* (Princeton: Van Nostrand, 1963).

would be the abolition of money.[40] Engels agreed fully with Marx on this point.[41] There would be no money and no debt; debt is a form of economic slavery, and it could never exist in the new society (I, 827-29; III, 703). It followed from this, in Marx's mind, that bankers are nothing more than "honourable bandits" (III, 641). Merchants' capital is simply "a system of robbery" (III, 389). None of this will exist in the world beyond the Revolution.

Thus, Marx's system contains multiple theories concerning the breakdown of capitalism. The falling rate of profit is one cause, and another is the supposed contradiction between production and consumption. There is overproduction of both capital goods and consumer goods; simultaneously, there is a shortage of the basic necessities for the masses of society. The overexpansion of credit is a third cause. Wherever Marx looked, he saw contradictions, all of which pointed to the inevitable coming conflagration and the restoration of a society free from the pains of alienated production. The proletariat would seize the reins of production from the capitalist class, and in doing so, the workers would remake society. Nothing could save capitalism, and nothing should save it. It has fulfilled its purpose in the overall world history by expanding vastly the productive capacity of industrial society, but its contradictions will permit it to exist only for a short time. Capitalism, both he and Engels argued, has shown men how to arrange *production* socially in the factory; now the proletariat will be able to organize *distribution*

---

[40] Marx, "On the Jewish Question" (1844), in T. B. Bottomore (ed.), *Karl Marx: Early Writings* (N. Y.: McGraw-Hill, 1964), 34-40. For Marx's general analysis of credit and money under capitalism, see *Capital,* III, chs. 25-36. Here is the central flaw of all socialist systems: how can the allocation of scarce resources take place in a society devoid of money? See the appendix on "Socialist Economic Calculation" for a more extended discussion of this problem.
[41] Engels, *Herr Eugen Dühring's Revolution in Science* [*Anti-Dühring*] (London: Lawrence and Wishart, [1877] 1934), 338-43. This section of *Anti-Dühring* was published separately under the title, *Socialism: Utopian and Scientific,* and it is available in a cheap paperback edition.

socially, removing the distribution process from the "anarchy" of the free market.[42] The anarchy of capitalist competition will be replaced by the order of social planning.[43] It was never explained exactly how society will be able to regulate production without a state and without monetary calculation, but Marx and Engels assumed on faith that the problem could be overcome eventually. They always claimed that they were not in the business of drawing up blueprints for the socialist future; it was enough for them merely to have demonstrated that the present system is corrupt and doomed to destruction. The inherent contradictions of capitalism will lead to a final resolution within a new social and economic form; in fact, the very contradictions are the source of the desired changes. As he wrote in volume I of *Capital*, "the historical development of the antagonisms, immanent in a given form of production, is the only way in which that form of production can be dissolved and a new form established" (535). It was convenient for Marx that the social system which he believed was a moral necessity would come inevitably out of the system which he had always hated. It is always

---

[42] On the supposed contradiction between "socialized factory production" and "anarchistic market distribution," see *Capital*, I, 391; III, 673, 1027. Engels made this a fundamental point in his explication of the Marxian system: *Anti-Dühring*, 296-301. Murray N. Rothbard has commented on this supposed separation: " 'Personal distribution' — how much money each *person* receives from the productive system — is determined, in turn, by the functions that he or his property performs in that system. There is no separation between production and distribution, and it is completely erroneous for writers to treat the productive system as if producers dump their product into some stockpile, to be later 'distributed' in some way to the people in the society. 'Distribution' is only the other side of the coin of production on the market." *Man, Economy and State*, II, 555.

[43] *Capital*, I, 90-91; III, 220-21, 673, 954. Engels, *Anti-Dühring*, 169, 311. The "anarchy" of the market somehow sees to it that each morning one receives his newspaper and milk, an incredible feat when one considers the intricate complexity of the whole operation. A remarkable order is displayed for such an "anarchistic" system.

pleasant to discover that one's moral goals can be proven as historically inevitable by one's neutral, scientific analysis. And once his tools are accepted as being scientifically accurate and valid, his logic and his empirical data will drag the reader to his inescapable conclusion. His conclusions follow from his presuppositions; in reality, his conclusions are determined from the start by his presuppositions. There is no escape, given the first principles he sets forth.

### Böhm-Bawerk's Criticism

It was Marx's misfortune that one of his contemporaries was Eugen von Böhm-Bawerk, perhaps the most logically rigorous and scholarly economist of the last century. Shortly after Marx died, Böhm-Bawerk's *History and Critique of Interest Theories* was published, and it contained a devastating section on Marx's exploitation theory, i.e., surplus value. This was in 1884. The third volume of *Capital* appeared in 1894; two years later Böhm-Bawerk published his classic essay on the Marxian system. The Marxists never recovered from this blow, in spite of seven decades of their attempts to reply to it. The basic problem which has proved impossible to solve is that Marx's law of value contradicts the empirically obvious fact of an average rate of profit in industry. Böhm-Bawerk had pointed this out in his preliminary chapter in 1884, and he elaborated on the subject in 1894. Between 1884 and 1894, Engels actually conducted a literary contest (aimed primarily at the followers of Roberdtus) in order to discover someone who could provide a solution to the problem. No one in the decade ever succeeded in carrying off the prize.[44]

The issue which faced Marx was simply this: his definition of the rate of surplus value did not conform to his explanation of the rate of profit. He had defined surplus value as that additional labor

---

[44] A list of these essays is found in Böhm-Bawerk's 1896 essay, which is generally translated as *Karl Marx and the Close of His System*. I am using a more recent edition, "Unresolved Contradiction in the Marxian Economic System," in *The Shorter Classics of Böhm-Bawerk* (South Holland, Ill.: Libertarian Press, 1962), I, 210n.

time in the production process over and above the labor necessary to produce the laborer's minimum subsistence wage. The capitalist appropriates the value of this extra labor, and this is the sole source of his profits. The rate of surplus value was defined as the surplus value divided by the wage: $\frac{s}{v}$. The rate of profit is something completely different. It was defined by Marx as the ratio between the surplus value and the *total* capital invested, including the constant capital: $\frac{s}{c+v}$. In other words, the capitalist calculates his returns not in terms of surplus value as such, but in terms of the profits of his industry in comparison to his overall capital outlay. Obviously, if he employs only one man to run a multi-million dollar machine, he can extract his profit only from the surplus living labor time contributed by that one man; the capitalist would be out of business very quickly if Marx's theory were correct. This raises a distinct problem, as Böhm-Bawerk pointed out with such devastating effect.

Consider, Böhm-Bawerk said, Marx's favorite example: an industry exists in which the workers earn their salaries in the first six hours of labor, yet they are forced to work an additional six hours for the capitalist. The rate of surplus value is $\frac{s}{v}$, or $\frac{6 \text{ hrs.}}{6 \text{ hrs.}}$, or 100%. We know, however, that different industries have different organic compositions of capital. One industry may be labor intensive, with 20 c (constant capital) and 80 v (wages). Others may be machinery intensive: 70 c and 30 v. Modern industry, of course, tends to fit into the latter category. Marx was aware of the problem, and he constructed several tables to demonstrate it and his supposed solution. The first table explored industries with equal rates of surplus value.

| Capitals | Rate of Surplus Value | Surplus Value | Value of Product | Rate of Profit |
|---|---|---|---|---|
| I.   80 c   20 v | 100% | 20 | 120 | 20% |
| II.   70 c   30 v | 100% | 30 | 130 | 30% |
| III. 60 c   40 v | 100% | 40 | 140 | 40% |
| IV.  85 c   15 v | 100% | 15 | 115 | 15% |
| V.   95 c    5 v | 100% | 5 | 150 | 5% |

Source: *Capital,* III, 183. A composite of this graph and another appears in Böhm-Bawerk's "Unresolved Contradiction," 221.

Böhm-Bawerk commented on this graph and its implications: "We see that this table shows in the different spheres of production where the exploitation of labor has been the same, very different rates of profit, corresponding to the different organic composition of the capitals" (221). Yet such a phenomenon is unheard of in industry. The profit rates of the various industries in the graph vary from 5% to 40%. Why would any intelligent capitalist stay in a highly mechanized industry which yields only 5% profit, when he can invest his money in some labor intensive project and reap a 40% return? As Böhm-Bawerk argued: "His theory demands that capitals of equal amount, but of dissimilar organic composition, should exhibit different profits. The real world, however, most plainly shows that it is governed by the law that capitals of equal amount, without regard to possible differences of organic composition, yield equal profits" (220).

There is absolutely no doubt that Marx recognized this contradiction very early. He did not need a Böhm-Bawerk to point it out for him. He admitted it in a letter to Engels in 1868, and he believed that he had discovered a solution to it.[45] He devoted all of part II of volume III of *Capital* just to this question (III, 168-246). In fact, Marx's own statement of the problem was as forceful as Böhm-Bawerk's, and Böhm-Bawerk quoted it in full (220):

We have demonstrated, that different lines of industry may have different rates of profit, corresponding to differences in the organic composition of capitals, and, within the limits indicated, also corresponding to different times of turn-over; the law (as a general tendency) that profits are proportioned as the magnitudes of the capitals, or that capitals of equal magnitude yield equal profits in equal times, applies only to capitals of the same organic

---

[45] Marx to Engels, 30 April, 1868: *Marx-Engels Selected Correspondence,* 243.

composition, with the same rate of surplus-value, and the same time of turn-over. And these statements hold good on the assumption which has been the basis of all our analyses so far, namely that commodities are sold at their values. On the other hand there is no doubt that, aside from unessential, accidental, and mutually compensating distinctions, a difference in the average rate of profit of the various lines of industry does not exist in reality, and could not exist without abolishing the entire system of capitalist production. It would seem, then, as though the theory of value were irreconcilable at this point with the actual process, irreconcilable with the real phenomena of production, so that we should have to give up the attempt to understand these phenomena (III, 181-82).

Then Marx issued the challenge to himself: "How is the equalization of profits into an average rate of profit brought about, seeing that it is evidently a result, not a point of departure?" (III, 205). He used two additional charts to show what was involved. The first one showed that it was necessary to find an average rate of profit for industry, and therefore he assumed that an average organic composition of capital had to exist in theory, though not in fact:

| Capitals | Rate of Surplus Value | Surplus Value | Rate of Profit | Used Up c | Value of Commodities | Cost Price | |
|---|---|---|---|---|---|---|---|
| I.   80 c + 20 v | 100% | 20 | 20% | 50 | 90- | 70 | |
| II.  70 c + 30 v | 100% | 30 | 30% | 51 | 111 | 81 | |
| III. 60 c + 40 v | 100% | 40 | 40% | 51 | 131 | 91 | |
| IV.  85 c + 15 v | 100% | 15 | 15% | 40 | 70 | 55 | |
| V.   95 c + 5 v | 100% | 5 | 5% | 10 | 20 | 15 | |
| 390 c +110 v | | 110 | 100% | | | | Total |
| 78 c + 22 v | | 22 | 22% | | | | Average |

In this chart, Marx set forth a more realistic assumption, that all the constant capital was not used up in one period; hence, the used up constant capital in industry I is not the full 80 c but merely 50 c. The total value of commodities in the example is therefore 90: 50 c (constant capital used up) + 20 v (wages) + 20 s (surplus value accruing to capitalist). The cost price, of course, is the price minus the surplus value, or 70. By adding the total capital invested in all the industries, we find a figure of 500. The total surplus value accruing to capitalists as a group is 110. The profit rate, then, is

$$\frac{s}{c+v} = \frac{110}{500} = 22\%.$$ This is the average profit rate for all industries, and it must assume the existence of an average ratio of constant capital to variable capital: 78 c and 22 v. This assumption, however, is an impossibility; the whole problem is that such an average organic composition of capital cannot exist in the real world.

The third chart assumes that the average rate of profit, 22%, is in operation throughout the industries. It is here that the labor theory of value collapses; if labor is supposed to be the sole source of value, and prices must reflect this value directly (since equal values are supposed to be exchanged for equals), then there should be no deviation of prices from values. Unfortunately, there is.

| Capitals | Surplus Value | Value | Cost Price of Commodities | Price of Commodities | Rate of Profit | Deviation of Price From Value |
|---|---|---|---|---|---|---|
| I.   80 c + 20 v | 20 | 90 | 70 | 92 | 22% | + 2 |
| II.  70 c + 30 v | 30 | 111 | 81 | 103 | 22% | − 8 |
| III. 60 c + 40 v | 40 | 131 | 91 | 113 | 22% | −18 |
| IV.  85 c + 15 v | 15 | 70 | 55 | 77 | 22% | + 7 |
| V.   95 c +  5 v | 5 | 20 | 15 | 37 | 22% | +17 |

Source: both of the last two charts appear in *Capital*, III, 185.

The cost price of commodities in example I is 70. The average rate of profit is 22%. Thus, the market price must be 92: 70 + 22 (.22 × 100). In the preceding chart, it was demonstrated that the real value of the commodities is 90 (50 c + 20 v + 20 s). Thus, the deviation of the *actual price* of 92 from the *value price* of 90 is +2. If the labor theory of value were correct, there could be no such deviation.

In explaining this obvious contradiction, Marx appealed to the idea of a "price of production" theory. This same escape had been used by both Adam Smith and David Ricardo, although Marx rejected their use of a similar approach (III, 233-34). First, he admitted the problem: "One portion of the commodities is sold in the same proportion above in which the other is sold below their

159

values" (III, 185). This statement is in absolute opposition to his basic assumption in volume I: "The creation of surplus-value, and therefore the conversion of money into capital, can consequently be explained neither on the assumption that commodities are sold above their value, nor that they are bought below their value" (I, 179). Marx went on: "And it is only their sale at such prices which makes it possible that the rate of profit for all five capitals is uniformly 22%, without regard to the organic composition of these capitals." Yet by his own definition, profit can be computed only in terms of the organic composition of capital: $\dfrac{s}{c+v}$. "The prices which arise by drawing the average of the various rates of profit in the different spheres of production and adding this average to the cost-prices of the different spheres of production, are the *prices of production*. They are conditioned on the existence of an average rate of profit, and this, again, rests on the premise that the rates of profit in every sphere of production, considered by itself, have previously been reduced to so many average rates of production" (III, 185). Finally, he defined his terms: "The price of production of a commodity, then, is equal to its cost-price plus a percentage of profit apportioned according to the average rate of profit, or in other words, equal to its cost-price plus the average rate of profit" (III, 186). He then used the analogy of a huge national stockholding company in order to resolve the problem; this crude aggregate was his basic answer:

> While the capitalists in their various spheres of production re-cover the value of capital consumed in the production of their commodities through the sale of these, they do not secure the surplus-value, and consequently the profit, created in their own sphere by the production of these commodities, but only as much surplus-value, and profit, as falls to the share of every aliquot part of the total social capital out of the total social surplus value, or social profit produced by the total capital of society in all spheres of production. . . . The various capitalists, so far as profits are concerned, are so many stockholders in a stock com-pany in which the shares of profit are uniformly divided for every 100 shares of capital, so that profits differ in the case of the individual capitalists only according to the amount of capital invested by each one of them in the social enterprise, according

to his investment in social production as a whole, according to his shares (III, 186-87).

But what kind of answer is this? Capitalists, except in the case of very limited cartels, never act in this fashion. They compete with each other, receiving their profits or taking their losses according to the competitive position of their *individual* establishments. If capitalists actually did act as if they were members of a huge stock company, then why should any of them receive losses? If the company is a part of a huge aggregate, automatically receiving its share of the average rate of profit, then it should never fail. But one of the main tenets of the Marxist faith is that capitalists become increasingly competitive, driving their competitors out of business whenever possible. The "cut-throat" competition of these "ruthless" industrialists — the vision which captivated Marx in volume I — now appears in a modified form: shareholders of one happy company can receive, automatically, their share of the average profits. Böhm-Bawerk exploded this aggregate argument forever: there is no such national sum of common profit from which each capitalist cuts his share (230-35). It is a totally static conception of profit.

Marx admitted only that "The foregoing statements are indeed a modification of our original assumption concerning the determination of the cost-price of commodities" (III, 194). It was more than a modification; it was a total refutation of his earlier position. He had argued before that the value of a commodity and its price had to be equal; his theory of surplus value was offered precisely as a solution to the problem of capitalism's profits arising in an economy where equal values *must* be exchanged for equals. Yet in volume III he offered as a mere modification the statement that "the price of production may vary from the value of a commodity . . ." (III, 194). Böhm-Bawerk pinpointed the issue, since he was unwilling to permit Marx to escape from an absolute contradiction as if the later revision were merely a modification of the earlier:

> There are two possible alternatives. The first alternative is that a permanent system of exchange is really established whereby goods are exchanged at values which are in proportion to the labor that the respective goods represent, and whereby, further-

more, the magnitude of the surplus proceeds to be derived from production is really determined by the quantity of labor expended. If that alternative obtains, then any equalization of the ratio of surplus proceeds to capital is an impossibility. The second alternative is that such an equalization does take place. If that alternative obtains, then products cannot possibly continue to be exchanged at values which are in proportion to the labor they represent. . . (226).

He then delivered the intellectual *coup de grâce:* "I cannot help myself; I see here no explanation and reconciliation of a contradiction, but the bare contradiction itself. Marx's third volume contradicts the first. The theory of the average rate of profit and of the prices of production cannot be reconciled with his theory of value" (228). He then went on to demolish Marx's four pathetic attempts to find some kind of solution, and the reader is referred to those rebuttals for further study (229-56).

Böhm-Bawerk's position has never been successfully rebutted. There have been numerous attempts by Marxists and others to redefine Marx's economics in order to avoid Böhm-Bawerk's telling criticisms, but none has carried the day; Marxists have never agreed upon any of these various alternatives. One of the more famous of these attempted reconstructions was presented by L. von Bortkiewicz near the turn of the century. His answer was very detailed and complex, dealing with a difficult portion of the more obscure volume II of *Capital*. Paul Sweezy, America's foremost living Marxist economist, has seized upon this solution in a desperate hope of salvaging Marx's system, but Paul Samuelson has shown the insufficiency of Bortkiewicz's attempt. In fact, Samuelson concludes that Bortkiewicz's theory of production is not far removed from Böhm-Bawerk's![46]

---

[46] Paul Samuelson, "Wages and Interest: A Modern Dissection of Marxian Economic Models," *American Economic Review,* XLVII (1957), 890-92. Cf. Paul M. Sweezy, *The Theory of Capitalist Development* (N. Y.: Monthly Review Press, [1942], 1964), 115-25. Sweezy included one of Bortkiewicz's essays in his edition of Böhm-Bawerk's *Karl Marx and the Close of His System* (N. Y.: Augustus Kelley, 1949). Another attempt along these lines is

G. D. H. Cole has argued that Marx's theory of value was not an explanation of prices at all! It was merely a theory of capitalist exploitation.[47] He fails to mention that Marx's theory of exploitation was written only in terms of a theory of capitalist prices. It would have surprised Marx to have learned that all of his time spent in computing price data, pouring over statistics in the British Museum, and formulating his theory of exchange — a system based on the pricing mechanism — was spent in vain. Cole's argument is certainly unique.

Perhaps the most startling revision is Sweezy's most recent contribution. Not only was Marx not talking about a theory of prices, he was not really interested in explaining the capitalist economy in terms of classical economic theory: "The first nine chapters of *Capital*, it is now widely recognized [!?!], are not primarily concerned with exchange value or prices in the sense of either classical or neoclassical economics but rather with what today might be called economic sociology."[48] Poor Marx; he actually imagined that his system was a total one. He thought that he had constructed a theoretical framework which demonstrated all the contradictions of capitalism, whether economic or social. He actually believed that he was an economist who used the very presuppositions of Adam Smith and Ricardo in order to demonstrate with their own intellectual tools that capitalism is doomed. But his followers have proven to their own satisfaction that Marx really had not accomplished this, even that he had not attempted to do so; he was a sociologist primarily, and not a classical economist. Odd, under these circumstances, that Marx was so concerned in volume III with his hopeful demonstration of the basic validity of volume I's economic outline. For a sociologist who was not supposed to have been interested in price theory, he certainly struggled for many pages with a problem which would not

Ronald L. Meek, "Some Notes on the 'Transformation Problem'," *The Economic Journal*, LXVI (1956), 94-107. This essay has been reprinted in Spengler and Allen, *Essays in Economic Thought*.

[47] Cole, *The Meaning of Marxism*, 210.

[48] Paul Sweezy, "Professor Cole's *History of Socialist Thought*," *American Economic Review*, XLVII (1957), 990.

have arisen except for the fact that it involved the problem of relating classical value theory to capitalism's price mechanism.

The attempted revisions of Marx's system are a testimony to at least two things: (1) the absolute contradiction in the original Marxian economic system; and (2) the unwillingness of Marxist scholars to face this basic truth. Since they cannot resolve the problem, they try to argue that Marx was never concerned with such matters, or that such matters, even if present in Marx's mind, were not fundamental to his outlook, in spite of the fact that Marx considered them to be of enormous importance. Scholarship, in this century, has not always been faithful to the idea of rigorous truth — even a truth defined by the canons of secular thought. As Samuelson advises: "Marxolaters, to use Shaw's term, should heed the basic precept valid in all societies: Cut your losses!"[49]

Gottfried Haberler, one of America's most respected economists, has offered this evaluation of Böhm-Bawerk's efforts: "In my opinion Böhm-Bawerk's is to this day the most convincing and lucid analysis of the Marxist theory of value, price, capital and interest. . . . Böhm-Bawerk's criticism which goes, of course, beyond the demonstration of an internal contradiction to showing the basic flaws of theory, is altogether convincing and has never been refuted."[50] No more fitting compliment could be paid to a master economist by one of his peers; it is a long-deserved memorial to a brilliant logician after a half century of garbled "refutations" and open villification by those whose Marxist presuppositions have interfered with their reasoning processes.[51]

---

[49] Samuelson, *op. cit., A.E.R.* (1957), 892.

[50] Haberler, "Marxist Economics in Retrospect and Prospect," in Milorad M. Drachkovitch (ed.), *Marxist Ideology in the Contemporary World — Its Appeals and Paradoxes* (N. Y.: Praeger, 1966), 115.

[51] In a letter to me dated 4 March, 1967, Professor Hans Senholz writes: "It's an indication of the incredible shallowness of contemporary thought that respected economists can deny the Marxian contradictions of fact and reality. Surely Marxian error is as important today as it was 85 years ago when Böhm-Bawerk wrote his rejoinders.

Marx sought for a solution to the profit question, and as we have seen, he was unable to find it. He assumed the existence of a national rate of profit which is produced by the competition of all capitalists. The solution was no solution at all, but it placed the idea of capitalist competition at the forefront of his economic analysis.

Throughout most of his economic analysis, as Bober has pointed out, Marx took a dim view of the functions of the capitalist-entre- preneur.[52] As capitalism develops, Marx believed, the capitalist as entrepreneur would begin to lose his function: "An industrial army of workmen, under the command of a capitalist, requires, likes a real army, officers (managers), and sergeants (foremen, overlookers), who, while the work is being done, command in the name of the capitalist. The work of supervision becomes their established and exclusive function" (I, 364). A statement made by Engels was even more explicit:

> If the crises revealed the incapacity of the bourgeoisie any longer to control the modern productive forces, the conversion of the great organizations for production and communication into joint- stock companies and state property shows that for this purpose the bourgeoisie can be dispensed with. All the social functions of the capitalists are now carried out by salaried employees. The capitalist has no longer any social activity save the pocketing of revenues, the clipping of coupons and gambling on the Stock Exchange, where the different capitalists fleece each other of their capital. Just as at first the capitalist mode of production displaced the workers, so now it displaces the capitalists, rele- gating them, just as it did the workers, to the superfluous popu-

---

If Marx were right for the 'aggregate' then in my belief capitals of equal amount and similar organic composition anywhere in the world would have to bear equal yields. A Mexican capital and American of identical composition would have to produce the same return, which again contradicts reality. To seek refuge in macro-economics to escape micro-economic deductions is to admit the lack of a logical answer."

[52] M. M. Bober, *Karl Marx's Interpretation of History,* 281-83.

lation, even if in the first instance not to the industrial reserve army.[53]

As capitalism advances, the salaried manager replaces the capitalist-entrepreneur: this is the basic thesis of Marxism in regard to the function of entrepreneurship. Marx made no functional distinction between the entrepreneur and the manager. This has always been a fatal flaw in Marxism, since it makes it impossible for the Marxist to explain the nature and function of profit in an economy.[54]

Marx's view of capitalistic profits hinged upon his belief that all profit stems from the exploitation of living human labor. But on this presupposition, Marx was unable to explain such phenomena as interest, profits accruing to the owners of unimproved land, and the high value of diamonds and other precious gems which have, in their natural state, virtually no human labor present in them. He had, in short, no theory of capitalist profits that would fit the economic facts. The only one which he had was effectively scrapped in volume III of *Capital* when he abandoned the rigid theory of surplus value which he had formulated in volume I. His "price of production" *assumed*

---

[53] Engels, *Anti-Dühring,* 306.

[54] Lenin's view of entrepreneurship was especially naive. Economics is reduced by him to mere accounting: "Accounting and control — these are the *chief* things necessary for the organizing and correct functioning of the *first phase* of Communist society. *All* citizens are here transformed into hired employees of the state, which is made up of the armed workers. *All* citizens become employees and workers of *one* national state 'syndicate.' All that is required is that they should work equally, should regularly do their share of work, and should receive equal pay. The accounting and control necessary for this have been *simplified* by capitalism to the utmost, till they have become the extraordinarily simple operations of watching, recording and issuing receipts, within the reach of anybody who can read and write and knows the first four rules of arithmetic." This he wrote in *State and Revolution* in 1917 [(N. Y.: International Publishers, 1943), 83-84]. It is little wonder that after four years of economic management run on this belief, the economy of the new Soviet Union collapsed, making necessary the reintroduction of at least limited private ownership and planning under the New Economic Policy (NEP).

a prevailing rate of profit without doing anything to explain its origin (apart from simple competition).

Modern economic theory sees profit as the result of entrepreneurial planning. This theory has been expounded forcefully by Frank H. Knight in his monumental *Risk, Uncertainty and Profit* (1921).[55] It offers the argument that pure profit stems from the ability of some entrepreneurs to *forecast* the state of the market more accurately than their competitors. They are thus able to reap an excess of income over capital, wage, and interest expenditures. *Profit*, in other words, stems from the fact of *uncertainty*. Without this entrepreneurial function — the task of guessing accurately about the future and planning accordingly — there could be no profits under capitalism's free market.[56] The *manager's* task is merely to carry out the decisions made by the entrepreneurs. While the function of management is in part entrepreneurial (just as the entrepreneur's function is in part managerial), the managers do not perform the basic task in a profit-seeking establishment.

Under this theory, the entrepreneur's success is directly dependent upon his ability to predict the future and plan for it. The least successful at the job will be forced out of business through the endless competition of the open market. In this view, all societies need entrepreneurs; so long as men are not omniscient concerning the future needs and wants of the population, the entrepreneurial function must be performed by someone. The free market, with its incentives of profit and loss, has been the most successful in meeting the desires of the public at the least possible expenditure. So far, it has proven to be the most efficient means of stimulating men to bear the risks of economic forecasting and planning.

Marx wrote, in regard to profit, that "the rate of profit of the individual capital is determined, not by the market price of a commodity, but by the difference between the market-price and the cost-price" (III, 434). This is true enough, but he neglected to

---

[55] Frank H. Knight, *Risk, Uncertainty and Profit* (N. Y.: Harper Torchbook, 1964), esp. chs. 8-10.

[56] Cf. Ludwig von Mises, *Human Action*, 286-307.

offer an explanation for this difference, other than his surplus value formulation. This concept involved the idea of the absolute minimum subsistence wage level — a fact not borne out by either subsequent economic developments in theory or in fact. The whole theory collapsed with the labor theory of value's demise; in fact, Marx's own writings called it into question. The fact that Marx abandoned the labor theory for a cost of production approach testified to the inapplicability of the labor theory and the surplus value theory of profit.

As we have already seen, both Marx and Engels de-emphasized the role of the entrepreneur. At best, the capitalist performs a small function of the "superintendence of labor." In short, capitalists command factory production (III, 450-51). But the coming of cooperative production has shown the uselessness of the capitalist. As he said, "not the industrial capitalists, but the industrial managers are 'the soul of our industrial system' " (III, 454). Ultimately, "only the functionary remains and the capitalist disappears from the process of production as a superfluous person" (III, 456). Then who will predict the nature of consumer demand in the future? If the managers do it, then they have, in effect, taken over the role of the capitalist; if they are not entitled to the resulting profit (i.e., that residual income remaining after the other factors of production have been paid for), then what incentive will they have to forecast as accurately as possible? A basic conservatism — the unwillingness to assume responsibility for losses — is notorious among salaried bureaucrats. Knight has referred to this fact: "The great danger to be feared from a political control of economic life under ordinary conditions is not a reckless dissipation of the social resources so much as the arrest of progress and the vegetation of life."[57] If there are

---

[57] Knight, *op. cit.,* 361. Cf. Mises, *Socialism,* 205-10. As Mises writes: "Success has always been attained only by those [joint stock] companies whose directors have predominant personal interest in the prosperity of the company. . . . Socialist-etatistic theory of course will not admit this. . . . It refuses to see in those who guide the company anything except officials, for the etatist wants to think of the whole world as inhabited only by officials." *Socialism,* 208-09.

no capitalist-entrepreneurs, how will the economy avoid total bureaucratic, "managerial" stagnation?

What Marx found abhorrent in capitalism was its dynamic character. Some firms failed, others profited, and all seemed caught up in the 19th century's scramble for increased production. Capitalism fluctuates too much. It is anarchistic. What it needs is collective planning, where all uncertainty is removed (III, 220-21). This has been the dream of all socialist thinkers. They have criticized the capitalist system because of its dynamism which, in the eyes of the socialists, is anarchistic because there is no board of planners directing all phases of economic life. Capitalism permits failure. This, of course, must be true of capitalism, since the free market economy accepts the necessity of losses for those firms and individuals who cannot supply the needs of consumers more effectively than their competitors. Capitalism operates under the assumption that men are neither omnipotent nor omniscient. Man, in short, is not God; capitalism recognizes this fact, and it tries to regulate production and distribution as efficiently as possible, given this basic limitation on mankind. Mises puts it very nicely: "That Socialism would be immediately practicable if an omnipotent and omniscient Deity were personally to descend to take in hand the government of human affairs, is incontestable."[58] The socialist has such a Deity: the state planning board. Marx had his: the "association."

Without a proper concept of entrepreneurship, Marx had no valid theory of profit. It is not surprising, as Haberler has pointed out, that "Marxist economics has proved operationally completely sterile in both capitalist and Communist countries."[59] Marx's concept of supply and demand was essentially static: once supply and demand "balance," i.e., once market prices correspond to prices of production, "these forces cease to operate, they compensate one another . . ." (III, 419). As if supply and demand were not always constantly in flux, a fact which Marx readily admitted in other places (III, 150, 190, 230). Supply and demand are dynamic fac-

---

[58] *Ibid.*, 207.
[59] Gottfried Haberler, "Marxist Economics in Retrospect and Prospect," in Drachkovitch (ed.), *Marxist Ideology*, 116.

tors; even at those points where market prices do equal cost prices, there is no cessation of economic forces.[60] At the point of perfect balance, there could be no profits in Marx's system of analysis, since costs and market prices are identical. Then why should he criticize the capitalist system? Capitalism uses the entrepreneur to forecast the future state of the market; if all capitalists were to succeed, all profit would disappear. Marx, therefore, had nothing but contempt for the very men whose function tends toward the conquest of uncertainty. He never saw capitalism for what it is: the response of sinful and limited men to make the best of an uncertain, imperfect and fallen world. Marx demanded an economic paradise where there would be no scarcity, no uncertainty, and no capitalist entrepreneurship. It is only this kind of world which can dispense with profits. Marx wanted heaven on earth, or more accurately, he wanted an escape from time and the curses which time has brought. His vision of socialism ultimately required a static universe in which there would be no change whatsoever, or at least where all change could be accurately predicted and controlled. Because the capitalist system failed to meet this requirement, he rejected it as the creation of alienated mankind, a temporary period which would come to an end with the Revolution. He castigated the capitalist for deviating from the utopian conception of a perfect world.[61]

## Conclusion

Marx began with the assumption that the labor theory of value is operative in capitalist economic affairs. A good must contain an equal quantity of human labor with any other good if an exchange is to take place. Prices, therefore, should be in direct proportion to the quantities of labor contained in the respective products. This theory in turn led Marx to formulate (or borrow from Roberdtus) the idea of surplus value: the presence of unpaid labor in the process of production gives the capitalist the power to exchange equals for

---

[60] See Böhm-Bawerk's remarks in "Unresolved Contradiction," 280-85.
[61] Cf. Bober, *Karl Marx's Interpretation of History,* ch. 14.

equals and still reap a profit (assuming the validity of his erroneous minimum subsistence wage concept). The surplus value issue raised still another problem: how could profits be equal on all equal capital investments if the only source of profit is living human labor? Would not the firm using more living labor in the production process reap far greater profits than a firm using machinery extensively? Yet this obvious conclusion stood in absolute contradiction with the economic facts. And if, as Marx finally had to admit, all capitals do return equal profits on equal capitals invested (in the long run), then the original presupposition of the Marxian system is destroyed: factors of production other than human labor time apparently create value and are therefore entitled to a return. Constant capital is obviously receiving an equal return with labor under these circumstances; the capitalist's profit does not depend strictly on the quantities of living labor present in the productive process. Hence, the labor theory of value collapses under its own weight.

What, then, of Marxian economics? Haberler offers his opinion, and it seems to be a sound one:

> I conclude that Böhm-Bawerk's prediction has come true. The Marxist economic system has slowly lost its influence and has no future. But the close of the Marxist system does not mean the end of socialism, and Marxist economics will always maintain a prominent place in the history of the social sciences and the intellectual history of the nineteenth and twentieth centuries. The historian of economic thought will never cease rummaging in the voluminous writings of Marx and the specialist will find flashes of insight and even genuine analytical discoveries, bits and pieces of usable scrap. People will always marvel as Böhm-Bawerk did, at the boldness of the whole lofty construction, but Marxism as an economic system is closed and will not be reopened.[62]

Nevertheless, the vision which Marx and his followers have held cannot be refuted by a step-by-step dissection of his economic system. Communists have never held to the system merely because of its particular insights into the nature of capitalist production and

---

[62] Gottfried Haberler, in Drachkovitch (ed.), *Marxist Ideology*, 124-25.

distribution. The system is held in faith because it promises a better world for secular, apostate men. Marxism fulfilled the needs of 19th century industrial men who were ready to destroy the system under which they lived. It provided an aura of scientific infallibility in an age which worshiped science. It simultaneously appealed to a side of man's nature which is never wholly absent: his desire for total destruction of the present. *Men want to escape from history,* since they believe that it is history which has limited them. Their world is filled with uncertainty, scarcity, and death; that this has been the result of man's apostacy and disobedience to God is something which they dare not admit. If they did, it would demand repentance. Throughout history, the cosmology of chaos has appealed to such men, for it offers the promise of total liberation from the bondage of time. Liber, in fact, was a Roman god of chaos, and it is from his name that we derive the word "liberty." Thus, the popularity of the hammer as a revolutionary symbol: it is the means of shattering the present world order. Marxism, in combining the two myths of scientific infallibility and revolutionary action, offered hope to those who have sought to escape from history. This is the essence of Marx's religion of revolution; it is the same appeal which has dominated all the chaos cults as far back as recorded history extends.

## APPENDIX A

> *The problem of economic calculation is the funda-*
> *mental problem of Socialism. That for decades people*
> *could write and talk about Socialism without touching*
> *this problem only shows how devastating were the*
> *effects of the Marxian prohibition on scientific scrutiny*
> *of the nature and working of a socialist economy.*
>
> Ludwig von Mises (1922)[1]

## VI.

## SOCIALIST ECONOMIC CALCULATION

What is economic science? This question has baffled even the best of economists for at least two centuries. Airtight definitions are, of course, impossible; no matter what the object of a definition may be, neither human language nor thought permit absolutely rigorous definitions. Nevertheless, we can at least approach a definition narrow enough to be useful, excluding enough extraneous material to allow some kind of understanding. In the past, many definitions of economics have been popular: the science of wealth, the study of welfare, and the science of human avarice.[2] In this century, Lionel Robbins has provided us with the most generally accepted definition: economics is the science of *economizing;* it is the study of the allocation of scarce resources among competing

---

[1] Ludwig von Mises, *Socialism* (New Haven, Conn.: Yale University Press, [1922] 1951), 135.

[2] Israel M. Kirzner surveys the various definitions of economics in his book, *The Economic Point of View* (Princeton: Van Nostrand, 1960).

ends. His book, *The Nature and Significance of Economic Science* (1932), has become the standard work on the epistemology of economics. He spells out his position in no uncertain terms: "But when time and the means for achieving ends are limited *and* capable of alternative applications, *and* the ends are capable of being distinguished in order of importance, then behavior necessarily assumes the form of choice. Every act which involves time and scarce means for the achievement of one end involves the relinquishment of their use for the achievement of another. It has an economic aspect."[3] His basic presupposition is simple: "Scarcity of means to satisfy ends of varying importance is an almost ubiquitous condition of human behavior."[4] Therefore, he concludes, "Economics is the science which studies human behavior as a relationship between ends and scarce means which have alternative uses."[5] It is the science of human choice.

The economist's task is supposedly neutral observation and explanation. He must at all times remain "scientific." Given a certain end, what is the most economical way to achieve it? How can a given end be attained with a minimum expenditure of scarce resources; alternatively, with a given quantity of scarce resources, how great a quantity of goods can be produced, and which kinds? In popular (though imprecise) terminology, economics is the study of the laws governing that ancient task, "getting the most from the least." It must make two very basic assumptions: (1) resources are scarce; (2) humans *can* organize these resources rationally in order to achieve their goals (although they *may* refuse to act in a rational manner).

In order to plan rationally, men need to have knowledge of certain economic and technological laws of production and exchange;

---

[3] Lionel Robbins, *The Nature and Significance of Economic Science* (2nd ed.; London: Macmillan, 1935), 14. Kirzner's attempt to differentiate Robbins's definition from Mises's *praxeology* (the science of human action) seems strained. There is nothing in Mises's view that is not at least implied by Robbins. Kizner, *op. cit.,* 161-62.
[4] Robbins, *op. cit.,* 15.
[5] *Ibid.,* 16.

174

additionally, they must have access to the various data of the particular case in question. They need both *theory* and *facts*. This is basic to all human knowledge, but it is especially relevant to rational economic action. Human beings have *wants;* they can satisfy them only through proper *action*. It requires both volition and knowledge. It is not surprising that Mises has entitled his major work *Human Action,* for it deals with what he calls *praxeology:* the science of human decisions and action in a world of limited resources. *Given* the ends of any particular society (or individual), the economist is supposed to be able to offer advice as to how human plans can be expedited with the least cost. It is the belief of Mises and those who have been influenced by him — Hayek, Röpke, and Robbins, among others — that the pricing mechanism of the free market economy is by far the most efficient means of satisfying human wants. The market's competitive framework places a premium on accurate forecasting and efficient planning. Those who fail to plan accurately suffer losses and, if they refuse (or are unable) to change their ways, they will be driven out of business. They can no longer gain control of scarce resources which could otherwise be used to satisfy more important consumer wants (or satisfy them more cheaply).[6]

---

[6] Mises, *Human Action* (New Haven, Conn.: Yale University Press, 1949); *The Free and Prosperous Commonwealth* (Princeton: Van Nostrand, [1927] 1962). Hayek, *The Road to Serfdom* (University of Chicago Press, 1944); *The Constitution of Liberty* (University of Chicago Press, 1960); *The Pure Theory of Capital* (London: Routledge and Kegan Paul, 1941). Röpke, *Economics of the Free Society* (Chicago: Regnery, 1963); *Civitas Humana* (London: Hodge, 1948); *International Economic Disintegration* (London: Hodge, 1942). Wilhelm Röpke, before his death in 1964, was acknowledged to have been the theoretical force behind Germany's post-war economic revival. He had a sense of the spiritual side of man which was unique among advocates of the free market; he saw what the effects of mass urbanization could do to society, whether or not urbanization is "sanctioned" by the free market. See especially his book, *A Humane Economy* (Chicago: Regnery, 1960). One economist who preceded Mises in time, but who shared his perspective

The price system is the heart of the free market economy. It is the mechanism by which supply is balanced with demand (assuming that there is no inflation of the currency by either the banking system or the civil government).[7] It informs the consumer of the relative availability of economic goods; simultaneously, it alerts the entrepreneur to the success or failure of his previous economic planning. The private firm is able to operate in a rational manner because prices provide the vital data concerning demand, interest rates, alternative possibilities for investment, and the present cost of labor and raw materials. From the point of view of the entrepreneur, prices are indispensable; they enable him to estimate the value of future sales, and this in turn permits him to make a rational decision concerning the purchase of capital goods — goods of the so-called "higher order." The overall economic system can thus allocate its scarce resources according to consumer demand; a balance of production can be established between consumers' goods and producers' goods. Without this pricing mechanism, men would be almost blind in their economic decisions; nothing beyond a very primitive subsistence economy could be possible. Long run economic planning of any complexity would be out of the question.

Of fundamental importance to the price system is *a common medium of exchange*. It requires, in short, the existence of *money*. Money has taken many forms throughout history, but it must display four qualities: scarcity, divisibility, durability, and portability. For large payments, of course, gold has fulfilled these demands most efficiently, since it is very scarce, extremely durable (it does not

---

on many issues, was Philip Wicksteed; Mises has said that he was the last great English economist. His most important work was *The Common Sense of Political Economy* (rev. ed.; London: Routledge and Kegan Paul, 1933). The best introduction to Mises's perspective is Murray N. Rothbard, *Man, Economy and State* (2 vols.; Princeton: Van Nostrand, 1962), although Rothbard's philosophical anarchism is not shared by Mises.

[7] Cf. Mises, *The Theory of Money and Credit* (New Haven, Conn.: Yale University Press, 1953), ch. 7; *Human Action,* ch. 20.

corrode), divisible (it can be cut with a knife), and relatively portable. But whatever form money takes, it must be present in any economic system that is based on the division of labor, for without it, there would be no common unit for making comparisons of relative cost. It is the most important of all exchange goods on a market, since it is, by definition, the most exchangeable good. Without it, economic society as we know it would not exist.

Marx saw this fact very early in his career. He realized the interdependence of money and the division of labor, and his absolute hostility against the division of labor led him to reject the use of money in his coming post-Revolutionary society. He expressed his objections to money in his early essay, "On the Jewish Question," which appeared in the *German-French Yearbooks* in 1844. He characterized the Jew of his day in the worst (for him) possible terms: the Jew is the ultimate bourgeois figure. "What is the profane basis of Judaism? *Practical* need, *self-interest*. What is the worldly cult of the Jew? *Huckstering*. What is his worldly god? *Money*."[8] Money, for the Jew, has become his instrument of economic control and social power: "The Jew has emancipated himself in a Jewish manner, not only by acquiring the power of money, but also because *money* had become, through him and also apart from him, a world power, while the practical Jewish spirit has become the practical spirit of the Christian nations. The Jews have emancipated themselves in so far as the Christians have become Jews."[9] Thus, he wrote: "In the final analysis, the *emancipation* of the Jews is the emancipation of mankind from *Judaism*."[10] In other words, the true freedom of the Jew can be attained only when the Jews' source of power is removed: money. With it, of course, capitalist production must also be destroyed.

Money, for Marx, became a kind of symbol of capitalism. He saw it as capitalism's worst feature. "Money is the alienated essence

---

[8] Marx, "On the Jewish Question," in T. B. Bottomore (ed.), *Karl Marx: Early Writings* (N. Y.: McGraw-Hill, 1964), 34.
[9] *Ibid.*, 35.
[10] *Ibid.*, 34.

of man's work and existence; this essence dominates him and he worships it."[11] In this early essay, he presented a theme which was never to be wholly absent from his writings from that time on: the idea of the alien, hostile force above man and his labor.

> Objectification is the practice of alienation. Just as man, so long as he is engrossed in religion, can only objectify his essence by an *alien* and fantastic being; so under the sway of egoistic need, he can only affirm himself and produce objects in practice by subordinating his products and his own activity to the dominion of an alien entity, and by attributing to them the significance of an alien entity, namely money.[12]

The conclusion was inescapable for Marx: the communist society would abolish all alienation, all division of labor, and all use of money.

> As soon as society succeeds in abolishing the *empirical* essence of Judaism — huckstering and its conditions — the Jew becomes *impossible,* because his consciousness no longer has an object. The subjective basis of Judaism — practical need — assumes a human form, and the conflict between the individual, sensuous existence of man and his species-existence, is abolished.[13]

This was not just the product of his youthful Hegelian speculation. He set forth the same goal in volume II of *Capital:*

> In the case of socialized production, the money-capital is eliminated. Society distributes labor-power and means of production to the different lines of occupation. The producers may eventually receive paper checks, by means of which they withdraw from the social supply of means of consumption a share corresponding to their labor-time. These checks are not money. They do not circulate.[14]

This returns us to one of the basic problems which Marx never faced: how can the total wealth of nature be released under socialism without the use of mass production methods that require the division

---

[11] *Ibid.,* 37.

[12] *Ibid.,* 39.

[13] *Ibid.,* 40.

[14] *Capital* (Chicago: Charles H. Kerr & Co., 1909), II, 412.

of labor? Perhaps even more fundamental, how can the socialist planning board allocate scarce resources efficiently without some kind of pricing mechanism involving the use of money? Socialist men, Marx wrote, must bring "the productive process under their common control as a law understood by the social mind" (III, 301). Apart from some vague metaphysical conception as the "social mind," how are the planners to accomplish this feat? On what possible basis can they make economic calculations?

Several economists had raised the question of socialist economic calculation before 1920, but it was in that year that Ludwig von Mises stated the problem in its most compelling form. It was only after the publication of his essay, "Economic Calculation in the Socialist Commonwealth," that socialists began to take note of the whole issue, a fact admitted by Oskar Lange, one of the socialist economists who accepted Mises's challenge. As Lange put it, only half in jest: "Both as an expression of recognition for the great service rendered by him and as a memento of the prime importance of sound economic accounting, a statue of Professor Mises ought to occupy an honorable place in the great hall of the Ministry of Socialization or of the Central Planning Board of the socialist state."[15]

Mises attacks the problem in two ways. First, he assumes that the socialist planning board will have to make use of some sort of price system. This, he says, is not really consistent with socialist hopes, but it will be necessary. Second, he shows that Marx's ultimate vision for society — a world without money — is absolutely unworkable in the real world. His arguments in both cases are based upon his belief that rational economic planning, apart from a truly free price mechanism which is founded on private ownership, is not possible.

---

[15] Oskar Lange, *On the Economic Theory of Socialism* (N. Y.: McGraw-Hill, 1964), 57-58. This is a reprint of Lange's articles that appeared in the *Review of Economic Studies,* IV (1936-37). The book also contains Fred M. Taylor's essay, "The Guidance of Production in a Socialist State," which was published originally in the *American Economic Review,* XIX (1929). It is one of the standard works defending the view that the socialist community can escape the criticisms raised by Mises.

The heart of the problem, Mises argues, is the problem of valuation. How can producers know how valuable any economic good is? Even more to the point, how can they evaluate the worth of a factor used in the production process? The good is not directly in demand by consumers, so how can its importance for production be estimated? Socialism is defined as the ownership of the means of production by the state. In this very definition lies the problem: there is no market for production goods. "Moreover, just because no production-good will ever become the object of exchange, it will be impossible to determine its monetary value. Money could never fill in a socialist state the role it fills in a competitive society in determining the value of production-goods. Calculation in terms of money will here be impossible."[16]

Economic theory since the 1870's has shown clearly that there is no objective, fixed standard of value (e.g., labor). It is the subjective preference by the particular individual that is the foundation of economic value. But, as Mises writes: "Judgments of value do not measure; they merely establish grades and scales."[17] In the calculation and comparisons involved in all valuation, money is an indispensable tool:

> In an exchange economy the objective exchange-value of commodities enters as the unit of economic calculation. This entails a threefold advantage. In the first place, it renders it possible to base the calculation upon the valuations of all participants in trade. The subjective use-value of each is not immediately comparable as a purely individual phenomenon with the subjective use-value of other men. It only becomes so in exchange-value, which arises out of the interplay of the subjective valuations of all who take part in exchange. But in that case calculation by exchange-value furnishes a control over the appropriate employment of goods. Anyone who wishes to make calculations in

---

[16] Mises, "Economic Calculation in a Socialist Commonwealth," in F. A. Hayek (ed.), *Collectivist Economic Planning* (London: Routledge & Kegan Paul, [1935] 1963), 92. This volume is basic to an understanding of the problem of economic calculation. It contains essays by Hayek, N. G. Pierson, Georg Halm, and Enrico Barone, in addition to the one by Mises.

[17] *Ibid.*, 96-97.

regard to a complicated process of production will immediately notice whether he has worked more economically than others or not; if he finds, from reference to the exchange-relations obtaining in the market, that he will not be able to produce profitably, this shows that others understand how to make a better use of the goods of a higher order [production goods — G.N.] in question. Lastly, calculation by exchange-value makes it possible to refer values back to a unit.[18]

Money, in sort, makes possible production based on the division of labor in society, and this includes an *intellectual division of labor*. This intellectual division of labor is absolutely vital, given the assumption that no single man or group of men can ever be omniscient.

No single man can ever master all the possibilities of production, innumerable as they are, as to be in a position to make straightway evident judgments of value without the aid of some system of computation. The distribution among a number of individuals of administrative control over economic goods in a community of men who take part in the labour of producing them, and who are economically interested in them, entails a kind of intellectual division of labour, which would not be possible without some system of calculating production and without economy.[19]

Yet Marx would have us abolish the use of money in the final stage of communism, forcing upon us the necessity of calculating *in natura* — in terms of the physical goods themselves, without any reference to a monetary standard. This would destroy all rational production in a society which went beyond a bare subsistence form of simple economy. "Calculation *in natura,* in an economy without exchange, can embrace consumption-goods only; it completely fails when it comes to deal with goods of a higher order."[20] But production goods are the basis of the large-scale productivity that has provided the modern world with its wealth. Without such capital investment, we would find ourselves in the same conditions found in the underdeveloped nations; capitalization through saving is the very foundation of modern economic life.

---

[18] *Ibid.,* 97-98.

[19] *Ibid.,* 102.

[20] *Ibid.,* 104.

"Economic relations between production-goods," Mises argues, "can only be established on the basis of private ownership of the means of production."[21] In other words, "Where there is no free market, there is no pricing mechanism; without the pricing mechanism, there is no economic calculation."[22] Mises then lays down the gauntlet for the socialists:

> Thus in the socialist commonwealth every economic change becomes an undertaking whose success can be neither appraised in advance nor later retrospectively determined. There is only groping in the dark. Socialism is the abolition of rational economy.[23]

Understandably, the article produced a storm of protest from the socialists. T. J. B. Hoff has surveyed these attempted rebuttals in his important study, *Economic Calculation in the Socialist Society* (1949), and he offers convincing arguments to demonstrate their impracticability. In fact, he often uses the various solutions of these socialist economists against each other, since many of them are mutually contradictory. In all of the arguments, certain themes and assumptions keep occurring: the omniscience of the planners, the static condition of the economy in regard to consumer tastes and technological development, and the possibility of establishing an arbitrary price system based upon the planners' value systems rather than public demand.[24]

The argument has been extended by Georg Halm. As he shows, the whole question of saving and interest rates cannot be solved by socialism except by arbitrary (and ultimately irrational) declarations by the authorities. The planners must decide how much of the

---

[21] *Ibid.*, 112.

[22] *Ibid.*, 111.

[23] *Ibid.*, 110.

[24] T. J. B. Hoff, *Economic Calculation in the Socialist Society* (London: Hodge, 1949). Cf. Walter Eucken, "On the Theory of the Centrally Administered Economy: An Analysis of the German Experiment," *Economica*, XV (May & Aug., 1948); reprinted in Morris Bornstein (ed.), *Comparative Economic Systems: Models and Cases* (Homewood, Ill.: Irwin, 1965), 157-97.

presently available capital should be devoted to consumers' goods, and how much to producers' goods. The *time preference* factor is, of course, basic to these calculations: how much are present goods valued by the public in comparison with future goods? Under capitalism, the interest rate allocates savings, and this in turn establishes the quantity of capital available for investment in productive activities. Such a free capital market cannot exist under socialism.

> Because capital is no longer owned by many private persons, but by the community, which itself disposes of it directly, a rate of interest *can* no longer be determined. A pricing process is always possible only when demand and supply meet in a market, when the competition of many offerers and demanders, the mutual out-bidding on the part of the buyers and under-cutting on the part of the sellers, leads by trial and error to the gradual emergence of a price, which may be called normal because it is that price at which the available supply, no more and no less, can be exactly disposed of. . . . In the socialist economy such a process of interest-determination would be impossible. There can be no demand and no supply when the capital from the outset is in the possession of the intended user, in this case the socialistic central authority.
>
> Now it might perhaps be suggested that, since the rate of interest cannot be determined automatically, it should be fixed by the central authority. But this likewise would be quite impossible. It is true that the central authority would know quite well how many capital-goods of a given kind it possessed or could procure by means of a compulsory restriction of consumption; it would know the capacity of the existing plant in the various branches of production; *but it would not know how scarce capital was.* For the scarcity of the means of production must always be related to the demand for them, whose fluctuations give rise to variations in the value of the good in question, in this case capital, even if the supply of it remains constant.[25]

Is it not possible for the state's authorities to set prices arbitrarily? Of course, says Halm: "This has, in fact, been explicitly demanded

---

[25] Georg Halm, "Further Considerations on the Possibility of Adequate Calculation in a Socialist Community," in Hayek (ed.), *Collectivist Economic Planning,* 162-63.

as far as the rate of interest is concerned. But if this were done, the case would be one of central planning without regard to the controlling element of consumers' choice."[26] The whole question of who is to control production according to whose value preferences is the vital one for Halm:

> For either production is planned, in which case freedom of consumers' choice must be abolished; or else consumption is left free, in which case production must be accommodated to it. The only way in which freedom of consumption can be interfered with, with even comparative safety, is by the extension of collective demand and the consequent artificial restriction of individual demands. Roads, parks, or playing-fields can be constructed, for instance, and the necessary resources secured by restricting the branches of production that satisfy the demands of individuals; and this, under capitalism, ultimately means increased taxation, and, under socialism, appropriate central direction. But what is not possible is on the one hand to allow freedom of consumption and on the other hand to produce according to a plan. Planning and freedom of choice cannot possibly be realized simultaneously.[27]

Profit, as we have already seen, is an increment which is the result of effective foresight and planning on the part of the entrepreneur. It is not some given percentage of sales that can be imputed beforehand in the overall production process. Under socialism, the calculation of profit is not possible, if by profit we mean a measurement of the accuracy of previous estimations of consumer demand and factor costs. The reason for this is that the state's production is *totally monopolistic.*

> Unified accounting in all branches of industry would necessarily be a task so difficult as to be practically insoluble, if only because the enterprises concerned would be so extremely numerous and the different kinds of organization and production technique so varied. . . . Thus the decisive question is whether it is possible to determine net profits at all within individual branches of industry. The problem is one of comparing commodity-prices with costs. The difficulty arises from the reciprocal monopoly relation-

---

[26] *Ibid.,* 187.
[27] *Ibid.,* 149-50.

ships. Even in the commodity markets, real competition prevails only on the demand side; supplies are in the hands of monopolists who determine the extent of production and so the level of prices. In these circumstances, even if costs could be assumed as known, it would be uncommonly difficult to decide whether profits were due to an efficient organization of production, a correct estimate of demand, or a monopolistic exploitation of consumers.[28]

Profits arise from the fact that the world is not static. It is constantly changing: knowledge grows, technology develops, the tastes of consumers change, and the skills an individual may possess will vary over time. In contrast to this apparent optimism, there can also be retardation; social advance can reverse itself, and this is also something which an entrepreneur must consider, especially if he is planning for long-run capital investment. His profits will be based on his ability to take change into consideration. But if there is no way to measure profit, then how can the appropriateness of planning be evaluated? Hayek points to many of these problem areas. Has a particular entrepreneur run too many risks? How can the central authority be sure?[29] If the state permits a kind of pseudo-profit to be made, how can the size of it be estimated? This can only be determined if a definite value can be assigned (imputed) to the existing plant, something which cannot be known in a world devoid of capital markets.[30] How much capital should be given to any particular enterprise or any particular entrepreneur within a given industry?[31] In short, how can the socialist planning board reap the fruits of competition (or, what is simply another word for the same thing, co-operation) apart from some kind of success indicators? This is precisely the problem that has bedeviled the planners of the Soviet Union, and no generally accepted alternative to free market competition has been found.[32]

---

[28] *Ibid.,* 194-95.
[29] F. A. Hayek, "The Present State of the Debate" (1935): *ibid.,* 234.
[30] *Ibid.,* 235.
[31] *Ibid.,* 236.
[32] A. Nove, "The Problem of 'Success Indicators' in Soviet Industry," *Economica,* XXV (1958); reprinted in Wayne A. Leeman (ed.),

Socialism, Hayek argues, is not some form of imitation capitalism, and it cannot be organized as if it were. Those socialist proposals that plan to establish some kind of competitive structure which would resemble capitalism's institutional framework are doomed to failure. In so far as Marx expected to preserve the capitalist system of mass industrial production and wealth, Hayek's criticism applies. To the extent that Marx did not expect to see any remnants of capitalism in the world beyond the Revolution, the more basic criticisms apply: how can there be economic calculation without a monetary system; how can there be mass production without the division of labor; how can the planners deal effectively with economic change? Assuming, for the moment, that Marx's first stage of communism (socialism) will preserve prices (thereby indicating scarcity in the world), Hayek's criticism of socialism's "quasi-competition" will stand:

> It will rest with the central authority to decide whether one plant located at one place should expand rather than another plant situated elsewhere. All this involves planning on the part of the central authority on much the same scale as if it were actually running the enterprise. And while the individual entrepreneur would in all probability be given some definite contractual tenure for managing the plant entrusted to him, all new investment will necessarily be centrally invested. This division in the disposition over the resources would then simply have the effect that neither the entrepreneur nor the central authority would be really in a position to plan, and that it would be impossible to assess responsibility for mistakes. To assume that it is possible to create conditions of full competition without making those who are responsible for the decisions pay for their mistakes seems to be pure illusion. It will at best be a system of quasi-competition where the person really responsible will not be the entrepreneur but the official who approves his decisions and where in consequence all the difficulties will arise in connection with freedom of initiative and assessment of responsibility which are usually associated with bureaucracy.[33]

*Capitalism, Market Socialism, and Central Planning* (Boston: Houghton Mifflin, 1963), 78-90.

[33] Hayek, *Collectivist Economic Planning*, 236-37.

In a socialist community, there is a constant tension between the goals of the macroeconomic planning of the whole economy and the microeconomic planning of the firm. Either the plan is made at the top apart from a price system based on microeconomic competition, or else private firms use competitive prices to determine production, to the detriment of the calculations made by the central planning agency. There is a continual fluctuation back and forth between centralization and decentralization. The Soviet Union is a classic example of this confusion; it has never been able to achieve a balance between the two forms of planning. The overall plan established by the central planning body is threatened by local intransigence and lethargy; local production units will not work efficiently unless they can plan according to local needs and conditions. But when the economy is permitted to shift to a more decentralized condition, the local firms tend to ignore national needs and concentrate on local wants and production for local profits. Centralized planning is inefficient; decentralized planning is less subject to political direction and manipulation.[34]

The problem of planning has been sketched by Mises in his study, *Bureaucracy* (1945). There are two forms of bureaucratic administration. The first form is the type associated with private capitalistic production. It is the decentralized type, since its primary requirement is that each level of the organization must produce a profit. It is left to the local managers to make the decisions which will produce that profit. This does not mean that no general rules are set down by the highest level; this level is the area of the greatest entrepreneurial power. But so long as the managers produce profits, they can be left to themselves without too much danger. There is therefore considerable flexibility for local decision-making. The second form of bureaucracy is the state bureaucracy. The situation

---

[34] On this tension, see Alec Nove, "The Soviet Industrial Reorganization," in Abraham Brumberg (ed.), *Russia Under Khrushchev* (N. Y.: Praeger, 1962), 189-204. Cf. Gregory Grossman, "Notes for a Theory of a Command Economy," in Bornstein (ed.), *Comparative Economic Systems,* 135-56.

here is totally different. The state's bureaucracy is limited by fixed appropriations. Flexibility at the lower levels must be curtailed if the total structure is to stay within its fixed budget. The bureaucratic planners must see to it that each dollar that is allocated for a specific purpose does, in fact, reach its destination. If the state's programs are to be brought to fruition, then there cannot be very much latitude in what is permitted to the bureaucracy's subsidiaries. The nature of the type of control is determined, in other words, by the source of the bureaucracy's operating funds. Private businesses are not faced with fixed appropriations; they can suffer losses or make profits, but they do maintain a far higher degree of local flexibility. The state's bureaucracy is not subject to the whims of the free market, since it does not operate on the basis of profit and loss. Hence, its decisions must be fixed in advance as much as possible and its activities must be executed according to the preconceived plan. Uncertainty is reduced, but so is the freedom of movement.[35] The two bureaucracies are very different, and their rules of conduct are not interchangeable. This is why each must be restricted to its proper realm.[36]

Another important problem for the socialist planners is that associated with technological development. Science and technology are at the mercy of the state's political planners. The latter hold their offices in terms of political desires and needs, and not primarily in terms of the notion of economic productivity (although the economic

---

[35] Mises, *Bureaucracy* (London: Hodge, 1945; New Haven, Conn.: Yale University Press).

[36] In so far as socialistic planning becomes the basis for producing a nation's goods, local industries will resemble less and less the sketch of private bureaucracies made by Mises. This is one of the chief defects of the discussion of bureaucracy made by Van Riessen: he does not differentiate between the two types. Consequently he ascribes the evils of the centralized state bureaucracy to the private sphere. He fails to mention that the reason that the private bureaucracies are beginning to become totalitarian in nature is at least in part due to the fact that they are becoming arms of the state under a so-called "mixed economy." Cf. H. Van Riessen, *The Society of the Future* (Philadelphia: Presbyterian and Reformed Pub. Co., [1952]), 135 ff.

aspect is one side of the political sphere, in so far as the voting public expects economic benefits to accrue to them as voters). On what basis will the planners make decisions concerning the development of science and technology? Obviously, they must decide, at least in part, in terms of the political ends of the ruling power. There have been a number of studies made concerning the retardation of scientific progress by politically motivated state bureaucrats, and when the state is the one source of research and development funds (as it is under a socialist régime), there are few alternatives open to the prospective developer.[37] Hayek has commented at length on this issue:

> In the discussion of this sort of problem, as in the discussion of so much of economic theory at the present time, the question is frequently treated as if the cost curves were objectively given facts. What is forgotten is that the method which under given conditions is the cheapest is a thing which has to be discovered, and to be discovered anew, sometimes almost from day to day, by the entrepreneur, and that, in spite of the strong inducement, it is by no means regularly the established entrepreneur, the man in charge of the existing plant, who will discover the best method. The force which in a competitive society brings about the reduction of price to the lowest cost at which the quantity salable at that cost can be produced is the opportunity for anybody who knows a cheaper method to come in at his own risk and to attract customers by underbidding the other producers. But, if prices are fixed by the authority, this method is excluded. Any improvement, any adjustment, of the technique of production to changed conditions will be dependent on somebody's capacity of convincing the S.E.C. [Supreme Economic Council — G.N.]

---

[37] One of the startling facts in history is that both the early telegraph and the first crude television were developed in Russia. In both cases, the refusal of the state's bureaucrats to finance the projects resulted in the stifling of the projects. This, of course, happened under Czarist rule, but the principle is the same under any statist system: beware of the political monopoly of investment; it leads to a monopoly of invention. On the telegraph-television point, see James R. Philips, "Russia's Strength in Science," *The Freeman*, XII (April, 1962), 18-25; cf. Mitchell Wilson, *American Science and Invention* (N. Y.: Simon & Schuster, 1954), 119, 400.

that the commodity in question can be produced cheaper and that therefore the price ought to be lowered. Since the man with the new idea will have no possibility of establishing himself by undercutting, the new idea cannot be proved by experiment until he has convinced the S.E.C. that his way of producing the thing is cheaper. Or, in other words, every calculation by an outsider who believes that he can do better will have to be examined by the authority, which in this connection will have to take over all the functions of the entrepreneur.[38]

The results of such a system can be safely predicted in advance. It will create a nation of frightened bureaucrats who fear all change because it forces them to make decisions — decisions which may result in more than financial losses if the supreme political authorities decide to make an example of the bureaucrat's error of judgment. It was Lange, against whose theory of economic planning Hayek is arguing, who had to admit that *"the real danger of socialism is that of a bureaucratization of economic life,"* and on this point Hayek was in full agreement.[39] Hayek's conclusion seems inescapable:

> The success of the individual manager will, however, to a large extent not only depend on the action of the planning authority; he will also have to satisfy the same authority that he has done as well as was possible. Either beforehand, or more likely retrospectively, all his calculations will have to be examined and approved by the authority. This will not be a perfunctory auditing, directed to find out whether his costs have actually been what he says they have been. It will have to ascertain whether they have been the lowest possible ones. This means that the control will have to consider not only what he actually did but also what he might have done and ought to have done. From the point of view of the manager it will be much more important that he should always be able to prove that in the light of the knowledge which he possessed the decision actually taken was the right one than that he should prove to be right in the end.

---

[38] F. A. Hayek, "The Competitive 'Solution'," *Economica*, VII, New Series (1940); reprinted in Hayek, *Individualism and Economic Order* (University of Chicago Press, 1948), 196-97.

[39] Oskar Lange, *On the Economic Theory of Socialism*, 109.

If this will not lead to the worst forms of bureaucracy, I do not know what will.[40]

The task which would face the central planning authorities is a monumental one. Enrico Barone, whose "solution" to the problem of economic calculation in socialism is in fact only a statement of the problem, realized clearly the magnitude of the planning operation.[41] An enormous job of collating all the data concerning technological methods presently available (let alone estimations of the state of future technology, which the capitalist entrepreneur must take into account if he is to stay in business), the tastes of the public, the capital available, and a host of other data must be accomplished by the planning agency. Large scale experiments would have to be conducted by the planners in order to discover the cheapest methods of production. This is mandatory: ". . . it has no other means of determining *a priori* the technical coefficients most advantageous economically, and must of *necessity* resort to experiments on a large scale in order to decide *afterwards* which are the most appropriate organizations, which it is advantageous to maintain in existence and to enlarge to obtain the collective maximum more easily, and

---

[40] Hayek, *Individualism and Economic Order,* 198-99.

[41] Enrico Barone, "The Ministry of Production in the Collectivist State," (1908), in Hayek (ed.), *Collectivist Economic Planning,* 287-90. In regard to this article, it is important to refer to a statement made by Hayek in another context: "Professor Schumpeter is, I believe, also the original author of the myth that Pareto and Barone have 'solved' the problem of socialist calculation. What they, and many others, did was merely to state the conditions which a rational allocation of resources would have to satisfy and to point out that these were essentially the same as the conditions of equilibrium of a competitive market. This is something altogether different from showing how the allocation of resources satisfying these conditions can be found in practice. Pareto himself (from whom Barone has taken practically everything he has to say), far from claiming to have solved the practical problem, in fact explicitly denies that it can be solved without the help of the market." Hayek, "The Use of Knowledge in Society," *American Economic Review,* XXXV (1945); reprinted in Hayek, *Individualism and Economic Order,* 90n.

which, on the other hand, it is best to discard as failures."[42] Barone ridicules Marx's idea that collectivist planning would somehow avoid the kinds of decisions made under "anarchistic" capitalism. Hayek is more pessimistic than Barone, and after surveying the number of problems which would face the planning board, he concludes that in an advanced society the decisions to be made by the board before embarking on any production plan would "be at least in the hundreds of thousands."[43] Lionel Robbins regards Hayek's estimate as overly optimistic. The task is overwhelming: "It would necessitate the drawing up of millions of equations on the basis of millions of statistical tables based on many more millions of computations. By the time the equations were solved, the information would have become obsolete and they would have to be calculated anew."[44] But Robbins and Hayek are clearly pikers in their evaluation of the problem. They are free market advocates who have never been connected with any major socialist planning project. In order to gain an idea of the real problem facing the planners, we must go to an expert, Victor M. Glushkov, the head of the Soviet Union's research program in cybernetics. Unless there is a radical reform in planning methods in the U.S.S.R. in the near future, Glushkov estimates that the planning bureaucracy will have to grow 36-fold by 1980, requiring the services of the entire Soviet population![45] If the central planners of the Soviet Union persist in the idea that every nail and screw of all factories under construction or already built must be known to them in advance, then there is no hope for them. There has to be a reform. Leon Smolinski reports on the discussion of the problem made by Glushkov:

---

[42] Barone, *op. cit.*, 286-87.

[43] Hayek, *ibid.*, 212.

[44] Lionel Robbins, *The Great Depression* (London: Macmillan, 1934), 151.

[45] Reported by Leon Smolinski, "What Next in Soviet Planning?" *Foreign Affairs*, XLII (1964); reprinted in Morris Bornstein and Daniel R. Fusfield (eds.), *The Soviet Economy: A Book of Readings* (Homewood, Ill.: Irwin, 1966), 329.

The attempt is utopian. As V. M. Glushkov has recently shown, it implies that the central planners would have to consider several quintillion relationships among the various products, probably the largest integer ever considered in economic analysis. Glushkov adds that even if high-speed electronic computers performing 30,000 operations a second were harnessed to the task, it would require one million computers working without interruption for several years. And, of course, the economy would not remain frozen, waiting for the computations to be completed.[46]

The other problem is hardly mentioned: what guarantee would the planners have that the data supplied by the various data-gathering centers is, in fact, accurate? *Total* central planning, in short, is a silly dream of deluded thinkers. It cannot be done.

In the final analysis, the problem comes down to this: men are not omniscient. For this reason, a productive society requires an intellectual division of labor. This is why we must have decentralized planning by men who are responsible economically for their errors, but who can reap profits for their successful endeavors. This, in short, is why every advanced society needs money: rational economic calculation is impossible without monetary calculation. It means that a free market must be present in order to provide the institutional framework for the price mechanism. And this, finally, returns us to the original issue raised in the very early pages of this book: economics, like philosophy, is not a neutral investigation. If the free market's goal of rational, economical, and productive calculation is accepted, then the free market must be accepted as the only means for attaining the goal. This presupposes a moral and theological framework: the free market cannot operate apart from certain basic moral prerequisites, including the willingness of the population to abstain from the theft involved in outright socialistic redistribution. It means that the members of the society must turn to production rather than to theft as a means of social advance. It means that men must accept personal responsibility for their actions in all areas of life, and this in turn presupposes a framework of *law*. Law is never neutral; it rests on fundamentally moral and religious foundations.

---

[46] *Ibid.,* 335.

The institutional framework of capitalism, based as it is on private ownership and the right to profits, cannot exist in a moral vacuum. The moral framework which supports it has been in all cases a Christian one. A society which rejects the basic social requirements of the Decalogue (Ex. 20:1-17) cannot expect to build a capitalist economic system, and it cannot hope to attain the economic growth and benefits that only capitalism can provide. There are no economic fruits without the religious roots.

Private property must be respected by the state's authorities because private property is basic to the Christian social framework. The civil government which refuses to honor these rights can expect the judgment of God, even as Ahab's treatment of Naboth resulted in the collapse of his authority and his death (I Kings 21; II Kings 9:26). The same end can be expected by all those economists who think that they can establish an intellectual and institutional economic framework in defiance of biblical justice; they have said in their "neutral" hearts that there is no God, and like the fools of old, they shall perish, along with those who have listened to them. The warning of the God who gave Jeremiah his dismal prophetic task should be in our ears:

> Shall I not visit for these things? saith the Lord: shall not my soul be avenged on such a nation as this? A wonderful and horrible thing is committed in the land; The prophets prophesy falsely, and the priests bear rule by their means; and my people love to have it so: and what will ye do in the end thereof? (Jer. 5:29-31).

## APPENDIX B

*The seizure of the means of production by society
puts an end to commodity production, and therewith
to the domination of the product over the producer.
Anarchy in social production is replaced by conscious
organisation on a planned basis. The struggle for
individual existence comes to an end. And at this
point, in a certain sense, man finally cuts himself off
from the animal world, leaves the conditions of animal
existence behind him and enters conditions which are
really human.*

Frederich Engels (1877)[1]

## VII.

### SOVIET ECONOMIC PLANNING

For almost half a century, Ludwig von Mises has maintained that
his analysis of the problem of economic calculation under socialism
is a correct one. Pure socialism — an economic system without a
free market based on private ownership of the means of production
— cannot allocate scarce resources efficiently; too many resources
will be used to create a given quantity and quality of economic goods.
From the standpoint of economic theory, his basic argument has
never been successfully challenged (Oskar Lange notwithstanding).
Yet how is it that in practice many ostensibly socialist nations can
compete economically with the United States and other relatively
free market societies? More specifically, how can the Soviet Union
continue to produce its goods (especially producers' goods) if Mises's
theory is more than just an intellectual exercize with little relation
to reality?

---

[1] Frederich Engels, *Herr Eugen Dühring's Revolution in Science
[Anti-Dühring]* (London: Lawrence and Wishart, [1877] 1934),
311.

195

The literature on the economic system of the Soviet Union is very large and constantly growing. It would be impossible to touch on more than just a fraction of this material in a short essay. Still, by limiting the survey primarily to those issues centering around the problem of allocation, valuation, and pricing, it is feasible to gain at least a brief picture of the Soviet economy.

For the beginner, it would be wise to consult Robert Campbell's excellent book, *Soviet Economic Power* (1966), which is notable for its lively style and solid treatment of a difficult subject in a comparatively small volume. From there, any number of studies would be useful, including Alec Nove's more detailed introduction, *The Soviet Economy* (1965) and Abram Bergson, *The Economics of Soviet Planning* (1964). There are several excellent collections of shorter articles, primarily limited to papers prepared by scholars for professional journals. The most adequate in this regard is probably Bornstein and Fusfield (eds.), *The Soviet Economy: A Book of Readings* (1966). Wayne A. Leeman's book, *Capitalism, Market Socialism, and Central Planning* (1963) provides some excerpts from important theoretical discussions in this whole area, as well as the usual comparative historical studies. For some insight into the Soviet side of the debate, a worthwhile introduction is Harry Shaffer (ed.), *The Soviet Economy: A Collection of Western and Soviet Views* (1963). For the more advanced student, the official translation of the Soviet periodical, *Problems of Economics,* published by the International Arts and Sciences Press, is very important. For more popular accounts, *Current Digest of the Soviet Press* provides English readers access to translations and summaries of Soviet newspapers, including many articles dealing with economic problems. The indispensable tool, as always, is the American Economic Association's *Index of Economic Journals.* Published by Richard D. Irwin, a company specializing in the fields of management and economics, the *Index* is a complete bibliography of all English language journals specifically devoted to economic theory and practice.

### Economic Growth

There can be no question of the fact that Soviet industrial production has increased vastly over the past five decades. However questionable their official statistics happen to be (especially the summary figures), by all possible measuring devices the Soviets have been able to attain high rates of growth in the areas of heavy industry and military armaments. Does this fact call Mises's basic theory into question? Does the Soviet experience refute the argument that socialist economic planning is inconsistent with the rational allocation of scarce resources?

The answer is difficult to ascertain. Mises was dealing with a problem of pure economic theory, and he had in mind a purely socialist economy. The Soviet Union has never attained such a stage of purity in its economic relations. The presence of such institutions as small privately owned agricultural units testifies to elements of "latent capitalism" in the USSR, and the use of money to facilitate economic exchanges is also a deviation from pure socialism — or at least pure Marxian socialism. To the extent that the Soviets use a system of centralized economic planning, the answer is no, their experience does not refute Mises. The waste, inefficiency, and general misallocation of scarce resources under the Soviet system are legendary. In fact, the very reluctance (or inability) of the Soviet leaders to allow total collectivization would indicate at least a partial realization on their part of the basic argument made by Mises: an absolutely socialistic, completely centralized, moneyless economy is an intellectual abstraction incapable of being put into practice.

Nevertheless, the fact of Russia's stupendous economic growth, or at least the growth of the statistical indices of industrial output, is still something which demands an explanation. Estimates vary widely among Western scholars, but Abram Bergson's figures are at least somewhat representative. He guesses that the gross national product of the Soviet Union has grown at a rate of some 4.5% per annum, and 5.2% if we exclude the war years, from 1928 to 1960 inclusive.[2] Given the basic weakness of the whole GNP concept, this may or may not be a relevant figure.[3] Even assuming its statis-

---

[2] Abram Bergson, *The Economics of Soviet Planning* (New Haven, Conn.: Yale University Press, 1964), 316.

[3] On the concept of Gross National Product, see Henry Hazlitt, *The Failure of the "New Economics"* (Princeton: Van Nostrand, 1960),

197

tical accuracy, the warning given by Naum Jasny should be considered: "The comparison of the economic potential of such greatly divergent countries as the USSR and the USA cannot be expressed in one figure."[4] Still, it does give us some idea, however crude, of the extent of Soviet development. G. Warren Nutter, whose estimate of Soviet growth tends to be conservative, has concluded that from 1928 to 1955, the USSR attained a 6.5% annual growth rate, a figure larger than any comparable 30 year period in United States history.[5] During the same period, the USA experienced, by Nutter's calculations, a 3.8% growth rate, a figure which should be tempered with the explanation that the 1928 base was so much larger for this country to start with; rapid growth rates are far easier, in terms of percentage figures, when one begins on a small base.[6] Soviet growth rates should also be counterbalanced by such considerations as the *quality* of their goods, since they are almost universally acknowledged as being inferior to free market goods, however defective the latter

---

410-11, 418. For relevant discussions of the problems of index numbers and other statistical aggregates, see Ludwig von Mises, *Human Action* (New Haven, Conn.: Yale University Press, 1949), 221-24; Mises, *The Theory of Money and Credit* (New Haven, Conn.: Yale University Press, [1924] 1953), 187-94; Louis M. Spadaro, "Averages and Aggregates in Economics," in Mary Senholz (ed.), *On Freedom and Free Enterprise* (Princeton: Van Nostrand, 1956), 140-60.

[4] Naum Jasny, *Soviet Industrialization, 1928-1952* (University of Chicago Press, 1961), 24.

[5] G. Warren Nutter, *Growth of Industrial Production in the Soviet Union* (A Study by the National Bureau of Economic Research [Princeton University Press, 1962]), 259-60.

[6] *Ibid.,* 289.

[7] *Ibid.,* 238-39. The low quality of Soviet goods is noted frequently in the Soviet press itself, television sets being a favorite for public criticism. In recent years, many goods have remained unsold on retailers' shelves. "This is an inevitable consequence of greater abundance and wider assortment, compared with the acute 'goods famine' which prevailed for so many years. Unsold stocks of unsaleable goods are causing worry to the authorities. The public is

may be at times.[7] But in the final analysis, the growth figures are impressive. How did this socialist nation accomplish the feat?

Naum Jasny, in the opening paragraphs of his monumental study, *Soviet Industrialization, 1928-1952,* offers one cogent explanation:

> The Bolsheviks came on the scene as fighters for socialism and against exploitation, for a great improvement in the well-being of everybody. What they achieved was a great increase in the rate of exploitation, reducing the people's share of the national income to an extent nobody believed possible. This strangulation of consumption put such large funds in the hands of the state as to permit extensive industrialization and even greater militarization, despite loss and waste of every kind caused by wars, internal strife, mismanagement, and so on.

> If one looks for figures as evidence of this revolution, there are probably no better ones than these: While the total personal income (calculated at constant prices) of the expanded population increased by about one-third from 1928 to 1952, the real value of the funds in the hands of the state for investment, military and other expenses, grew almost eightfold. This transformation must be considered a financial, economic, and social revolution.[8]

Without such a blatant repression of the rights and wants of the Soviet population, the statistics of industrial output would never have shown such a phenomenal growth rate. The costs were enormous in human misery. A million people starved in 1933.[9] Stalin's forced collectivization of the farms in the early 1930's resulted in at least five million people being shot or deported.[10] When the magnitude of such costs are considered, Rothbard's question does not seem out of place: "By what right do you maintain that people *should* grow faster than they voluntarily want to grow?"[11] It is a question which

---

becoming more choosy, as supplies and living standards increase." Alec Nove, *The Soviet Economy: An Introduction* (rev. ed.; N. Y.: Praeger, 1966), 184.

[8] Jasny, *Soviet Industrialization,* 1-2.

[9] *Ibid.,* 73.

[10] Robert W. Campbell, *Soviet Economic Power* (2nd ed.; N. Y.: Houghton Mifflin, 1966), 24.

[11] Murray N. Rothbard, *Man, Economy and State* (Princeton: Van Nostrand, 1962), II, 837.

the leaders of many "underdeveloped" countries ought to ask themselves.[12]

Another extremely important factor in the growth of Soviet industrial production was the ability of the Soviet planners to borrow from Western technology. This, as Gerschenkron points out, is the advantage which all underdeveloped nations possess, but the USSR has made use of it to an exceptional degree. After World War II, this massive theft of Western production methods slowed, but it is still going on in many cases.[13] Bergson concurs, arguing that Soviet borrowing has been on an "unprecedented scale."[14] It is Gerschenkron's belief that technology became a retarding factor after World War II, since the USSR had begun to catch up with Western Europe's basic technological methods, leaving less room for Soviet borrowing.[15] He is not followed in this by all scholars, however, since other factors are now present, such as an educational system which concentrates on turning out technologists, engineers, and theoretical scientists.[16] The real threat to Soviet growth is not technological, but institutional; they must learn how to implement their technology efficiently before

[12] For a discussion of the whole question of economic growth, see the essay by Colin Clark, originally published in *The Intercollegiate Review,* now distributed by the National Association of Manufacturers, *"Growthmanship": Fact and Fallacy* (1965). See also P. T. Bauer, *Economic Analysis and Policy in Underdeveloped Countries* (Durham, N. Carolina: Duke University Press, 1957); Bauer and Basil S. Yamey, *The Economics of Under-developed Countries* (University of Chicago Press, 1957).

[13] Alexander Gerschenkron, *Economic Backwardness in Historical Perspective* (Cambridge, Mass.: Harvard-Belknap Press, 1962), 8, 261-62.

[14] Abram Bergson, *The Real National Income of Soviet Russia Since 1928* (Cambridge, Mass.: Harvard University Press, 1961), 293.

[15] Gerschenkron, *Economic Backwardness,* 262.

[16] Jan S. Prybyla, "Soviet Economic Growth: Perspectives and Prospects," *Quarterly Review of Business and Economics,* IV (1964); reprinted in Morris Bornstein and Daniel R. Fusfield (eds.), *The Soviet Economy: A Book of Readings* (Homewood, Ill.: Irwin, 1966), 308-09.

they will be able to match Western standards of consumption and production.

Campbell's comments on the whole issue of borrowed technology in the Soviet command economy are enlightening:

> But the interesting thing is that, despite this advantage in being able to borrow technology, Soviet progress in productivity does not seem to have been exceptional. The rate of increase in resource productivity does not seem to differ much from that achieved in other countries. This obviously implies that exceptional growth should be attributed more to the ability of Soviet command planning to mobilize resources — i.e., to accumulate capital, to educate on a mass scale, to move people from low productivity occupations such as agriculture to high productivity ones such as industry, and to force increases in participation rates — than to any special ability to use resources efficiently and increase their productivity.[17]

Coercion, even more than borrowed technology, is the key to Soviet economic growth. It should never be forgotten, as Campbell points out, "It was in the name of industrialization that the totalitarian terror machine was perfected."[18] The extent of this coercion is reflected in the standard of living of the Soviet people during the four decade era of rapid industrialization.

### Standard of Living

Janet Chapman's exhaustive study of Soviet wages throws additional light on the usefulness of Soviet aggregate statistics of economic growth. In 1921, the Soviet government was forced to revert to some measure of private ownership in the areas of agriculture and small scale industry in order to regain the economic losses of the War and the "war communism" period of 1917-1921. The extent of those losses was staggering; production in 1921 had fallen to some 20% of 1914 output![19] For seven years, the economy experienced a surprisingly large rate of growth, so that by 1928, the pre-War level of production had been regained. If anything, the standard of living

[17] Robert W. Campbell, *Soviet Economic Power,* 128-29.
[18] *Ibid.,* 26.
[19] Campbell, *ibid.,* 14.

was somewhat above the 1913 level.[20] It was at this point that farm collectivization began in earnest; Stalin had consolidated his position and was ready to begin building the new society.[21]

First of all, it must be borne in mind that Russia in 1928 was far behind Western Europe in both production and consumption. Statistical measurement in this regard is rather difficult, but Bergson has estimated that the average per capita income of the Soviet Union in 1929 was approximately $170; the United States had achieved this level of per capita income in 1875.[22] Between 1928 and 1937, the rate of growth of the USSR's economy was extremely rapid, probably approaching 13% per annum.[23] The suffering of the peasants and even urban dwellers was enormous. The state had to institute rationing of consumer goods in this area (it ended in 1935); inflation (that "bourgeois" evil) was eating into money wages so rapidly that rationing had to be substituted for market pricing.[24] Despite the achievements in industrial output by 1937, real wages were actually *below* 1928 wages by a considerable margin. Even more chilling is the fact that, as Chapman shows, the 1937 levels of consumption "represent a considerable recovery from a drastic decline in the early 1930's."[25]

World War II naturally took a heavy toll of both Soviet manpower and production. At best, American economic aid kept the Soviet losses of capital equipment about even, while no aid could cover the loss of lives and the skills that went with them. In 1948, the net wages of the Soviet worker (after taxes and compulsory bond

---

[20] Janet Chapman, *Real Wages in Soviet Russia Since 1928* (Cambridge, Mass.: Harvard University Press, 1963), 6.

[21] For an account of Stalin's rise to power and the advent of this 1928 turning point in agriculture, see Isaac Deutscher, *Stalin: A Political Biography* (N. Y.: Vintage, [1949] 1960), ch. 8.

[22] Abram Bergson, *Real National Income,* 261.

[23] The figure is Gerschenkron's, and he cites other estimates which agree with his. The lowest figure is 10.6%. Gerschenkron, *Economic Backwardness,* 259-60.

[24] Chapman, *Real Wages,* 19.

[25] *Ibid.,* 146.

purchases) were some 63% of the 1937 wages (70%, if 1937 prices are used as the base rather than 1948 prices).[26] Only in 1952 did Soviet wages reach 1937 levels.[27] Since the figures for 1937 were about the same as 1928, and since the 1928 figures were in turn approximately equivalent to 1913, the conclusion is inescapable: *the per capita real wages in the USSR in 1952 were barely up to the 1913 pre-War levels!* On an hourly basis, real wages reached the 1928 point only in 1954. After surveying such factors as the drop in quality of goods after 1928 and the decline of production in all animal products (eggs, meats, leather, milk, etc.), Chapman concludes:

> Several arguments which I find persuasive have been presented for giving more credence to the index number of real wages using 1937 prices and showing the larger decline in real wages. Nevertheless, it remains true that the magnitude of the change in real wages between 1928 and 1937 eludes precise measurement and the alternative possibility of a less drastic decline in real wages might be kept in mind. But even the most favorable measure shows that the Soviet worker's real wage in 1954 exceeded that of 1928 by less than 15 per cent after taxes and bond subscriptions.[28]

She also alludes to the estimates made by Jasny concerning the production of edible animal products, and these statistics are worth repeating. In 1952, the production of edible animal products was down 30% from the 1928 level (the year prior to the collectivization of the farms). Only in 1955 did the 1928 level reappear.[29] Even in this case, much of this produce was supplied by the tiny one-half acre private agricultural plots permitted to collective farmers. In fact, only after 1960 did the collectivized system produce over 50% of the total supply of these goods.[30] Chapman's conclusion is interesting, to say the least:

---

[26] *Ibid.,* 147.

[27] *Ibid.,* 150.

[28] *Ibid.,* 152.

[29] *Ibid.,* 173.

[30] Alec Nove, *The Soviet Economy,* 29. Over half the meat and potatoes were produced by the private sector in 1959, and almost

The reader hardly needs to be reminded that the Soviet standard of living in 1928 was extremely low compared with American or Western European standards. But it may be startling to realize that, during the more than a quarter of a century in which the Russians have been engaged in full-scale socialist planning and have in other areas been gaining on the foremost capitalist countries, the material position of the Soviet worker has probably declined relative to that of workers in other countries.[31]

All of this by-passes the question of slave labor in the Soviet Union. Bergson estimates that at least 3.5 million people were in the "correctional re-education" units in the 1930's, and these pathetic creatures received only a quarter of the prevailing civilian wage.[32] The costs of rapid industrial growth were indeed very great.

One area of Soviet life which stands as a classic example of how consumers are slighted is public housing. Alexander Balinsky has made a thorough investigation into this question, and he has concluded, with some justification: "The housing shortage in the USSR is that country's most critical single economic problem."[33] Per capita living space (i.e., space not including kitchen, bath, etc.) in 1960 was barely over seven square meters, "or precisely what it had been in 1917."[34] Campbell's figures indicate an even greater lack: six

---

100% of the eggs, he goes on to say. It is likely that in 1956 some 30% of all agricultural output in the Soviet Union came from the small private plots. In fact, the "success" of the collective sector in finally outproducing the private plots in animal products after 1959 may have been in part due to new coercive measures against the private sector. Nove comments that "a gradual and cautious attempt has begun to be made to reduce private livestock holdings and private activity in general. Its success was slight up to 1959, but some reduction was achieved by 1960." Nove, "The Incomes of Soviet Peasants," *The Slavonic and East European Review,* XXXVIII (1960), 330.

[31] Chapman, *Real Wages,* 175.

[32] Bergson, *Real National Income,* 96.

[33] Alexander Balinsky, "Non-Housing Objectives of Soviet Housing Policy," *Problems of Communism* (U. S. Information Agency), X (July-Aug., 1961), 17.

[34] *Ibid.*

square meters (or about 64 square feet). This is compared to U. S. figures of about 200 square feet.[35] Housing is another case of state coercion; Balinsky shows how the state's control of housing has been used to achieve political objectives. Under Lenin, "parasitic" classes did not have access to co-operative housing units, and their own dwellings were expropriated by the state.[36] As late as 1953, 25% or more of the housing units was in the control of factory managers; they were thus able to enforce production norms on recalcitrant workers.[37] The rental costs for all housing are very low, since the state keeps laws on the books enforcing low rents. This, of course, has contributed to the shortage. Party membership is vastly more important in getting adequate housing than the mere ability to pay the rent.[38] As Balinsky says:

> There seems to be a general presumption in the Soviet philosophy on housing rights that everyone who is not an enemy of the state should be housed as well as possible. But it is the law defining *status,* and not the law of property or contract, which determines these rights. Within such a juridical framework, the Soviet regime has been able to distribute dwelling space in reward for real or presumed service to the state.[39]

G. Warren Nutter's findings should be mentioned at this point. While Soviet growth has been greater relative to U. S. growth in the last five decades, the absolute gap between the two countries has widened (since the U. S. started on such a far larger base in 1917 that our slower rates of growth have still enabled us to maintain the absolute output advantage).[40] His conservative estimate is that Soviet production in 1955 was only about 23% of the production of the U. S. Thus, the claims of Soviet planners that the Soviet Union has

---

[35] Robert Campbell, *Soviet Economic Power,* 137.
[36] Balinsky, *op. cit.,* 19.
[37] *Ibid.,* 21.
[38] *Ibid.,* 23.
[39] *Ibid.,* 22.
[40] G. Warren Nutter, *Growth of Industrial Production in the Soviet Union,* 239.

increased production by 26 times over 1913 are absurd. A figure something under a sixfold increase is closer.[41]

We have seen, in short, that Soviet economic growth has been paid for to a large extent by the enforced minimum consumption levels of the Soviet population. Until recently, these citizens have had very little to say concerning the allocation of scarce resources in their country — the resources which they have been responsible for producing. Certainly, gross output figures can be greatly increased when, as Bergson says, "gross investment absorbs nearly half the increase in output realized under the first two five-year plans, and 60.7 per cent of that achieved from 1940 to 1950."[42] To a limited extent, the economic tide has been turning in the Soviet Union, as the preferences of the consumers are being taken into consideration to a larger extent than before. Again, quoting Bergson: "The share of household consumption in the increase in output under the first two five-year plans is only 9.1 per cent. For 1940-50, the corresponding figure is 29.4 per cent, but from 1950 to 1955 it is 53.2 per cent."[43] Unfortunately for the official Soviet growth rate, this shift has caused (along with several other factors) a slowing down. Most non-Marxist Western observers agree that after 1958 the formerly high rates of growth began to taper off.[44] The old problem of economic life reasserts itself today in the Soviet Union: you cannot consume goods that are not produced. Campbell's evaluation is striking: "The Soviet Union is very, very, very far behind the United States in terms of the amount of consumption goods produced and, because of their larger population, still farther behind in terms of

---

[41] *Ibid.,* 268. The usually accepted figure is that the Soviet output is at one-third of the U. S. Jasny believes that Nutter's figures do not reflect Russia's potential economically, but Nutter is not concerned with potential as much as actual accomplishment. Cf. Jasny, *Soviet Industrialization,* 25. The sixfold increase up to 1955 is the accepted figure: Gerschenkron, *Economic Backwardness,* 267; Bergson, *Real National Income,* 216.

[42] Bergson, *Economics of Soviet Planning,* 311-12.

[43] *Ibid.,* 312.

[44] Nove, *The Soviet Economy,* 156.

per capita consumption."[45] So much for the Soviet consumer. He hastens to point out, however, that in other important areas, "ones which are really much more relevant to issues of international image making and military rivalry, the Soviet Union is much closer."

## Problems of Central Planning

If centralized state planning is to equal the efficiency of a decentralized free market economy, certain features of the free market's mechanism should be present within the planning bureau. First, planning should be based on a full *knowledge* of each product, including its true cost (i.e., its marginal cost or "cost-of-the-most-important-use-foregone"), its market, the productive apparatus necessary to create it, and the local environment in which it is produced. This knowledge must be at least comparable to that provided by the market's pricing mechanism to the local manager under capitalism.[46] Second, the planners must be able to *integrate* all the various supplies and demands with a smoothness comparable to that of the open market with its use of profit and loss to direct production into its most important uses. Third, the planners must be able to *foresee* the effects of new processes and products in all of the prospective markets. Errors in foresight should be registered as forcefully as they are when they are made on a free market. All of this involves the fourth, and perhaps most important problem of knowledge, the measurement of *profit and loss* in a market-less economy. It assumes, fifth, that there is such a thing as *economic law,* and that such laws can be known and used by planning agencies in their activities.

Alexander Gerschenkron, one of the foremost experts in the field of Russian economic history, has summarized the issue beautifully:

> The official view of the Soviet economy is premised upon the assumption of unrestricted knowledge and foreknowledge on the

---

[45] Campbell, *Soviet Economic Power,* 141.

[46] On the whole question of knowledge, economic planning, and the free market, see Hayek's masterful essay, "Economics and Knowledge," *Economica,* IV, New Series (1937); reprinted in Hayek, *Individualism and Economic Order* (University of Chicago Press, 1948), 33-56. This was his Presidential address before the London Economic Club.

part of the central planners. Needless to say, this assumption is far from realistic. The stream of paper reports that flows from the plants to the central authorities may belittle the majesty of the Volga River, but it provides no assurance of real insight into the conditions within the individual plant. The fundamental ignorance of the central authorities restricts their ability to enforce their will. Obversely, it is the knowledge of the manager that assures for him his area of freedom.[47]

In other words, the central planning of supply assumes the omniscience of the central planners. Without this omniscience, the system is faced with overwhelming difficulties. The main one Gerschenkron alludes to: how can the on-the-spot knowledge of the local manager be integrated into the overall central plan? Will not the freedom to allocate scarce resources at one level interfere with the planning activities of the other? This is the inescapable, inevitable, perpetual problem of the USSR's economic planners.

Only the most aggregative, general kind of planning is carried on at the center. Gosplan, the central planning agency, co-ordinates the production of a few major products and services. In an oft-quoted article, Herbert S. Levine has estimated that between 800 and 1500 commodities are totally planned at the center.[48] He outlines that planning process. First, a statistical analysis of the base period is made in the first half of the planning year (in preparation, of course, for the following planned year). A survey of the pervious year is made. Second, control figures are drawn up for a dozen or so of the chief products and investment targets. These serve as guideposts for economic units at a lower level. Third, and most important, is the confirmation of the plan by the political hierarchy, and a great deal of political maneuvering takes place at this point. This maneuvering appears at all levels of the economy and in all local districts. An

---

[47] Gerschenkron, *Economic Backwardness*, 287.
[48] Herbert S. Levine, "The Centralized Planning of Supply in Soviet Industry," *Comparisons of the United States and Soviet Economies* (Joint Economic Committee, Congress of the United States, 86th Con., 1st Session, 1959); reprinted in Wayne A. Leeman (ed.), *Capitalism, Market Socialism, and Central Planning* (Boston: Houghton Mifflin, 1963), 55.

extremely complicated and often varied process of surveying begins: local plants are supplied with forms relating to forthcoming production goals and supply needs; these forms, when completed, are sent to the Gosplan board for confirmation or revision. The ocean of data then is co-ordinated at the top into some kind of hopefully workable plan. Fourth, the detailed plan is returned to the firm for implementation.[49] Unfortunately, but very understandably, these final plans often arrive late, a constant complaint of enterprise managers.[50] Theoretically and ideally, this should never happen, but it does. Managers cannot always wait for the plan figures to arrive, so they begin on a tentative production plan. Naturally, it frequently needs drastic revisions when the official plan is delivered.

Jasny has argued that the very planning units — the Five Year Plans — were really propaganda devices, and that the annual and quarterly plans were the real basis of planning up until the advent of the Seven Year Plans in the mid-1950's.[51] For most of the history of Soviet planning, in other words, the long range plans were irrelevant for economic purposes. The goals of the 1930's were set so high that it would have been impossible to achieve them; this resulted in what he calls "bacchanalian planning."[52] Planning for long term goals was a function not of economic realities but rather of oratory. In a very real sense, Soviet planning in these years was, in Mises's provacative term, "planned chaos."

The magnitude of the statistical problem has been mentioned in Appendix A (notes 45, 46). The task grows continually less manageable. "Centralized planning," Nutter argues, "becomes less and less efficient as the number of products multiplies."[53] Peter Wiles and Leon Smolinski quote Soviet Acadamician Dorodnitsyn who has estimated that some four quadrillion relationships are present for the 20 million products of the Soviet Union. This, as the authors

---

[49] *Ibid.,* 55-58.
[50] *Ibid.,* 68.
[51] Naum Jasny, *Soviet Industrialization,* 25-27.
[52] *Ibid.,* 73ff.
[53] Nutter, *Growth,* 64.

point out, is an impossible task to co-ordinate, and the Gosplan USSR only prepares final plans (as distinguished from total planning from start to finish) of 18,000 products, or less than one-tenth of one per cent of the total Soviet output. Yet even this is bound to become more difficult, since, as they say, "the complexity of planning grows also with the square of the number of establishments; . . ."[54] Planning today is some 1600 times more complex than in 1928.[55] The conclusion is inescapable:

> It is thus obvious from the administrative point of view that planning must be decentralized if it is to exist at all. It always has been, and still is: the center draws up a general skeleton and the subordinate bodies put flesh on the bones. . . . Confining ourselves still to economics, it is plain that such technical planning desiderata as consistency and punctuality are compatible with, even possibly favored by, decentralization.
>
> One planning function, however, is very seriously disfavored: the rational allocation of resources. From this point of view decision-making should be *either* central *or* peripheral; a mixture is bad.[56]

Here we find the inevitable problem in operation: the constant tension between centralized, ministerial planning and localized decision-making. The Soviet economic planners constantly shift the locus of planning back and forth in their attempt to discover a solution to this problem of administrative balance. As Gregory Grossman says, "To put it schematically at the risk of oversimplification: overcentralization, imbalance, and autarky are the three corners of a triangle of hazards within which the Soviet-type economy seeks to find an organizational solution."[57]

---

[54] Peter Wiles and Leon Smolinski, "The Soviet Planning Pendulum," *Problems of Communism*, XII (Nov.-Dec., 1963), 24.

[55] *Ibid.*, 21.

[56] *Ibid.*, 24-25.

[57] Gregory Grossman, *Value and Plan: Economic Calculation and Organization in Central Europe* (Berkeley: University of California Press, 1960), 7-8. A list of the economic reorganizations and counter-reorganizations in Russia since 1957 is found in *Problems of Communism*, XII (May-June, 1963), 30-31. Cf. the accompanying

Alec Nove has surveyed this topic at some length. "The authorities that hand down plans," he writes, "are often unaware of the tasks already given that enterprise by other authorities."[58] He then quotes a statement made by I. Borovitski in *Pravda* (5 Oct., 1962). Borovitski, it seems, is a disgruntled enterprise manager:

> The department of Gosplan which drafts the production program for *Sovnarkhozy* [regional economic councils] and enterprises is totally uninterested in costs or profits. Ask the senior official in the production program department in what factory it is cheaper to produce this or that commodity? He has no idea, and never even puts the question to himself. He is responsible only for the distribution of production tasks. Another department, not really concerned with the costs of production, decides on the plan for gross output. A third department or subdepartment, proceeding from the principle that costs must always decline and labor productivity increase, plan costs, wages fund and labor on the basis of past performance. Material allocations and components are planned by numerous other departments. Not a single department of Gosplan is responsible for the consistency of these plans.[59]

In short, too many blind cooks are spoiling the soup. All of these planning problems are compounded by the constant meddling of Party officials at all levels of the economy.[60] This interference leads to irrationality in planning. "The problem is not, of course, new;

---

article by Rush V. Greenslade, "Khrushchev and the Economists," *ibid.*, 27-32. Z. M. Fallenbuchl's statement should be compared with Grossman's: "Hence the perennial dilemma of the Soviet economic organization: how to decentralize some economic activities without losing control over the economy and the possibility of central planning." His essay, "How Does the Soviet Economy Function Without a Free Market?" is reprinted in Bornstein and Fusfield (eds.), *The Soviet Economy,* 34-36. The statement appears on p. 35. Cf. Alec Nove, *The Soviet Economy,* ch. 2; he includes additional relevant discussions of this subject, 171, 202ff., 312.

[58] Nove, *The Soviet Economy,* 207.

[59] *Ibid.*

[60] Cf. Greenslade, "Khrushchev and the Economists," *op. cit.,* 193ff.

it is inherent in the separate existence of party and state hierarchies."[61] The Soviet planning system, in the words of Wiles and Smolinski, is "a crazy quilt of agencies organized according to several principles."[62] This has been the situation for five decades, as Wiles has argued elsewhere; the system is irrational:

> The possibility of the private consumer being irrational is of course an accepted cliche of Western economics. But none of this makes planners' preferences rational. It is astonishing that people with an intimate knowledge of how the Soviet system works should consider the possibility of operating on the assumption that planners' preferences are in fact rational in a Communist economy.[63]

Wiles, in this case, is considering a slightly different issue, i.e., the problem of planners' choices rather than the actual operational defects of the economy's institutional structure, but the point is the same: there are too many planning agencies, too many plans (none of which is guaranteed to be rational), and too many irrational decisions.

The almost incredible extent of the total bureaucratization of Soviet planning is evidenced by two frequently encountered examples. In one case, a plan for ball bearings had to go through so many agencies for approval that a staggering (literally) total of 430 lbs. of documents was generated.[64] In another instance, one "autonomous" Republic, the Tatar ASSR, had its investment plan changed almost 500 times in 1961.[65] Under these conditions, the task of enterprise management would be impossible were it not for some ingeneous (and often illegal) solutions worked out by factory managers.

---

[61] Alec Nove, "Revamping the Economy," *Problems of Communism,* XII (Jan.-Feb., 1963), 15.

[62] Wiles and Smolinski, "Pendulum," *op. cit.,* 25.

[63] Peter Wiles, "Rationality, the Market, Decentralization, and the Territorial Principle," in Grossman (ed.), *Value and Plan,* 186-87. Cf. Gerschenkron, *Economic Backwardness,* 287-88.

[64] Bergson, *Economics of Soviet Planning,* 150.

[65] Nove, "Prospects for Economic Growth in the USSR," *American Economic Review, Papers and Proceedings,* LIII (1963); reprinted in Bornstein and Fusfield (eds.), *The Soviet Economy,* 318.

The basic solution has been the creation of a vast network of "independent" supplies — a black market. This is the phenomenon known informally as *"blat."* Joseph S. Berliner, in his extremely valuable study, *Factory and Manager in the USSR* (1957), has described this process. Since official supply channels are often exasperatingly slow and frequently deliver the wrong or inferior goods, managers must turn to alternative sources of inputs if their production quotas are to be met (and their bonuses received). A plant may have an excess capacity in any given year; the additional goods may be traded to some other firm for some future service or present luxury. It aids not only those smaller firms whose plans are not so detailed or that are on a lower priority list for supplies, but it also helps the high priority industries in periods of crisis.[66] Certain "middlemen" with informal connections are employed, usually under a bogus administrative title, as the agents for the *blat* operations. They are the "pushers" whose activities co-ordinate the underground supply and demand. They are called *tolkatchi.* Some firms employ only part-time *tolkatchi,* especially the smaller organizations. In recent years, the government has eliminated the criminal sanctions that were once imposed upon such activities of unauthorized exchange or resale of supplies. In addition to this softening, the procedures for obtaining official authorization to purchase extra supplies have been eased.[67] The state planners have, in effect, recognized the necessity of these "capitalistic" practices. Production goals are sometimes more important than official ideology. These practices go on as long as the conditions of inefficient production and distribution remain. As Berliner says, "The *tolkatch* thrives in an economic soil watered by shortages and fertilized by unrealistic targets."[68]

Alec Nove's summary of the "centralization-decentralization" problem is to the point:

---

[66] Joseph S. Berliner, *Factory and Manager in the USSR* (Cambridge, Mass.: Harvard University Press, 1957), chs. 11, 12.
[67] Berliner, *"Blat* Is Higher than Stalin," in Abraham Brumberg (ed.), *Russia Under Khrushchev* (N. Y.: Praeger, 1962), 173.
[68] *Ibid.,* 175.

While centralized planning overburdens the organs charged with carrying it [the plan] out, decentralization — the obvious remedy — proves completely unworkable so long as planners' instructions are the principle criterion for local decisions. The modest attempt to devolve authority to territorial economic organs, in 1957, was inevitably followed by renewed centralization. Within the system as it is, only the center is in a position to know the needs of industry and of society at large, since these are not transmitted by any economic mechanism to any territorial authority. The latter is therefore unable to foresee the effects of its decisions on the economy of other areas, and, in the circumstances, decentralized decision making must lead to intolerable irrationalities. . . . Thus decentralization is both indispensable and impossible.[69]

## Basic Practical Problems

In the previous section, we have looked at several important problem areas of the Soviet economy, but the discussion has been confined primarily to the theoretical problems of central planning vs. decentralized planning. With this broad perspective in mind, it is now relevant to examine some of the actual practices of Soviet firms in their day-to-day activities. These are perennial problems which are usually discussed by all critics of Soviet economic institutions.

First, there is the question of the so-called "safety factor." Managers deliberately understate the productive capacity of their plants in all reports to higher planning authorities. Their motives are easy enough to understand; if their goals are set too high by the central planners, then they will not be able to meet the output goals. Consequently, they try to see to it that their goals are set lower, thus leaving some excess capacity in reserve to meet all unforeseen contingencies. The central planners, of course, are aware of this practice, and they in turn try to boost the output goals above the reported limits stated by managers. Thus, an honest manager would be destroyed (or at least he would be forced to take this chance); a statement of full capacity will not be taken very seriously at the top.

---

[69] Nove, "Prospects," *op. cit.,* 318.

This tendency to understate capacity is augmented by the fact that small increases above the required output levels are rewarded by bonuses. Thus, managers strive to attain an output of, say, 103% of the official plan. Under these conditions, it is advantageous for the manager to convince the authorities that what is really 95% capacity is 100%.

Second, the hoarding problem appears. The supply system is not trustworthy, so managers are encouraged to store up quantities of production goods in case there is some emergency. This problem is absolutely inescapable so long as the Soviet system denies that interest payments on scarce capital is in accord with socialistic principles. With no interest to pay, managers can keep excess quantities of goods in reserve, either for use in the *blat* system or for direct employment in production. Only recently has interest been introduced in the form of a "pay off period." Calculations are made to determine how long the savings of a particular piece of equipment will take to pay off its purchase price. This, of course, applies only to new machinery and is probably limited to large-scale projects, but not for basic raw materials. It is interest, as Campbell says, "brought in through the back door."[70] But the problem is not solved as yet, and productive machinery which might be used elsewhere often rusts away in some storage room.[71]

Third, there is the whole question of technological innovation. A key article on this problem is Gregory Grossman's study of inertia and pressure in the Soviet economy.[72] Bureaucracies, he argues, are by nature conservative. They resent any breaks in their daily routines. Grossman points to the paradox of an economy like the Soviet Union's which has experienced such rapid economic growth and that has simultaneously been "plagued by a strong and widespread re-

---

[70] Campbell, *Soviet Economic Power,* 58.

[71] For a discussion of many of these problems, see Harry G. Shaffer, "Ills and Remedies," *Problems of Communism,* XII (May-June, 1963), 18-26.

[72] Grossman, "Soviet Growth: Routine, Inertia, and Pressure," *American Economic Review, Papers and Proceedings* L (1960), 62-72.

sistance to the introduction of new products and techniques."[73]  Only extreme pressure from the higher political bodies has succeeded in overcoming this institutional resistance to innovation, an opinion shared by Barrington Moore.[74]  The progressive features of capitalism are absent in the Soviet Union: (1) competition among firms for a share of the market; and (2) sales efforts on the part of private capital goods industries. It is primarily the régime's decision to race the West — hence an *external* pressure of competition — which acts as the great stimulus to technological change.

The Soviet manager's position is one of constant flux. He is deliberately shifted from post to post every few years in order to prevent him from forming local alliances with local Party members and others who would be apt to aid him in escaping his responsibilities. This element of "familiness" is a problem for central administrators. Since the manager's goals of increased output are identical with the goals of the Party officials at the local or regional level (they, too, want high output figures to impress the hierarchy), the various interest groups work together and tend to cover up for each other's mistakes. The central planners do not want this to happen, and the result is a constant shifting of managers. Unfortunately, this encourages managers to base all production and innovation on a short run perspective. Technological innovation costs time, money, and materials; why risk the possible losses? If the manager should fail to meet output quotas due to the shift in resources into innovation and technological experimentation, then he is in trouble. Any real benefits, however, would accrue to his successor, since the latter would take over after the innovating manager had been transferred. Innovation involves risk with little chance of reward. The results are predictable: outmoded designs, wasted raw materials due to inefficient production methods, and lower overall long-run production. This problem has been a continuing one. It is precisely the one which Hayek had said would be inevitable under a socialist system. Since the decision-making function would be stifled by a fear of

---

[73] *Ibid.*, 64.
[74] Barrington Moore, *Terror and Progress in the USSR* (Cambridge, Mass.: Harvard University Press, 1954), 40, 71.

losses, the socialist commonwealth would inevitably be less efficient in this regard than a capitalistic one.[75]

## Success Indicators

The fourth basic weakness of Soviet practice deserves its own special section. How are the planners to evaluate the success or failure of their plans? On what basis can a measurement be made of such success or failure? The free market system uses profit and loss as its guide, but socialism cannot use this measuring device. To the extent that the Soviet Union does use this system of measurement, it is abandoning pure socialism.

Alec Nove has called attention to this issue in a now famous essay. The Soviets have no concrete rule for measuring success; their pricing system is irrational from the point of view of true profit and loss, supply and demand. Plan fulfillment, and essentially gross output fulfillment, is the basic economic goal. But this raises a problem: what is to be the target? If it is simply *weight,* for example, a nail manufacturing plant will concentrate on large, heavy nails to the exclusion of smaller sizes or tacks. If *number* is substituted, then tacks will be produced, with a few large construction nails. What about a *value* goal? If gross output value is the target, managers will see to it that more expensive raw materials are used in the construction of any particular product. If a "value added" by production method is used, then it will pay the manager to break up the production process into numerous and semi-autonomous units, thus creating several unnecessary production steps in order to profit from as many "value adding" steps as possible. The central planners have, for half a century, battled the lower stages of the bureaucracy on such problems as these, but the system is self-defeating. The enterprises are merely following the profit motive; whatever the centrally imposed targets may be, managers will operate to excess in terms of them.[76]

---

[75] Hayek, "The Competitive Solution," *Economica,* III, New Series (1940); in Hayek, *Individualism and Economic Order,* 196-99.
[76] Nove, "The Problem of 'Success Indicators' in Soviet Industry," *Economica,* XXV (1958); in Leeman (ed), *Capitalism, Market Socialism, and Central Planning,* 78-90.

For several years (especially after 1961), there has been considerable discussion of the possibility of instituting quasi-market pricing for some consumer goods. The name usually associated with this recommendation is Y. Liberman. He has called for three targets: volume of output, assortment variations, and delivery schedules. Enterprise profits are the only other guide to be followed, given these three basic considerations.[77] This would help to upgrade quality, thus insuring greater consumer satisfaction. He claims that this would still permit full central planning, but both domestic critics and foreign observers have argued that this system, once begun, could not be stopped.[78]

It is not clear as to where the Liberman experiments in the 130 enterprises will lead. Philippe Bernard believes that the status quo will stand; there will be no extension of the market into areas of industry besides textiles, fur, and clothing, where Liberman's recommendations are already prevailing.[79] Robert Campbell agrees; the 1965 reform was not really basic to the Soviet economy.[80] Prices are not really negotiable, since higher agencies still establish the prices. Supplies are still regulated by the old system. The bureaucrats are acting like bureaucrats and are dragging their feet, even interfering into areas supposedly "reformed." Vaclav Holesovsky's assessment is illuminating:

> It is rather futile to talk of price reforms in the presence of an accounting system that is designed to facilitate central control

[77] Shaffer, "Ills and Remedies," *op. cit.,* 22, gives a summary of the Liberman proposals.

[78] For examples of Liberman's writings with a scattering of some of his critics' essays, see Myron E. Sharpe (ed.), *Reform of Soviet Economic Management* (2 vols.; White Plains, N. Y.: International Arts & Sciences Press, 1966). Cf. the discussion by Marshall I. Goldman, "Economic Controversy in the Soviet Union," *Foreign Affairs,* XLI (1963); reprinted in Bornstein and Fusfield (eds.), *The Soviet Economy,* 339-51.

[79] Philippe Bernard, "Postscript," in his *Planning in the Soviet Union* (N. Y.: Pergamon Press, 1966), 295.

[80] Robert W. Campbell, "Economics: Road and Inroads," *Problems of Communism,* XIV (Nov. Dec., 1965), 28-33.

but is utterly unsuited for rational estimation of true production costs.

Genuine decentralization would mean compromising with the operation of market forces; the government would retreat from attempts at universal guidance of the production process toward the position of a buyer of final products. Is it likely that the Soviet Union will set out on such a course in the near future? In view of the implications involved, the answer would appear to be in the negative. At present, the government generally demands more from the economy than it can comfortably deliver. Should it surrender, even partially, its direct and comprehensive controls over the economy, it would be offering production managers a degree of freedom that would allow them to adjust to the actual capacities and true cost levels of their productive resources. By relaxing the 'command economy,' the state would thus lose the principle implement of pressure it exerts not only upon the resources, but also upon the people who produce them and use them.[81]

But it is Alexander Gerschenkron who has put his finger on the most fundamental issue: the *maintenance of political control.*

It is doubtful that a consumption economy can be established in Soviet Russia. A decentralized economic system geared to a steady rise in levels of consumption would leave the Soviet dictatorship without a social function, without a justification for its existence. It is much more likely that the dictatorship will continue the policy of willfully provoking one international crisis after the other and of maintaining a high rate of investment as the economic pendant to such a policy. There a renewed curtailment of such managerial freedoms as have been granted since Stalin's death, followed by a general reversal of the decentralization policy, should only be a matter of time, and enterprise and management in Russia should once more return to the normalcy of Soviet mercantalism, concealed beneath a generous veneer of of socialist phraseology.[82]

### Economic Law

The confusion over success indicators and pricing points to a basic flaw in Soviet economic life. There is no agreement among

---

[81] Vaclav Holesovsky, "Surveying the Soviet Economy," *Problems of Communism,* XII (Sept.-Oct., 1963), 59.

[82] Gerschenkron, *Economic Backwardness,* 294-95.

economists, managers, and political leaders as to what exactly constitutes an economic law. In the fall of 1964, for example, *Pravda* published an article by Academician V. Trapezinikov. The author came forward with a pro-profit proposal basically similar to the one presented by Liberman a few years earlier.[83] As the editors later admitted, this and other articles along the same lines created a considerable amount of interest among the readers, so much so, that some 600 letters and articles had poured into the offices of *Pravda* as a result. Most of these scholars, the editors admitted, were basically on Liberman's side. Nevertheless, the range of the various answers was enormous; no two seemed to agree on exactly how the system was to operate. One suggested a standard of "the effectiveness of output produced," by which he meant a graded series of standards including, quality, value, reliability, weight, service time, safety, convenience in use, productivity, convenience of use. How he expected central economic planners to draw up such a graded scale for all products he did not explain. Another argued that profit was not the best standard, but productivity of social labor (whatever that is) should be. A third wanted to compute such productivity in terms of savings in costs of production. A fourth letter argued that an index reflecting savings in living and social labor costs should be constructed; it should estimate the growth of volume of final output per employee and per unit of productive capital. In other words, theoretical economic chaos reigns in the academic circles of the Soviet Union.[84]

Under these circumstances, Bergson's evaluation of the nature of Soviet planning seems justified: it is *lawless*. It is, as he says, the domination of economics by politics: ". . . under Soviet socialism the government has always been held to be the master rather than the servant of 'economic laws.' "[85]

---

[83] *Current Digest of the Soviet Press,* XVI, #33 (9 Sept., 1964), 13-15.

[84] *Ibid.,* XVII, #7 (10 March, 1965), 28-29. From *Pravda,* 17 Feb., 1965. The preceding page includes the 20 Jan. announcement of the establishment of the Liberman proposals in the 128 enterprises.

[85] Bergson, *Economics of Soviet Planning,* 13.

I have referred previously to the reluctance of the government to commit itself to economic principles. This reluctance must be seen in relation to the attachment of the system's directors to centralized decision making generally. To have sanctified economic principles would have diminished the role and perhaps the authority of the system's directors.[86]

To some extent, this attitude is changing today, if only by the pressure of the overwhelming task of economic planning in a complex, industrialized society. Nevertheless, the arbitrariness of a lawless system still exists:

> When superior authorities are reluctant to commit themselves to principles, arbitrariness easily comes to be considered as something of a virtue in itself. . . . As principles lately have gained in force, this attitude has lost ground. Hostility to principle and a flair for arbitrariness are alike seen now as manifestations of a cult of personality that must be exorcised, though apparently such attitudes still prevail. . . .[87]

Economic theory is clearly a shifting thing in the Soviet Union. Marxian concepts have retarded its economy in many areas, but as the growing complexity of the economy forces Soviet planners to re-evaluate their presuppositions, some of these Marxian bottlenecks will probably be broken. This, at least, is the attitude of some Western observers.[88] Robert Campbell has shown how, in recent years, economic discussion in the USSR has begun to resemble Western value theory in many respects.[89] So political life may be "mellowing" in some peripheral areas, and economic theory may be one of them, but the country is still ruled by a monolithic Party

---

[86] *Ibid.,* 174.

[87] *Ibid.,* 271.

[88] Joseph S. Berliner, "Marxism and the Soviet Economy," *Problems of Communism,* XIII (Sept.-Oct., 1964); reprinted in Bornstein and Fusfield (eds.), *The Soviet Economy,* 18-33.

[89] Robert W. Campbell, "Marx, Kantorowich, and Novozhilov: *Stoimost'* versus Reality," *Slavic Review,* XX (1961); reprinted in Leeman (ed.), *Capitalism, Market Socialism, and Central Planning,* under the title, "Mathematics in Soviet Planning, and the Theory of Value," 102-18.

which is notorious for its unwillingness to accept any deviation from its prevailing policies. When we realize that no textbook in political economy appeared in the USSR from 1928 to 1954, and that it was found necessary to cease teaching economics classes in higher institutions of learning in these years, then we can better understand the realities of Soviet intellectual life.[90] It is not surprising that practical economics should suffer under such circumstances; economic theory is too cramped by political ideology.

## Soviet Statistics

Soviet statistics, all critics agree, are highly questionable in most cases. Just how valid they actually are, however, is a source of rather heated debate among Western observers. Naum Jasny is the great antagonist of the validity of Soviet statistics. He sees their statistics more as functions of the political desires of the ruling hierarchy than as reflections of Soviet economic life. "Neutral" statistics were sacrificed after 1929; from 1930 they reflected Stalin's personal whims:

> Since practically all leading statisticians favored unbiased statistics, the statistical organizations were fully reorganized, these statisticians disappearing in the usual Soviet manner within one or two years.[91]

The method of distortion most commonly employed is the refusal of the government to publish unfavorable statistics. When certain data do not conform to the impression which the Soviet leadership wishes to convey to the outside world and the domestic population, the figures are simply not published. This fact is recognized by virtually all non-Marxist observers. As a result, Jasny argues, and because he feels that deliberate distortion is also employed, "a careful student should not accept a single Soviet figure without thorough check."[92]

---

[90] On the suppression of economics textbooks and classes, see Nove, *The Soviet Economy*, 282.

[91] Naum Jasny, "Soviet Statistics," *The Review of Economics and Statistics*, XXXII (1950), 92.

[92] *Ibid.*, 93.

One classic example of such distortion came in the early 1930's. Half the livestock of Russia was lost in these years, due to the unwillingness of the peasant population to bring them into the collective farms; they preferred to eat the livestock instead. At 1926-27 prices, some four billion rubles worth of livestock perished. Yet the official Soviet statistics reported that a *gain* of a billion and a quarter rubles worth of livestock came into the economy. The way this figure was achieved was simple: only state-owned herds were counted! Jasny estimates that the official Soviet estimation of the agricultural contribution to national income in 1937 was exaggerated by 45%.[93]

Jasny's critics take the attitude that while the statistics may be misleading, they are not deliberately manipulated (except, perhaps, in the final summaries). Gerschenkron argues that Jasny's own work is based to a large extent on official published figures, and that any corrections which he has made in the official sources have themselves been derived from other, less publicized, Soviet sources.[94] Alec Nove is one of those who has looked at Soviet statistics with a somewhat less jaundiced eye.[95] Nevertheless, they all agree that extreme caution must be taken with the official statistics of the USSR.

Daniel Marx has made an interesting point which ought to be taken into consideration in making an evaluation of Soviet statistical methods:

> While no one would pretend that estimates made by Western European countries are infallible, the insistence that Eastern European estimates must be valid because they have 'the force of law' [the argument of one previously quoted Communist apologist] appears almost naive. This attitude, however, may help to explain the procedures employed by the Soviet Union in the compilation and presentation of their output statistics. If 'plans' have the force of law, the results *must* agree with the

[93] *Ibid.*, 94.

[94] Alexander Gerschenkron, "Comments on Naum Jasny's 'Soviet Statistics'," *The Review of Economics and Statistics,* XXXII (1950),

[95] Nove, "A Note on the Availability and Reliability of Soviet Statistics," published as an appendix in *The Soviet Economy,* 323-30. Cf. Lynn Turgeon, "On the Reliability of Soviet Statistics," *The Review of Economics and Statistics,* XXXIV (1952), 75-76.

forecasts or run the risk of illegality and all that such a discrepancy implies.[96]

Jasny's hostility stems from what he considers "the all-important issue," namely, "that the achievements of the socialized planned economy, in industrialization and other respects, are only a fraction of the 'statistical' ones and that the sacrifices in consumption levels are vastly greater than those according to official 'statistics' and their official commentators."[97] As he has said elsewhere, "It is as a rule impossible to decide whether a Soviet economist is making a wrong statement against his better knowledge, or whether he is not properly informed."[98]

## Conclusion

Agriculture, the old nemesis of all socialist planners, has not been discussed. The reader is referred to some of the easily available literature on the subject.[99] It is enough to point out that agriculture and housing are invariably the two weak spots of any industrialized socialist nation. Poland has become the most productive farm area in the Soviet bloc; the solution was simple: Poland decentralized

[96] Daniel Marx, "Comments on Naum Jasny's 'Soviet Statistics'," op. cit., 251.

[97] Jasny, "Soviet Statistics," op. cit., 98.

[98] Jasny, Essays on the Soviet Economy (Munich: Institut zur Erforschung der UdSSR, 1962), 59. As he admits, the distorted statistics are in the minority, but in important sections, i.e., the summarizing sections. Ibid., 17.

[99] On the agriculture question, see Naum Jasny, The Socialized Agriculture of the USSR (Stanford, Calif.: Stanford University Press, 1949); Lazar Volin, A Survey of Soviet Russian Agriculture (Washington, D. C.: U. S. Dept. of Agriculture, 1951); Gregory Grossman, "Soviet Agriculture Since Stalin," The Annals, CCCIII (1956), 62-74; Lazar Volin, "Agricultural Policy of the Soviet Union," Comparisons of the United States and Soviet Economies (Joint Economic Committee, Congress of the United States, 86th Cong., 1st Session, 1959), pt. I; excerpts in Bornstein and Fusfield (eds.), The Soviet Economy, 168-201; Nancy Nimitz, "Agriculture Under Khrushchev: The Lean Years," Problems of Communism, XIV (May-June, 1965); reprinted in Bornstein and Fusfield, ibid., 202-15.

agriculture almost completely. Farmers are relatively free to grow what they want. The Soviet Union will continue to suffer from low output per farmer until she follows Poland's lead.

In the final analysis, the theory of Mises, Hayek, and the others appears to be justified, or at least hardly disproved, by Soviet economic theory and practice. Most non-Marxist commentators are willing to admit that in terms of economic efficiency as such — low production costs, higher output, allocation according to demonstrated consumer preferences — the free market economies outperform the Soviet system. It must be borne in mind, of course, that the goals of the Soviet hierarchy have seldom been consumer preference oriented; the goal has been the establishment of political power. Waste was a less important consideration than the strengthening of the Party and the Soviet state. There has been growth, to be sure, especially in the areas of heavy industry and military armaments. In terms of economic growth as such, Bergson's restrained conclusion is certainly accurate enough:

> As it has turned out, the outstanding example of socialism that has yet to come into existence has distinguished itself not so much for effective use of resources as for the novel and strange ends imposed on a great state.[100]

But Jan Prybyla's comment comes closest to the mark:

> What the Russians have shown is that cockeyed economic growth at rapid rates can be achieved without economists and without economic science; but that after the economy outgrows its teenage crisis, elusive and subtle problems of resource allocation among an increasing number of competing "priority" ends demand an economic science for their solution.[101]

How they propose to solve these problems remains to be seen, but it seems clear that without decentralization economically and the advent of a consumer economy based upon private ownership and profit,

---

[100] Abram Bergson, *Economics of Soviet Planning,* 358.

[101] Jan S. Prybyla, "Soviet Economic Growth: Perspectives and Prospects," *op. cit.,* in Bornstein and Fusfield (eds.), *The Soviet Economy,* 314.

the basic issues will remain unsolved. The economy will shift back and forth between planning at the top and localism, growing more and more irrational as the complexity of the planning task grows ever greater. The system, in good Marxian terminology, contains the seeds of its own destruction.

# VIII.

## BIBLIOGRAPHY

I.   ORIGINAL WRITINGS BY MARX AND ENGELS

1. *Basic Writings on Politics and Philosophy,* edited by Lewis S. Feuer. Garden City, New York: Doubleday Anchor, 1959. This collection stresses the political side of Marx, in addition to his philosophy of history. It deemphasizes the economic writings, and it takes little notice of the early manuscripts dealing with human alienation.

2. *Capital: A Critique of Political Economy.* New York: Modern Library, n.d. This is a reprint of the Charles H. Kerr edition of volume I of *Capital,* 1906. In this volume, Marx presented his basic critique of the capitalist economic system.

3. *Capital: A Critique of Political Economy.* Chicago: Charles H. Kerr & Co., 1909. The second volume of Capital, entitled *The Process of Circulation of Capital.* The least important of the three volumes, assembled after Marx's death by Engels.

4. *Capital: A Critique of Political Economy.* Chicago: Charles H. Kerr & Co., 1909. Volume three of the study, *The Process of Capitalist Production as a Whole,* was also assembled by Engels. It attempts to clear up some of the theoretical difficulties raised in volume one. Some commentators (notably Böhm-Bawerk) have argued that it abandons the principles set forth in the first volume.

5. *A Contribution to the Critique of Political Economy.* New York: International Library Publishing Co., 1904. This is the N. I. Stone translation of the 1859 volume. Here was the first contribution which Marx considered to be fully scientific economic reasoning, as contrasted to his political and philosophical speculations and his commentaries on contemporary events.

227

The introduction contains one of his most famous statements of economic determinism.

6. *Dialectics of Nature* (Engels). New York: International Publishers, 1940, 1960. These manuscripts were published posthumously. They contain many of his excursions into the field of the physical sciences, which he attempted to explain in terms of dialectical reasoning. The Soviet Marxists consider them to be integral to the original Marxian system, but many Western commentators (Lichtheim, R. C. Tucker) believe that these essays are foreign to the Marxian outlook.

7. *The Economic and Philosophic Manuscripts of 1844.* New York: International Publishers, 1964. At the age of 26, Marx wrote these manuscripts dealing primarily with human alienation and the society which fosters it. In the last decade, these essays have been "rediscovered" by scholars, both in the East and the West, and they have been the focus of numerous articles and books.

8. *The German Ideology.* London: Lawrence & Wishart, 1965. This edition is the first full translation into English of this important early manuscript. It was written in the year following the *EPM 1844,* and like the latter, it was published only in this century. The first section outlines his theory of economic determinism in its earliest form, and it contains a lengthy critique of several of Marx's left-Hegelian opponents, most of them long forgotten.

9. *Herr Eugen Dühring's Revolution in Science* (*Anti-Dühring*). London: Lawrence & Wishart, 1934. In 1877, Engels wrote the first edition of this volume. It is most famous for its center section which was later published separately as *Socialism: Utopian and Scientific.* It continues many of the speculations concerning natural science, and in this sense it is the companion to his *Dialectics of Nature.*

10. *The Holy Family.* Moscow: Foreign Languages Publishing House, 1956. The only English translation of the 1845 manuscript. This was the first book jointly authored by Engels and Marx (primarily the latter). It is a typical diatribe against

some of Marx's former German colleagues, and it represents his earlier philosophic position. For some reason, it is out of print and extremely difficult to locate.

11. *The Housing Question* (Engels). New York: International Publishers, n.d. Written as a series of articles in 1872, these represent attacks on the Proudhonist faction of European socialism.

12. *Karl Marx: Early Writings,* edited by T. B. Bottomore. New York: McGraw-Hill, 1964. Bottomore has translated some of the important 1843 and 1844 writings of Marx, including the famous essay, "On the Jewish Question," in which he castigates bourgeois European Jews as the essence of the capitalist system. It also includes translations of the *Economic and Philosophic Manuscripts of 1844.*

13. *Karl Marx: Selected Writings in Sociology and Social Philosophy,* edited by T. B. Bottomore and M. Rubel. New York: McGraw-Hill, 1964. Published first in 1956, these fragments of the early Marxian essays launched the new interest in the "alienation" theme in Marx. It also includes relevant fragments from the later Marxist studies.

14. *Letters to Americans, 1848-1895.* New York: International Publishers, 1953. One of several collections of correspondence between the two founders of Marxism and their American followers.

15. *Letters to Kugelmann.* New York: International Publishers, 1934. Correspondence between Marx and Dr. Kugelmann went on for a dozen years, between 1862 and 1874. Marx comments on current social and political trends, his own economic condition, and on the socialist movement in general.

16. *Ludwig Feuerbach and the Outcome of Classical German Philosophy* (Engels). New York: International Publishers, 1941. Here Engels traces the development of German philosophy from Hegel to Feuerbach. He sees Feuerbach as the chief contributor to materialist philosophy before Marx, although he criticizes Feuerbach's passivistic view of man. In transcending

Feuerbach, Marx launched scientific socialism, according to Engels.

17. *Malthus,* edited by Ronald Meek. New York: International Publishers, 1954. These fragments by Marx and Engels deal with the population problem, especially as treated by Malthus, whom they characterized as an apologist for the bourgeois class.

18. *Marx-Engels Selected Correspondence, 1846-1895,* edited by Dona Torr. New York: International Publishers, 1935. This is the most influential selection of Marx and Engels' correspondence that is in English. It includes most of the famous letters that are frequently quoted by students of the Marxian system.

19. *Marx-Engels Selected Works,* 2 vols. Moscow: Foreign Languages Publishing House, 1962. This set contains most of the more important shorter works by Marx and Engels, including the *Communist Manifesto, The Civil War in France,* and the *Critique of the Gotha Program.*

20. *On Colonialism.* Moscow: Foreign Languages Publishing House, n.d. A collection of the articles written between 1850 and 1888 by Marx and Engels on the subject of colonialism, especially British colonialism in Asia. Many of these essays were published in the New York Daily Tribune, Horace Greeley's liberal newspaper, for which Marx was a European correspondent.

21. *The Poverty of Philosophy.* Moscow: Foreign Languages Publishing House, n.d. This was written by Marx in 1847 as a reply to Proudhon. He outlines some of the themes which were to mark his later researches: criticism of the division of labor, the acceptance of the labor theory of value, and the revolutionary quality of science.

22. *Pre-Capitalist Economic Formations,* edited by E. J. Hobsbawm. New York: International Publishers, 1964. These are posthumously published fragments from his later career (1857-58). It traces the development of property and the growth of economic productive units. It contains a treatment of feudalism,

one of the very few times he ever strayed from his central theme: the analysis and criticism of capitalism.

23. *Revolution and Counter-Revolution or Germany in 1848.* Chicago: Kerr & Co., 1896. These were essays written in 1851 and 1852 for the *New York Daily Tribune,* and they can be considered as companion studies alongside of his more famous essays on France in the period 1848-52.

24. *Revolution in Spain.* New York: International Publishers, 1939. These are articles which were written for the *New York Daily Tribune* concerning the 1854 insurrection in Spain. It rounds out the essays on the mid-century European revolutions that Marx and Engels penned.

25. *Theories of Surplus Value.* Moscow: Foreign Languages Publishing House, n.d. This is the first section of the so-called fourth volume of *Capital.* It surveys the teachings of early economists, including Adam Smith, David Hume, and the Physiocrats.

II.  BIOGRAPHIES OF MARX

26. Berlin, Isaiah. *Karl Marx: His Life and Environment.* New York: Oxford University Press, 1963. This is perhaps the best known biography, and it deserves recognition for its balance of ideas, biographical details, and its evaluation of the Marxian system.

27. Carr, E. H. *Karl Marx: A Study in Fanaticism.* London: Dent, 1935. Perhaps the best overall biography of Marx, unfortunately out of print.

28. Lewis, John. *The Life and Teaching of Karl Marx.* New York: International Publishers, 1965. The latest "official" biography of Marx. It is the only one which pays attention to the early manuscripts by Marx; for this reason it is important. It stresses Marxism as a philosophy of voluntary activism as contrasted to the idea of Marxism as scientific prediction.

29. Mehring, Franz. *Karl Marx.* Ann Arbor: University of Michigan Press, 1962. This is a reprint of the classic biography. It is the key "official" biography, and it is the one most devoted

to the details of Marx's day-to-day struggles for the Revolution. It is least adequate in the area of ideas and philosophy.

30. Nicolaievsky, Boris and Maenchen-Helfen, Otto. *Karl Marx: Man and Fighter*. London: Methuen & Co., 1936. A sympathetic treatment of Marx. An adequate study, but not particularly distinguished.

31. Rühle, Otto. *Karl Marx: His Life and Work*. New York: New Home Library, 1943. A sympathetic, but not blindly favorable, study of Marx. Perhaps the best introduction to Marx as a person. It also contains solid and useful observations on Marx's teachings.

32. Schwartzschild, Leopold. *Karl Marx: the Red Prussian*. New York: Universal Library, 1947. The one really hostile biography on Marx. The author often drifts into polemics, but it offers certain correctives to the sympathetic treatments, especially in regard to his self-proclaimed triumphs as a student in college. The author is most eager to show how often Marx's predictions failed, something which his protagonists tend to ignore.

## III. Commentaries on the Marxian System

33. Böhm-Bawerk, Eugen Von. *Shorter Classics of Böhm-Bawerk,* vol. I. South Holland, Ill.: Libertarian Press, 1962. This book includes his famous essay on the contradictions within the first and third volumes of *Capital*.

34. Bober, M. M. *Karl Marx's Interpretation of History*. New York: Norton, 1965. A reprint of the 1948 edition of this important study. Bober stays away from peculiar or original views of Marx, and this is the strength of the book. It summarizes the Marxian system.

35. Carew-Hunt, R. N. *The Theory and Practice of Communism*. Baltimore: Penguin, 1964. Originally published in 1950, this is perhaps the best one volume introduction to Marx's thought. The first half deals with Marx and Engels, while the second half covers later conntributions to Marxism: Lenin, Stalin, post-Stalinist thought. Like Bober, Carew-Hunt does

not offer any startling theses about Marx; he simply comments intelligently on the system as a whole, clarifying and expanding the implications of Communism.

36. Cole, G. D. H. *The Meaning of Marxism*. Ann Arbor: University of Michigan, 1964. A reprint of the 1948 study. Cole tries to summarize Marxism, while reworking the original Marxian ideas so that the serious criticisms made by hostile commentators will not be so telling. He does not make a total apology, however; where he believes Marx to be clearly in the wrong, he says so. It is a very ponderous book to read; Cole's style of writing does not lend itself to quick skimming. Nevertheless, a serious student must read it.

37. Cornforth, Maurice. *Marxism and the Linguistic Philosophy*. New York: International Publishers, 1965. Cornforth, one of the most influential of America's Marxist philosophers, continues his studies of the Marxian philosophical approach. The first sections of the book are somewhat technical, dealing with problems of language and the theory of communication. The concluding section is very important, especially the chapter on "Socialist Humanism," where he spells out the ultimate implications of Marxism.

38. Dunayevskaya, Raya. *Marxism and Freedom*. New York: Bookman Associates, 1958. A confused book by an American Trotskyite. Its importance in 1958 was in the translation of several fragments of Marx's early 1844 manuscripts, which have subsequently been published in full.

39. Dupre, Louis. *The Philosophical Foundations of Marxism*. New York: Harcourt, Brace, & World, 1966. A useful introduction to Marx's early philosophical thought and its Hegelian background.

40. Fromm, Erich. *Marx's Concept of Man*. New York: Ungar, 1964. Fromm offers an introductory essay on the implications of the Marxian alienation theme for modern thought. Marx, in Fromm's eyes, is a traditional humanist. It is not surprising that Fromm tends to ignore Marx's call for total revolution, and Marxist commentators have not been lax in

calling this to Fromm's attention. The book also includes Bottomore's translation of the *Economic and Philosophic Manuscripts of 1844.*

41. Fromm, Erich (ed.). *Socialist Humanism: An International Symposium.* Garden City, New York: Anchor, 1966. Fromm assembles a series of essays by many scholars (most of them from Eastern Europe) dealing with the Marxian conception of alienation. It demonstrates what a profound impact the early Marxian writings have had on modern humanists, or at least how happy they have been in discovering that such an influential scholar as Marx was really in the humanist camp all along.

42. Gray, Alexander. *The Socialist Tradition.* New York: Longmans, Green and Co., 1946. This is a classic study of the history of socialist thought. Its importance lies in its treatment of pre-Marxian socialists from whom Marx drew many of his economic ideas.

43. Hook, Sidney. *From Hegel to Marx.* Ann Arbor: University of Michigan, 1962. A reprint of the 1950 edition in which Hook traces the development of left-wing Hegelianism which culminated in the Marxian system. The chapters on Feuerbach are especially important.

44. Hook, Sidney. *Towards an Understanding of Karl Marx.* New York: John Day, 1933. One of Hook's early analyses of Marx. It pictures Marx as basically a pragmatist, and it is as much a reflection of Hook's views at the time as it is of Marx's. Still, it is a well-written piece.

45. Lenin, V. I. *The Teachings of Karl Marx.* New York: International Publishers, 1964. A short introduction to the Bolshevik view of Marx, published first in 1917.

46. Lichtheim, George. *Marxism: An Historical and Critical Study.* New York: Praeger, 1963. Probably the most important recent study of Marxism. Lichtheim offers several new theses concerning the development of the system. He distinguishes Marx's contributions from Engels' later additions; he divides Marx's own thought into chronological periods; and he tries

234

to argue that after 1850 Marx was not really interested in revolution.

47. Marcuse, Herbert. *Reason and Revolution: Hegel and the Rise of Social Theory*. Boston: Beacon Press, 1964. This book throws light on the Hegelian conception of alienation, and it contrasts this with the idea of alienation which the young Marx held. Both emphasized the salvation of man in terms of labor: Hegel saw the process as mental labor; Marx saw it as material, social labor.

48. *Marxism and Alienation: A Symposium*. New York: American Institute for Marxist Studies, 1965. Included are several essays on the general theme of human alienation as it relates to art, philosophy, and the American social order. The bibliography in the last chapter is very useful. All the contributors are Marxists, or at least men highly sympathetic to Marxism.

49. Meyer, Alfred G. *Marxism: The Unity of Theory and Practice*. Ann Arbor: University of Michigan, 1963. Meyer, whose study of Leninism is superior to this work, traces several themes in Marx's thought. He sees the theme of the unity of theory and practice as the central idea in Marx: revolution is the synthesis of the dualism between mind and matter, thought and action.

50. Parkes, Henry Bamford. *Marxism: A Post-Mortem*. London: George Allen and Unwin, 1940. A liberal's criticism of Marxism which rests on the argument that Marxism is hostile to liberal democracy and therefore cannot bring human freedom into being. It was published in America under the title, *Marxism: An Autopsy,* which the University of Chicago reprinted as a paperback in 1964.

51. Popper, Karl R. *The Open Society and its Enemies,* vol. II. Princeton: Princeton University Press, 1963. Written in 1945, this study of Marx has met with mixed reactions. Carew Hunt considers it to be a classic: Marxists and non-positivists consider it to be absurd. It is primarily a criticism of Marx's historicist methodology: the idea that the historical process provides its own laws of interpretation and prediction. Popper

is a positivist, and he accepts Marx's claim that he (Marx) favored freedom and liberalism. Popper only argues that Marx's historicism led him away from the goal.

52. Schumpeter, Joseph A. *Capitalism, Socialism, and Democracy*. New York: Harper Torchback, 1962. Originally published in 1942, Schumpeter's book stands as one of the classic examinations of Marx. His basic argument seems to be that Marx's overall prediction of the collapse of capitalism may come true, but not for the reasons Marx used. He provides illumination on Marx's theory of classes, his economics, and on his historical impact. It is a difficult book to read, but its importance makes the effort expended worthwhile.

53. Sweezy, Paul M. *The Theory of Capitalist Development*. New York: Monthly Review Press, 1964. A reprint of the 1942 work. Sweezy presents a one volume summary of Marx's economics. The author is a Marxist, and for this reason the book is indispensable. He tries to show that Marx is still relevant in spite of modern developments in economic science that would appear to refute Marx's economics.

54. Tucker, Robert C. *Philosophy and Myth in Karl Marx*. Cambridge: The University Press, 1964. Written in 1961, this book, along with Lichtheim's, has been important in reevaluating Marx's early writings in terms of the alienation theme. Tucker sees Marx as essentially a religious figure who was concerned with questions of man's estrangement, salvation, and progress on earth. The importance of this study cannot be overemphasized.

55. Wilson, Edmund. *To the Finland Station*. Garden City, New York: Doubleday Anchor, 1953. A literary critic's intelligent history of Marx and his revolutionary heirs.

56. Wolfson, Murray. *A Reappraisal of Marxian Economics*. New York: Columbia University Press, 1966. A mediocre survey of some of the basic doctrines of the Marxian economic system. It is probably a simpler introduction than Sweezy's *Theory of Capitalist Development*.

57. Wright, David McCord. *The Trouble With Marx*. New Rochelle, N. Y., 1967. An introductory study of Marxism-Leninism. Not very systematic, and it is concerned only with Marxian economics at the simplest level. Some useful insights are presented.

# INDEX

scarcity, 113n
Berliner, Joseph, 213
Bernstein, Eduard, 105
Birch, Una, 90n
Black market, 213
*Blat,* 213, 215
Bloch, Ernst, 91n
Bloch, J., 77
Bober, M. M.
  accidents, 82
  democracy and revolution, 105n
  Marx and entrepreneurship, 165
  Marx's predictions, 97
  misery of proletariat, 142n
  relativism in Marx, 68n
  scarcity, 113n
Bogomils, 90
  Böhm-Bawerk, Eugen von
  criticism of Marx, 155ff.
  Marx's definitions, 129
  relevance today, 171
  theory of exchange, 126n
Borovitski, I., 211
Bortkiewicz, L., 162
Bottomore, T. B., 45n
  division of labor, 60n
  elites, 75n
  Marx as scientist, 83
Brozen, Yale, 147n
Buber, Martin, 104, 107n
Buonarroti, Filipo, 91n
Bureaucracy
  conservative nature, 168, 215
  Hayek on, 190
  hippies vs., 37
  in USSR, 212
  Mises on, 187
  two kinds, 187
Burns, Arthur R., 139n
Burroughs, William, 89

Caillois, Roger, 87, 93
Calculation *in natura,* 181
Calling, 56, 57.
Calvinism, 16
Campbell, Robert
  borrowed technology in USSR, 201
  economic gap, USA vs. USSR, 206
  economic theory in USSR, 221
  Liberman, 218
Capital
  constant, 133
  organic composition of, 135, 160
  overproduction of, 148
  variable, 133
Capitalism
  anarchy of, 154, 195
  contradictions in, 153
  duhumanizing all men, 59
  dynamic character, 169
  man into commodity, 57
  moral foundations of, 194
  reform of, 110
Capitalist accumulation, 136ff.
Carew-Hunt, R. N., 79
Cathars, 90
Central planning; see Planning, centralized
Chain of payments, 149
Chance
  control vs., 75
  economic determinism and, 73, 80
  Engels on, 78
  foundation of Marx's thought, 68
  individuals vs., 73
  philosophy, 34, 35
Chamberlain, Gary L., 65n
Change and profits, 165ff., 185

Kugelmann, Dr., 27
Kuhn, Thomas, 123n

Labor
  alienated (estranged), 58
  homogeneous, 127
  skilled, 127
  see also Calling
Labor power, 131
Labor theory of value, 166ff.
  creation doctrine and, 124
  Marx's modifications of, 130
Lange, Oskar, 179, 190, 195
Lassalle, Ferdinand, 28
Law
  abolition of, 88
  Christian view, 98, 118
  creation and, 120
  economic, 66ff., 219
  Engles' view, 101
  flux and history, 66ff.
  flux vs. static law, 34
  humanistic law, 118
  impersonal vs. personal, 40
  Nature, 35
  neutrality and, 193
  static law denied by Marx, 67
League of the Just, 24
Left Hegelians, 41
  see also Young Hegelians
Lenin
  entrepreneurship theory, 166n
  housing policy, 205
  tactics, 106
Levine, Herbert, 208
Lewis, C. S., 74
Lewis, John, 79
Liber, 172
Liberman, Y., 218, 220
Lichtheim
  dialectical materialism, 101n
  later Marx as determinist, 78n

Marx as Social Democrat,
  96n, 104n, 106
Linear history, 100
Lissagaray, 92n
Lowe, Donald, 15, 97n
Löwith, Karl, 83
Lozovsky, A., 104n, 106n

Machinery, 133
Magic, 9
Man
  as God; see God, man as
  autonomous, 47, 119
  Biblical view of, 120
  creator, 47ff., 124
  fall of; see Fall of man
  measure of all things, 47
  relationship with God, 98, 110
  see also Autonomy, Creation,
    Humanism
Manager
  in USSR, 209, 214
  vs. entrepreneur, 166ff.
Mantoux, Paul, 52n
Marcuse, Herbert, 38
Marginalist economics, 123ff.
Markovic, Mihailo, 46n
Márkus, György, 79n, 122
Marx, Daniel, 223
Marx, Elanor, 25, 92n
Marx, Heinrich (father), 21, 22
Marx, Karl
  alienation, 51ff., 85
  anti-communist period, 23
  anti-Semitism, 29ff.
  antinomies in system, 67ff.,
    73ff., 80, 116ff.; see also
    Antinomies
  apriorism, 49
  Archimedean point, 49
  atheism, 48
  autonomy of man, 49, 119;

246

revolution theme, 85n
Mazdak, 89
Means, Gardiner C., 139n
Means of subsistence: see Subsistence, means of
Measurement of economic growth, 197, 202, 224
Medieval philosophy, 35
Meek, Ronald, 141n, 143n, 163n
Mehring, Franz, 22n
Menger, Carl, 123, 126n
Meyer, Alfred G.
  Marx's Promethian view of man, 50
  Marx's revolution theory, 102n
  scarcity theory, 113n
Mises, Ludwig von
  bureaucracy, 187
  division of labor, 56n
  economic calculation, 173, 179
  psychology and economics, 126
  Marx and Mises on crises, 152
  statist officials, 168n
Mode of production, 64, 81
Money
  alienation and, 178
  defined, 176, 177
  division of labor and, 177ff.
  Judaism and, 177ff.
  Marx on, 115, 152, 177ff.
Monopoly, 138, 184
Moralism, 109, 110, 122
Moxon, Cavendish, 65n
Mueller, Gustav, 40n
Murray, John, 110n

Naboth, 194
Nature, 35, 47
Nature-freedom antinomy, 36, 59, 88, 116ff.
Necessity, 39, 74, 117; see also

Inevitability
Nef, John U., 53n
Neutrality
  economics and, 174, 194, 195
  Marx and, 49, 122ff.
New humanity, 85, 111
New Morality, 37
Niel, Mathilda, 75n
Nimitz, Nancy, 224n
Nisbet, Robert A., 15
  alienation theme, 52n
  conservatives vs. industrialism, 52n
  definitions, 26n
  Marx as statist, 118
  Rousseau, 55n
North, Gary
  inflation and centralization, 137n
  specie hoarding, 151n
Nove, Alec, 211n
  centralized planning, 214
  low quality goods in USSR, 198n
  Soviet agriculture, 204n
  success indicators in USSR, 217
  text recommended, 196
Nuttall, Jeff, 89
Nutter, G. Warren
  centralized planning in USSR, 209
  economic gap, USA vs. USSR, 205
  growth rate in USSR, 198

Odajnyk, Walter
  dualism in Marx, 79
  dialectical materialism, 102n
  man as I.B.M. machine, 116
Omniscience, 181, 207ff.
Overproduction, 142ff.